HARRY TRUMAN'S
Excellent Adventure

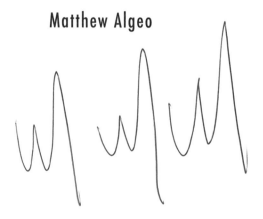

HARRY TRUMAN'S
Excellent Adventure
The True Story of a Great American Road Trip

Matthew Algeo

CHICAGO
REVIEW
PRESS

Library of Congress Cataloging-in-Publication Data
Algeo, Matthew.
  Harry Truman's excellent adventure / Matthew Algeo. — 1st ed.
    p. cm.
  Includes bibliographical references and index.
  ISBN-13: 978-1-55652-777-7
  ISBN-10: 1-55652-777-2
  1. Truman, Harry S., 1884–1972. 2. Truman, Harry S., 1884–1972—
Travel—United States. 3. Automobile travel—United States. 4. Truman,
Harry S., 1884–1972—Finance, Personal. 5. Presidents—Retirement—
United States. 6. Presidents—United States—Biography. I. Title.

  E814.A75 2009
  973.918092—dc22
  [B]   2008040136

Interior design: Jonathan Hahn
Map design: Chris Erichsen

Published by Chicago Review Press, Incorporated
814 North Franklin Street
Chicago, Illinois 60610
ISBN 978-1-55652-777-7
Printed in the United States of America
5 4 3 2 1

To Allyson, the best girl ever.

I like roads. I like to move.
—Harry S. Truman

Contents

Preface

On the afternoon of July 5, 1953, a slightly bored state trooper named Manley Stampler was patrolling a lonely stretch of the Pennsylvania Turnpike near the town of Bedford, about one hundred miles east of Pittsburgh. Around three o'clock, Stampler spotted a gleaming black Chrysler ahead of him in the left lane, with a line of cars behind it. The Chrysler was blocking traffic. It wouldn't move over to the right lane. Pennsylvania law required—still requires, in fact—that traffic keep right, except to pass. Stampler zipped up the right lane, pulled alongside the Chrysler, and motioned for it to pull over. It was, in the trooper's estimation, as routine as a routine traffic stop could be.

The Chrysler obediently moved to the right shoulder and slowed to a stop, its tires crunching on the loose gravel. Stampler passed the car and parked in front of it. He stepped out of his cruiser, adjusted his wide-brimmed hat, and slowly strode back toward the Chrysler. When he reached the driver's window, he bent down and peered inside. Behind the

1

wheel was a white male, mid- to late sixties, round face, big round-rimmed glasses, close-cropped gray hair. Seated next to him was a matronly woman, presumably his wife, looking slightly perturbed. Stampler immediately recognized the couple as Harry and Bess Truman. Until very recently they had been the president and first lady of the United States of America. Now they were in the custody of Trooper Manley Stampler.

"Shit," Stampler thought to himself. "What am I gonna do now?"

Harry Truman was the last president to leave the White House and return to something resembling a normal life. And in the summer of 1953 he did something millions of ordinary Americans do all the time, but something no former president had ever done before—and none has done since. He took a road trip, unaccompanied by Secret Service agents, bodyguards, or attendants of any kind. Truman and his wife, Bess, drove from their home in Independence, Missouri, to the East Coast and back again. Harry was behind the wheel. Bess rode shotgun. The trip lasted nearly three weeks.

One night they stayed in a cheap motel. Another night they crashed with friends. All along the way, they ate in roadside diners. Occasionally mobs would swarm them, beseeching Harry for an autograph or just a handshake. In towns where they were recognized, nervous local officials frantically arranged "escorts" to look after the famous couple.

Sometimes, though, the former president and first lady went unrecognized. They were, in Harry's words, just two "plain American citizens" taking a long car trip. Waitresses and service station attendants didn't realize that the friendly, well-dressed older gentleman they were waiting on was, in fact, America's thirty-third president (or thirty-second—Harry himself could never understand why Grover Cleveland was counted as two presidents).

Everywhere they went, the Trumans crossed paths with ordinary Americans, from Manley Stampler to New York cabbies. But their trip also took them to the upper reaches of society in mid-twentieth-century America. In Washington, Harry had lunch with two young up-and-coming senators, John Kennedy and Lyndon Johnson, and ran into the new vice president, Richard Nixon. Bess had tea with Woodrow Wilson's widow. In New York, the couple took in the most popular shows on Broadway, and Harry appeared (albeit quite by accident) on a new television program called the *Today* show.

It was a long, strange trip, and, after nearly eight hard years in the White House, Harry Truman loved every minute of it. As one newspaper put it, he was "carefree as a schoolboy in summer." It would stand out as one of the most delightful and memorable experiences in his long and exceedingly eventful life. It was also an episode unique in the annals of the American presidency, and it helped shape the modern "ex-presidency," which has become an institution in its own right.

Today ex-presidents get retirement packages that can be worth more than a million dollars a year. When Harry Truman left the White House in 1953, his only income was a small army pension. He had no government-provided office space, staff, or security detail. Shortly before leaving office, he'd had to take out a loan from a Washington bank to help make ends meet. One of the reasons he and Bess drove themselves halfway across the country and back was that they couldn't afford a more extravagant trip.

Harry and Bess Truman's road trip also marked the end of an era: never again would a former president and first lady mingle so casually with their fellow citizens. The story of their trip, then, is the story of life in America in 1953, a time of unbridled optimism and unmitigated cold war fear. It is also the story of the monumental changes that have occurred since then.

Between fall 2006 and summer 2008, I retraced the Trumans' trip in stages, sometimes alone, sometimes with my wife, Allyson. I drove where the Trumans drove, ate where they ate, and slept where they slept. I saw the sights they saw and, whenever possible, met with the people they met with.

In the following pages, I have included stories from my travels if, in my estimation, they help illuminate my account of the Trumans' trip. I have also included a few stories from my travels simply because I find them interesting or amusing. For this I beg your indulgence.

Like Harry, I crossed paths with ordinary Americans everywhere I went. None but a very few refused my requests for help. Many have become my friends. I have used their real names. For reasons of privacy, however, some surnames are omitted.

Also like Harry, my travels took me to the upper reaches of society. I stayed in some of the country's most exclusive hotels. I met a former president of the United States. I even made my own appearance on the *Today* show.

Most important, by retracing his trip with Bess, I discovered a Harry Truman not often found in the pages of history books. A Harry Truman who drove too fast. A Harry Truman who was a pretty good tipper. A Harry Truman who loved fruit. I mean, he really loved fruit. And Bess might have loved it even more.

But enough with the preface already. Let's hit the road with Harry and Bess!

1

Washington, D.C., Inauguration Day, 1953

On January 20, 1953—his last day in the White House—Harry Truman awoke at five-thirty, as usual. He skipped his customary morning walk and, after breakfast, attended to the final business of his presidency. His last official act was the signing of a letter to James A. Campbell, the president of the American Federation of Government Employees, on the occasion of the seventieth anniversary of the federal civil service system. (The system was instituted after one of Truman's unlucky predecessors, James Garfield, was assassinated by Charles Guiteau, the proverbial "disappointed office seeker.") In the letter, Truman decried what he called "recent reckless attacks" on civil servants, referring to Republican charges that the federal bureaucracy was infested with communists.

At 8:45, the president began saying good-bye to the White House staff, bounding from room to room, shaking hands with every stenographer, cook, maid, doorman, secretary, mailroom clerk, and telephone operator. The good-byes were heartfelt. Few presidents were as beloved by the White House help. Truman remembered their birthdays. He called them when they were sick. "He has been a wonderful guy to work for," one unidentified White House employee told a reporter that day. "You just wanted to do things for him."

Around eleven o'clock, Truman retired to the Red Room. An eighteenth-century French clock on the mantelpiece loudly ticked off the seconds as Truman and his wife, Bess, waited for his successor to arrive. The Trumans had invited Dwight and Mamie Eisenhower to join them inside the White House for coffee before riding to the inauguration. It was a tradition that stretched back nearly 150 years, to 1809, when Madison called on Jefferson. It wasn't always convivial or comfortable, particularly when the presidents were from different parties, but it symbolized, palpably, the peaceful and democratic transfer of power.

Awaiting Eisenhower, Truman's emotions must have been mixed. The two men had once been cordial, even friendly. Truman had admired Eisenhower, the general who'd done so much to win the war that Truman had unexpectedly inherited as commander in chief. When Eisenhower announced his candidacy for the Republican presidential nomination early in 1952, Truman was effusive, notwithstanding Ike's party affiliation. Eisenhower was "a grand man," Truman told reporters soon after Ike's announcement. "I am just as fond of General Eisenhower as I can be."

But the presidential campaign had soured their relationship. At a campaign stop in Wisconsin, Eisenhower had redacted from his speech a tribute to General George Marshall, who had served Truman as secretary of state and, later, as secretary of defense. Marshall, who would win the Nobel Peace Prize later that year, was a favorite target of Senator Joseph McCarthy, who called him all but a traitor for the "loss of China" to Mao's communist forces. Eisenhower apparently expunged the tribute to avoid alienating McCarthy in his home state. (Unbeknownst to Ike, an unedited copy of the speech had been distributed to reporters beforehand.) When

Truman, who considered Marshall closer to God than most men, heard this, he was apoplectic. In Utica, New York, Truman, campaigning for the Democratic candidate, Adlai Stevenson, told a crowd, "I had never thought the man who is now the Republican candidate would stoop so low." Privately, Truman called Eisenhower a "coward" for kowtowing to McCarthy.

Truman and Eisenhower had even had a hat spat: Eisenhower wanted to wear a homburg to his swearing in. Truman thought the occasion befitted a more formal top hat, but, conceding it was Ike's prerogative to choose the headgear for his inauguration, he wore a homburg. (John F. Kennedy would turn the tables on Eisenhower eight years later. JFK donned a silk top hat, forcing Ike to wear one too. Since then the presidential hat wars have abated markedly.)

At eleven-thirty, the president-elect's limousine finally pulled up to the White House. Ike sent word inside that he and Mamie would not be joining the Trumans for coffee. Tradition be damned: Ike didn't want to step foot inside the executive mansion until he was the executive. It was a snub, plain and simple, a "shocking moment," according to the newsman Eric Sevareid, who was there. Truman was furious, but he walked outside and greeted Eisenhower with all the faux warmth he could muster. "Truman was gracious," Sevareid told Truman biographer David McCullough. "He showed his superiority by what he did."

Truman joined Eisenhower in an open limousine, a huge black Lincoln, for the short ride to the Capitol. Their wives (and the Trumans' daughter, Margaret) rode behind them in a separate car. Truman and Eisenhower smiled and waved to the crowds lining Pennsylvania Avenue, but barely spoke to each other.

After a ride that must have seemed much longer than the two miles it actually was, the limousine pulled up to the east side of the Capitol, where a temporary platform had been constructed for the inauguration ceremonies. Truman climbed up to the dais and was seated in a plush leather chair just behind the podium.

Photo by Sammie Feeback, courtesy of the Harry S. Truman Library

Bess, Harry, and Margaret Truman, photographed in 1953. Harry called Bess "the Boss." Margaret was "the Boss's Boss."

Eisenhower's running mate, Richard Nixon, was sworn in first. While repeating the oath, Nixon failed to repeat the word *support* when he was supposed to swear to "support and defend the Constitution of the United States." The omission was barely noticed. At twelve-thirty—a half-hour late—Eisenhower was sworn in by Chief Justice Fred Vinson. (Vinson had been appointed by Truman, and he is still the last chief justice appointed by a Democrat.) Eisenhower was now president of the United States. Truman, as he had put it in his farewell address five days earlier, was now "a plain, private citizen."

After a brief prayer, Eisenhower began his inaugural address. "My fellow citizens," he intoned. "The world and we have passed the midway point of a century of continuing challenge. We sense with all our faculties that forces of good and evil are massed and armed and opposed as rarely before in history. . . ."

Truman slumped in his chair ever so slightly. He later admitted he'd found it difficult to focus on Eisenhower's words. His mind began to wander. Perhaps his thoughts turned back to the summer of 1922. Back then—a little more than thirty years earlier—he was thirty-eight, married just three years, and living in his mother-in-law's house in Independence, Missouri. The haberdashery that he had opened with his friend Eddie Jacobson in nearby Kansas City had failed earlier that year, and it would take him fifteen years to pay off the debts. He was, for all intents and purposes, unemployed. "Broke and in a bad way"—that's how Harry summed up that summer many years later.

It was an old army buddy named Jimmy Pendergast who came to Truman's rescue. Jimmy's uncle, Tom Pendergast, was Kansas City's political boss, and he was looking for a good candidate to run for eastern judge of Jackson County, a position akin to county commissioner. Jimmy recommended Truman. As a Baptist, a Mason, and a former farmer, he fit the bill perfectly. Running as the "good roads" candidate, Truman won the election that fall.

In 1934 the Pendergast machine helped Truman get elected to the U.S. Senate. For years he was known derisively as "the senator from Pendergast," but he eventually distinguished himself by chairing a commission that uncovered waste in military spending.

At the 1944 Democratic National Convention in Chicago, party leaders decided to kick Vice President Henry Wallace off the ticket. They regarded Wallace, a plant geneticist who dabbled in mysticism and astrology, as far too liberal, something of a loose cannon, and, well, a little strange. Truman, who always insisted he never campaigned for the job, was chosen to replace Wallace, largely because the other contenders were either too liberal or too conservative. "I had never even seen Truman in my life before he was nominated," remembered Democratic National Committee Chairman Edward J. Flynn. "All I knew was that no one could do Roosevelt any good, and it was a question of who would do him the least harm." Franklin Roosevelt, who didn't even bother to attend the convention, went along with the choice, though he complained he hardly knew the senator. Truman's candidacy was, reporters joked, another "Missouri Compromise." Bess Truman, who already thought the family was spending far too much time away from Independence, was not happy. After the convention, Harry, Bess, and Margaret drove home. The atmosphere inside the car, Margaret later recalled, was "close to arctic." It was the last long drive Harry and Bess would take for many years.

A month later, Roosevelt invited Truman to the White House for lunch. Truman, who hadn't even seen the president in a year, was shocked by his appearance. "I had no idea he was in such a feeble condition," Truman confided to a friend. "In pouring cream in his tea, he got more cream in the saucer than he did in the cup." In photographs taken of the two men that day, Roosevelt is hunched and haggard, with dark bags beneath his eyes. Truman is beaming, vibrant. It was hard to believe that Roosevelt was only two years older than Truman.

The Roosevelt-Truman ticket won the 1944 election in a landslide. Roosevelt died on April 12, 1945. Truman had been vice president eighty-two days. Apart from cabinet meetings, he had met with Roosevelt just twice.

Truman would win the White House in his own right in 1948, famously upsetting Thomas E. Dewey and most political prognosticators.

His presidency had encompassed some of the most monumental events of the twentieth century: World War II, the founding of the United Nations, McCarthyism, Korea, the cold war.

Sitting on that dais on that winter's day in 1953, the summer of 1922 must have seemed like a very long time ago to Harry Truman.

Eisenhower droned on: "Freedom is pitted against slavery; lightness against the dark . . ."

Truman's mind wandered still. Perhaps he pondered his uncertain future. He was sixty-eight now, but quite hale. On most mornings he still walked two miles before breakfast, at his old army pace of 120 steps per minute. And longevity was in his genes: his mother had lived to be ninety-four. (His father had died at sixty-two of complications from surgery for a hernia.) By any estimation, Harry Truman had a lot of life left.

But what to do with it? Truman, a student of history, well knew that ex-presidents often faded into obscurity, irrelevancy—or worse. There were notable exceptions, of course. After their presidential terms, John Quincy Adams was elected to the House of Representatives and William H. Taft was appointed chief justice. But, more often, an ex-president's life was one of disappointment and disillusionment. Martin Van Buren and Theodore Roosevelt both tried to regain the presidency without success. John Tyler was elected to Congress—the Confederate Congress. He died before he could take office, but most Northerners considered him a traitor, and his passing was barely noted in Northern newspapers. Franklin Pierce, a raging alcoholic, reportedly said there was nothing to do but "get drunk" after the presidency. This he did with astonishing abandon, until it killed him, though hardly anybody noticed.

Herbert Hoover, seated just a few feet from Truman on the dais that day, was the only other living member of the ex-presidents club. After his humiliating defeat in 1932, Hoover had lived in political isolation—until his career was resuscitated by Truman himself.

Hoover, at least, was rich. He'd made a fortune in mining before going into politics. At the time, ex-presidents received no pension, and some had died broke. Thomas Jefferson was forced to sell his beloved library to make ends meet. James Monroe was so destitute he had to move in with his daughter and her husband. Ulysses S. Grant, his life savings lost in a swindle, had just eighty dollars in the bank at one point. He was saved from penury only by selling his memoirs to Mark Twain. "They just . . . let them starve to death," Truman complained of the country's treatment of its ex-presidents soon after he left the White House.

Truth was, Harry Truman didn't know what to do with the rest of his life. He had no specialized training, nothing more than a high school diploma. (He is the last president without a postsecondary degree.) There was speculation that he might make another run for office, perhaps as a senator or governor back in Missouri. He could even run for the White House again if he wanted to: he was the last president eligible to serve more than two terms. Theoretically, anyway, in four years he could be standing once more in the very spot where Eisenhower now stood.

One thing was certain, though: Harry Truman needed money. He wasn't destitute, but he was far from rich, and he knew his post-presidential expenses would be considerable. He had already rented an office in Kansas City, and he would need at least two assistants just to answer the mail. Besides, he felt obligated to maintain a certain standard of living, if only to uphold the dignity of the office he had just vacated.

Yet his only income would be a pension for his service as an officer in France during World War I. That pension amounted to $111.96 a month, after taxes. Ironically, he did not receive credit for his nearly eight years as commander in chief.

Truman had come to the presidency with little personal wealth. When he took office, the salary was seventy-five thousand dollars a year, but out of that he was expected to pay all White House expenses. One year he netted just forty-two hundred dollars. In 1949 the salary was raised to a hundred thousand dollars plus fifty thousand for expenses, but this was still barely enough to cover the growing cost of running the White House, and Truman was able to save little. A few months before leaving office, Truman had met with Martin Stone, a lawyer–turned–television mogul, to discuss his post-presidential job prospects. "The president was frank that he'd be needing money when he returned to his modest home," Stone recalled.

Finally, Eisenhower concluded his inaugural address: "The peace we seek . . . is nothing less than the practice and fulfillment of our whole faith among ourselves and in our dealings with others. . . . This is the work that awaits us all, to be done with bravery, with charity, and with prayer to Almighty God. My citizens, thank you." The speech had lasted nineteen minutes.

A wave of applause rolled toward the dais, snapping Truman out of his reverie.

After the ceremony, the Trumans were driven to the home of Dean Acheson, Harry's erstwhile secretary of state, for a farewell luncheon. As his driver negotiated the teeming Inauguration Day streets of Washington, the new ex-president experienced his first taste of civilian life: the long black White House limousine obeyed all traffic signals. It was the first time in nearly eight years that Harry Truman had stopped for a red light.

After lunch, the Trumans stopped by the home of Harry's longtime personal secretary, Matthew Connelly, where Harry took his customary afternoon nap. Around 4:00 P.M., they were driven to Union Station to catch the train back home to Independence.

At the station, Harry and Bess bade farewell to their Secret Service detail. Just as they received no pensions, ex-presidents at that time received

As president, Harry often took walks around Washington. Here he is in 1950, walking from his temporary home in the Blair House to the White House, accompanied by Secret Service agents. (The White House was being renovated at the time.)

Photo by William E. Carnahan, Silver Spring, Maryland, courtesy of the Harry S. Truman Library no government-financed bodyguards. The Trumans were no longer, in Secret Service parlance, protectees. They were on their own now.

The Trumans would ride home in the presidential railcar, the *Ferdinand Magellan*, which was attached to the end of the Baltimore & Ohio Railroad's regular National Limited. Truman had undertaken his historic whistle-stop campaign on board the *Ferdinand Magellan* in 1948. The car was now at Eisenhower's disposal, of course, but the new president had offered it to the Trumans in an effort to mend fences. Truman appreciated the gesture, but for the time being, anyway, he kept the hatchet very much unburied.

Unexpectedly, a crowd of over three thousand had gathered at Union Station to see the Trumans off: senators, members of Congress, supreme court justices, generals, admirals, old friends, foreign diplomats, ordinary Washingtonians. They sang "For He's a Jolly Good Fellow" and "Auld Lang Syne." "Good-bye, Mr. President," they shouted. "Good-bye, Harry!" Many wept. Said prim Dean Acheson with uncharacteristic folksiness, "We're saying good-bye to the greatest guy that ever was." The Trumans were deeply moved by the impromptu going away party. "I can't adequately express my appreciation for what you are doing," Harry told the crowd from the rear platform of the *Ferdinand Magellan*. "I'll never forget it if I live to be a hundred—and that's just what I intend to do!" At six-thirty, the valves underneath the train hissed and the conductor called out, "All aboard." As the train slowly pulled out of the station, Harry and Bess stood waving from the back platform. They seemed reluctant for the moment to end. They kept waving as the train disappeared into the Washington night. "They've gone back to Missouri," a porter said wistfully as he watched the couple fade into darkness.

The twenty-six-hour ride home was reminiscent of the whistle-stop campaign. At each stop along the way, great crowds came out to say farewell to their erstwhile president. "Crowd at Silver Spring, Md., some three or four hundred," wrote Truman in his diary. "Crowd at Harpers Ferry, Grafton, and it was reported to me at every stop all night long.

Same way across Indiana and Illinois." The outpouring was touching. It was also surprising, because Harry Truman was not very popular when he left the White House, mainly due to the stalemate in Korea. In 1952 his approval rating in a Gallup Poll had sunk to 22 percent—a record low unmatched until 2008. On the eve of his departure, newspaper columnist Walter Trohan called Truman "one of the most mediocre men ever to inherit power. . . . Our Harry has rattled around in the White House like a peanut in a ball room and has floundered in the president's chair." Yet, as the outpouring of affection on the trip home attested, many Americans were beginning to realize just what they were losing.

Several times on the ride home Truman left the *Ferdinand Magellan* to stroll through the rest of the train, stopping frequently to chat with passengers. It was something he hadn't been able to do in eight years, to move about as he wished, unencumbered by Secret Service agents. When he walked into one car and the passengers began to rise in deference, Truman stopped them. "Don't get up," he said. "I'm no longer president."

At 7:15 on the morning after the inauguration—Truman's first full day as ex-president—the train stopped for a fifteen-minute layover in Cincinnati. Truman disembarked with the other passengers and waited patiently in line to buy the morning papers at the station's newsstand. A photographer spotted him and called out, "Look this way, Mr. President." "I'm not 'Mr. President' anymore," Truman answered with a smile. "I'm just plain Harry Truman." This was a point of etiquette unresolved at the time. America still didn't know what to call its former chief executives. "I don't care what people call me," Truman said when asked how he should be addressed. "I've been called everything." But Truman made it clear that he always called Herbert Hoover "Mr. President." "Like a five-star general or admiral," Truman explained, "[a president] doesn't have his former rank taken away on retirement." In time, it would become customary to address Truman and all other ex-presidents as "Mr. President."

The train reached Independence at 8:05 that night. The reception was positively tumultuous. More than eight thousand people swarmed the town's tiny depot to welcome Harry and Bess home. As they stepped from the *Ferdinand Magellan* for the last time and began making their way through the massive crowd, an American Legion band struck up "The Missouri Waltz" (never mind that Truman hated the song). The Trumans were overwhelmed with emotion. Standing behind a forest of microphones planted on the platform, Harry addressed the crowd. He joked about being in the "army of the unemployed"—though he was quick to add that it was a "small army."

"I can't tell you how much we appreciate this reception," he said. "It's magnificent—much more than we anticipated. It's a good feeling to be back home." Bess could barely speak. "I'm just delighted to be home," she said. "This is certainly a wonderful welcome." When they finally reached their house at 219 North Delaware Street, another fifteen hundred people were waiting to greet them. "Mrs. T. and I were overcome," Truman later wrote of that night. "It was the payoff for thirty years of hell and hard work."

Harry and Bess walked hand in hand into the house. The next morning Harry was asked what he planned to do. "Take the grips up to the attic," he said, using the old-fashioned word for suitcases.

Retirement, as it has come to be known, is a relatively recent concept. The first edition of Noah Webster's *American Dictionary of the English Language*, published in 1828, lists four meanings for the word, none of which mention age. You worked until you couldn't work anymore, in which case your family, probably large, provided for you. Or you worked until you died. No gold watches, no pensions, no Social Security.

But older workers had no place in the Industrial Revolution. They couldn't operate the newfangled machinery as nimbly as younger workers. And assembly lines were only as efficient as their weakest link, which was usually an older worker. The aged were simply in the way, and many employers began wondering how best to get rid of them.

The answer, suggested a Johns Hopkins professor named William Osler in a 1905 lecture, was "a peaceful departure by chloroform." Osler was being facetious (one hopes), but his point was serious. Osler believed men over forty contributed little to society. "Take the sum of human achievement in action, in science, in art, in literature—subtract the work of the men above forty and . . . we would practically be where we are today."

As for men over sixty, Osler thought them completely useless. His proposal, short of chloroform, was mandatory retirement. There would be an "incalculable benefit . . . if, as a matter of course, men stopped work at this age." (Osler, who was fifty-five at the time, would live another fifteen years—and never retire.)

But older workers couldn't afford to stop working. They needed the money. In response, some employers began offering pensions—in the name of efficiency, not altruism. Funded by younger, lower-paid employees, pensions gave older workers the means to retire—sometimes involuntarily. A foreman in a Connecticut textile mill recalled how one worker was "retired" in 1916:

> Old Mr. McGuire, Jim McGuire's father, used to make spools, and he was getting to be a pretty old man. He'd go over to the storage bin, and sometimes he'd only bring one spool at a time. . . . Well, finally, I spoke to [a supervisor], and I guess he mentioned it in the office because Mr. Shields come out. He got me and Mr. McGuire together, and he said, "We have decided that you have worked long and hard. And you always done good work too. And we think it is time you had a rest. So we have decided to pension you, and we will give you $55 a month, and you can have your house free as long as you live. But that doesn't mean your wife can have it free after that." . . . So the old man was pensioned

off. You know, it's a funny thing about them pensions. Practically everybody that gets one dies pretty soon after.

But by 1932, just 15 percent of American workers were eligible for private pensions. Not until the Social Security Act was signed by FDR in 1935 were most workers guaranteed at least some income after retirement.

As a government employee, however, Harry Truman did not qualify for Social Security. And he'd left the Senate too soon to qualify for a congressional pension.

His only income was that army pension.

2

Independence, Missouri, Winter and Spring, 1953

*N*o twentieth-century president retired to more humble surroundings than Harry Truman. When not traveling the world, Teddy Roosevelt returned to Sagamore Hill, his estate on Long Island. Woodrow Wilson retreated to a fashionable townhouse in Washington, the only ex-president to stay in the capital. Herbert Hoover eventually settled into a plush suite at the Waldorf-Astoria in New York. Gerald Ford would retire to the pristine golf courses of Palm Desert, California. Bill Clinton would choose tony Westchester County, New York (mainly so his wife could run for the Senate).

But when Harry Truman left the White House in 1953, he returned to the same rambling, slightly ramshackle, two-and-a-half-story Victorian that he and Bess had lived in since their marriage thirty-four years earlier. It had been painted white when he became president in 1945, and hadn't been painted again since. There was no air-conditioning. The only indication that it was the home of a luminary was the iron fence that surrounded the property. It had been erected in 1949 at the behest of Herbert Hoover, who had warned Truman that souvenir hunters would "tear the place down" otherwise. (Hoover said the doorknobs had been stolen off his childhood home in Iowa. Presumably he suffered no such thievery at the Waldorf.)

Known locally as the Gates-Wallace home, the house on Delaware Street was built, in fits and spurts, by George Porterfield Gates, Bess's maternal grandfather, between 1867 and 1895. Bess, her three brothers, and her mother, Madge Gates Wallace, moved into the house in 1904 after Bess's father committed suicide. After he married Bess, Harry moved into the already-crowded house as well. It was in their second-floor bedroom that their only child, Margaret, was born during a snowstorm on February 17, 1924. After Madge Gates Wallace died at age ninety in 1952, Harry and Bess bought out her brothers' shares of the property, and, for the first time in their lives, the Trumans owned their own home. They would never own another.

Today the Truman home is managed by the National Park Service as part of the Harry S Truman National Historic Site in Independence. (Truman had no middle name—the "S" was meant to honor both his grandfathers, Anderson Shippe Truman and Solomon Young—so the period after his middle initial is optional. The Park Service does not use one, unlike the National Archives and Records Administration, which runs the Harry S. Truman Library and Museum. Truman himself claimed to be neutral on the matter, though he usually used a period when signing his name.)

More than thirty thousand people visit the Truman home every year, but on my tour there were just two other people, a thirteen-year-old girl and her grandfather. The girl claimed her favorite subject was history, but thought the Germans had bombed Pearl Harbor and was unable to name Truman's predecessor in the White House. Her grandfather seemed unusually interested in the home's bathroom fixtures. Maybe he was a plumber.

Our guide was a friendly ranger named Norton, who looked exactly like Santa Claus with a ponytail and a Smokey Bear hat. The house looks much as it did when Harry and Bess returned from Washington in 1953. The kitchen is painted a bright apple green with cherry red accents. Against the wall is a small red Formica table where Harry and Bess took most of their meals, a Proctor-Silex toaster standing sentinel on top. The furnishings throughout the house are simple, almost Spartan. A small reading room is lined with bookshelves sagging under the weight of history tomes and murder mysteries. There are two well-worn upholstered chairs—his and hers. On the end table next to hers lies a Dorothy L. Sayers novel. In the front parlor, a massive black-and-white television set is parked incongruously against one wall, near a piano. Norton, our guide, explained that Bess liked to watch baseball games. (Bess was a good athlete in her own right. Harry liked to brag that she was "the best shortstop they ever had in Independence.")

The Trumans were frugal, a blessing to the home's preservationists. Norton pointed to a water-stained patch of wallpaper in the front parlor. It was being replaced by extra paper that Harry had saved and stored in the attic. In fact, the paper from the attic was so well preserved that it would have to be artificially aged before replacing the stained bit. But the Trumans' frugality had a downside, too. As Norton explained, when the Park Service took over the property in 1983, it was in such poor condition that the repairs cost several hundred thousand dollars. It was said that only the paint was holding the house together.

When they left the White House, there was speculation that the Trumans might move to Key West, where they had often vacationed when Harry was president, or New York, where Margaret lived. But they returned to Independence, partly out of principle. As Harry liked to say, "I tried never to forget who I was and where I'd come from and where I'd go back to."

There were practical advantages, too, to moving back to Independence. It was near the Truman farm in Grandview, Missouri, where Harry hoped to build his presidential library. And nobody made a big fuss over them. Visitors

from out of town would occasionally come to the house, asking for an autograph or a handshake, a request Harry always obliged. But, by and large, the
locals would leave the Trumans alone. Bess could drive to the library or push
her cart around the supermarket without causing a stir. Harry could take
his morning walks unmolested, often accompanied by Mike Westwood, an
Independence cop assigned to the former president part-time.

But the Trumans also came back to Independence because they couldn't
afford to live anywhere else. They already owned the house on Delaware
Street. Given their limited income, it just didn't make sense to move anywhere else.

Back in Independence, Harry soon settled into a routine. He awoke
every morning at five-thirty, dressed, read the morning papers (on the back
porch when the weather was nice), picked a cane from his collection of a

Photo by Sammie Feeback, courtesy of the Harry S. Truman Library

Harry headed out for one of his morning walks, November 18, 1954. "I was always
a walker," he said. "I never did believe in being afraid to go on foot to the corner
store, the way a lot of people are."

hundred or so, and took his walk. His route varied. Sometimes he would walk down to the town square, passing the Jackson County Courthouse, which had been built in 1934, back when he was the county's presiding judge. Other times he would meander through the residential neighborhoods around his home. An old newsreel shows Truman enjoying one of his walks when a small boy in a cowboy costume suddenly jumps out of the bushes and "shoots" the former president with a toy gun. Truman laughs and pats the irrepressible tyke on the head. Today, a Secret Service agent watching the film would likely suffer a heart attack, and the unlucky youngster who attempted such an ambush would perish in a hail of gunfire.

Back at the house, he had breakfast at the kitchen table with Bess (who did not share his penchant for early rising). Around nine he went into his office, a three-room suite on the eleventh floor of the Federal Reserve Building in Kansas City. Sometimes Mike Westwood drove him, but often he drove himself. "Harry S. Truman" was painted in black letters on the opaque glass of the door to the suite, just like a detective agency in a pulp novel. (Truman claimed the only reason he'd even put his name on the door was because people kept mistaking his office for a restroom.) He had two assistants: his private secretary, Rose Conway, who had served him in the same capacity when he was president, and Frances Myers, a receptionist who had also worked in the Truman White House. He paid their salaries out of his own pocket. Much of his day was spent answering mail. He received more than seventy thousand pieces in the first two weeks after he left the White House, and as many as a thousand a day thereafter: notes from well-wishers, invitations to everything from church suppers to national conventions, autograph requests. Budding politicians wrote him asking for advice (or endorsements). The founder of a new cult tried to recruit him. When Truman casually mentioned in an interview that he was looking for a silver dollar minted in 1924, the year of Margaret's birth, silver dollars poured in by the dozens. Truman estimated that less than one-half of one percent of the letters came from "crackpots," a statistic that surprised him. "I expected more," he said. "I had many chances to make people mad."

He answered each and every piece of mail because, he said, "I have always believed that if a person goes to the trouble of writing a letter, even a critical letter, I should answer or at least acknowledge it." The postage was, of course, solely his responsibility. At three cents a pop, it would cost him nearly ten thousand dollars in just his first year out of office.

Truman maintained an open-door policy, and just about anybody who dropped by was likely to get an audience with the former president. "Many people," he said, "feel that a president or an ex-president is partly theirs— and they are right to some extent—and that they have a right to call upon him." His office number was even listed in the Kansas City telephone directory: Baltimore 6150. (His home number was unlisted, probably in deference to Bess.)

When he wasn't answering mail, entertaining uninvited visitors, or taking unsolicited telephone calls, Truman was busy raising money—not for himself but for the grand library he planned to build on the family farm in Grandview. The library would serve as a repository for his papers, which, for the time being, were stored in four hundred four-drawer filing cabinets in a room on the fourth floor of the Jackson County Courthouse.

With his keen sense of history, Truman well understood the importance of preserving his papers. "Did you know that Millard Fillmore's son burned some of his papers?" he asked an interviewer. "A good many of Jackson's papers were lost—some were found again, but a good many were lost. . . Lincoln's son burned some of his papers. Think of it, some of Abraham Lincoln's papers burned! It's awful."

Truman envisioned the library as a "research center for the benefit of small colleges" in the Midwest. He wasn't interested in a memorial to himself, he insisted. "I'll be cussed and discussed for the next generation anyway." Besides, Truman didn't think much of memorials to the living. "You can never tell what foolishness they may get into before they get into a pine box and then the memorial sometimes has to be torn down."

A private corporation called the Harry S. Truman Library, Inc., had been established to raise money for the project—money that could not be used for Truman's personal or business expenses.

Around four o'clock he would go home. After dinner, he listened to a newscast or two on the radio. Then he retired to the reading room, where he indulged his passion for history. By ten o'clock he was in bed.

It was, in many respects, a perfectly ordinary life.

Truman, however, still needed money. He was, he wrote, under a "heavy burden of personal expense." He could have solved his financial problems overnight by accepting one of the many lucrative offers that came his way. A chain of clothing stores offered him a job for a hundred thousand dollars a year as a "sales manager." Another firm offered him an eight-year, eight-hundred-thousand-dollar contract requiring him to "work" just one hour a day. A sewing machine company offered him "a salary in six figures" for doing nothing more than making occasional public appearances. There were lucrative offers to appear on a radio program, or to put his name on a brand of soap. Truman refused them all. He would do nothing that would "commercialize" the presidency, he said, nothing that would exploit or trivialize the office in any way.

Occasionally he accepted modest fees for giving speeches, which he donated to his library fund. Beyond that, he refused to cash in on his status as a former president. It was a principle that future ex-presidents would abandon.

In early February, just a few weeks after leaving office, it was announced that Truman had agreed to sell his memoirs to Doubleday for an advance of six hundred thousand dollars. It was an astronomical sum, especially in 1953, when the average worker's annual salary was barely more than four thousand. It was assumed the former president's financial worries were over. Like Grant before him, he'd been saved from financial ruin by a book deal. But the truth was far different.

For one thing, the advance would be taxed as income, at a rate of 67 percent. Four years earlier, when Truman was in the White House, the IRS had allowed Dwight Eisenhower to claim his $635,000 advance on *Crusade in Europe* as a capital gain, rather than income, reasoning that the general was not a writer by profession. That reduced the tax on Ike's advance to 25 percent. When Truman asked the IRS for permission to claim his own advance as a capital gain, as Eisenhower had, his request was denied. This did little to improve relations between the ex-president and the incumbent.

Out of what remained of his advance, Truman would have to pay a small army of researchers, stenographers, and ghostwriters, not to mention his other expenses. Years later, Truman would declare—with more than a touch of bitterness—that out of that six-hundred-thousand-dollar advance, he had realized just thirty-seven thousand dollars.

Still, the book deal allowed him to splurge just a little bit. In March, he, Bess, and Margaret took a Hawaiian vacation, though Harry's friends Averill Harriman and Ed Pauley picked up most of the tab. And, even before that, Harry went shopping for a car. He needed one. Since returning to Independence he'd either been using Margaret's, which was stored in the garage, or borrowing his brother-in-law's.

Few presidents loved automobiles as much as Harry Truman did. His first car was a 1911 Stafford, which he purchased used in 1914 for $600 (or $650—accounts vary). Hand-built in Kansas City by a mechanic named Terry Stafford, it was a flashy car, black with brass accents, a thirty-horsepower engine, and a three-speed transmission. On a good road it was capable of speeds as fast as sixty miles per hour. This was no Model T. Legend has it that he bought the Stafford to impress Bess, whom he was courting at the time. It certainly made it easier for him to commute from his family's farm in Grandview to Bess's house in Independence. Previously, he had had to catch a train or a trolley. In the Stafford, Harry took Bess for afternoon drives, and Sunday picnics along the Little Blue River. When his National Guard unit was called up in 1917, he took the car with him to Camp Doniphan in Oklahoma, where he was stationed for training. Before he was shipped overseas, Harry reluctantly sold the Stafford to an army sergeant for two hundred dollars. "It was an excellent car," he wrote,

Photo courtesy of the Harry S. Truman Library

Harry behind the wheel of his first car, a 1911 Stafford, at a picnic around 1915. "It was an excellent car," he said. Seated next to him is Bess Wallace, the future Mrs. Truman. The other passengers are Bess's relatives.

"and would take an awful beating. You can be sure of that if one lasted me as long as three years, which that one did."

For the rest of his life, Truman bought nothing but Chryslers, Dodges, and Plymouths. In November 1940, he bought two: a gray 1941 Chrysler Royal Club coupe for himself and a gray Chrysler Windsor sedan for Bess. They were the last cars he had owned. After he became president, he gave the coupe to his sister and sold the sedan to a friend in Washington.

Shortly after he started shopping for a new car, Truman received a telephone call from K. T. Keller, the chairman of the Chrysler Corporation.

"Lincolns seemed to have had the inside track at the White House while you were there," Keller told Truman, referring to the presidential limousine fleet. "But we want you to use a Chrysler."

"What kind of a model do you suggest?" Truman asked.

"Our best model is the Imperial."

"That sounds a little too swanky for me. What else do you recommend?"

"Our New Yorker is next," Keller said. "However, Mr. President, I hope you realize that we want you to have this car with our compliments."

Truman demurred. "I'm a private citizen now," he said. "I don't think I should get any privileges that wouldn't come to any other private citizen. . . . I'm going to have a Chrysler all right. But I'm going to pay for it."

Much was made of the fact that Truman paid for his own car. Exactly how much he paid, however, is unknown. The list price was around four thousand dollars, but Truman probably paid much, much less. "I suspect the agreed price might have been one dollar," speculated a Chrysler offi-

Harry beams as he inspects his new 1953 Chrysler New Yorker at the Haines Motor Company in Independence, February 16, 1953. "It's got so many gadgets on it I'll have to go to engineering school to handle it," he said.

cial who was familiar with the transaction. Harry Truman was a man of scruples, to be sure, but some deals were simply too good to pass up.

Truman took delivery of the New Yorker at the Haines Motor Company in Independence on February 16, 1953. It was a black, four-door sedan with chrome wire wheels and whitewall tires. The interior was a beautiful tan velour. Powered by a 331-cubic-inch V-8 FirePower engine (later known as a Hemi), it boasted all the latest technological innovations, including a PowerFlite automatic transmission, power steering, and power brakes. "It's got so many gadgets on it I'll have to go to engineering school to handle it," Truman cracked. Chrysler sent a young engineer named Frederick Stewart to Independence to help Harry get acquainted with the vehicle. With Stewart driving, Harry in the passenger seat, and Bess in back, they spent about two hours driving the back roads of Jackson County, with Stewart explaining the car's many features.

Finally it was Harry's turn to get behind the wheel. "It was soon apparent that Mr. Truman hadn't done much driving recently," Stewart remembered, "so we sort of made this drive a little refresher course on driving the very latest in automobiles." Eventually Harry got the hang of things, and the three of them headed back into town. Driving past the Jackson County Courthouse, Truman told Stewart how there had been ten thousand dollars left over after the courthouse was built, so Truman arbitrarily decided to have a statue of his hero, Andrew Jackson, erected out front. It was, he told Stewart, the only thing he had ever done in his political career that he could have been put in jail for.

The next day, Truman sent K. T. Keller a thank you note. "That wonderful Chrysler arrived yesterday," he wrote. "It certainly is a peach of a car and I can't tell you how very much I appreciate the courtesies which you have extended to me. I'll think of you whenever I take a ride and that will be rather frequently you can be sure."

Harry Truman's 1953 Chrysler New Yorker is still out there somewhere, in a dusty garage or weathered barn. According to Mark Beveridge, the

Truman Library's registrar and unofficial "car guy," the Chrysler is owned by a collector who "wishes to remain anonymous." I was eager to see the car, of course, so I asked Beveridge if he would be willing to forward a letter from me to the anonymous collector. "No," he said apologetically. Beveridge hopes the collector will eventually donate the Chrysler to the museum, and he didn't want to do anything that might jeopardize that acquisition.

I wasn't about to give up that easily, so I placed ads in classic car newsletters—nothing. I posted pleas on Internet bulletin boards—still nothing. I even enlisted the help of a private investigator, again to no avail. My quest, however, did turn up another 1953 Chrysler New Yorker, much like Harry Truman's.

Back in 1971, Alan Hais was twenty-five years old and just starting his first job as an environmental engineer for the District of Columbia. He was looking for a cheap car to get him around town when he spotted an ad in the paper for a 1953 New Yorker. The asking price was three hundred dollars. Hais and a friend drove out to Fredericksburg, Virginia, to check out the then eighteen-year-old car, but when he learned it had ninety-seven thousand miles on it, Hais got cold feet. When he and his friend stopped for burgers on the way home, though, Hais reconsidered. "It was a good solid car," he remembered. "So I said, well, we might as well go back." Hais drove the car home, with his friend following just in case.

Since then, Hais has gone on to a long and successful career, mainly working for the Environmental Protection Agency. And the New Yorker has gone from his beater car to his pride and joy. Over the years he has lovingly restored it "piece by piece," rebuilding the carburetor, replating the chrome, replacing the brakes and exhaust system. He had it repainted its original color: "Hollywood maroon."

I went to visit Alan on a warm, humid spring day. The skies were cloudy, and when I pulled into the driveway of his home on Maryland's Eastern Shore, he was already outside waiting for me. He was eager to take the Chrysler out before it rained. He carefully backed the car out of his garage, the door of which was barely wide enough to accommodate it. I hopped in and we went for a drive.

Harry's New Yorker was a four-door sedan. Alan's is a two-door convertible, but in most other respects the cars are identical. It is a massive machine, measuring nearly eighteen feet in length and weighing around forty-three hundred pounds. The interior is gorgeous, especially the instrument panel, a half-circle with a speedometer surrounded by four simple gauges for gas, oil pressure, engine temperature, and amplitude. Directly above the ignition is a cigarette lighter.

As we cruised along country roads at forty to fifty miles per hour, Alan explained that 1953 was a transitional year for the automobile industry. Immediately after the war, most cars were just warmed-over versions of prewar models. But by 1953, automakers were beginning to innovate. "They were experimenting with a lot of things," Alan said. "But they didn't get them all quite right." I asked for an example. "Well," he said, "the power brakes are pretty unreliable." The laws of physics being immutable, this was not a comforting thought. "By 1955," Alan continued, "the horsepower race started, and you started to see the first traces of fins, which really went over the top in '57 and '58."

After a few minutes Alan turned to me. "Do you wanna drive it?" he asked. I hesitated. Of course I wanted to drive it. But I also didn't want to wrap his pride and joy with the unreliable brakes around a telephone pole. "Maybe up the driveway," I said. But Alan, to his credit, was insistent. "Drive it," he said, bringing the car to a stop in the middle of the road. "There's very little traffic."

I climbed behind the giant three-spoke steering wheel and put the car in gear. I don't know how Harry felt the first time he drove his New Yorker, with a Chrysler engineer sitting next to him in the front seat, but I was a bit self-conscious driving with Alan beside me. Alan, however, seemed to relish the rare opportunity to enjoy his New Yorker from the vantage point of a passenger. "Not many people have driven this car besides me," he said. "But you've got a special case."

Harry Truman loved cars. Here he is behind the wheel of a 1946 Ford, one of the first models produced after the war ended. In the passenger's seat is Henry Ford II.

It certainly didn't handle like the Toyota Corolla I'd rented for the drive out to Alan's place. The New Yorker had power steering, but when I moved the wheel, it seemed to take the car a moment or two to respond. This, apparently, was another one of the innovations they didn't get quite right in 1953. It was especially disconcerting when oncoming vehicles approached, but Alan was unfazed. "It's a little iffy to steer," he said a bit too nonchalantly. "That's just one of the things you've gotta get used to."

Alan said he likes to take the car to shows, but admitted that Chrysler collectors can be "oddballs." "We're a little more quirky," he explained. "You go to a show, you can see loads of General Motors cars and loads of Ford cars, but there's just not nearly as many Chryslers out there, particularly of this era." Chrysler collectors, he speculated, "go for the underdog."

I was greatly relieved when I safely pulled the big car into his driveway. Inside his house, Alan showed me an issue of *Consumer Reports* from 1953. Of the New Yorker, the magazine said, "The steering is precise."

Steering issues notwithstanding, Harry Truman loved his New Yorker. With its wire wheels, whitewall tires, and gleaming chrome trim—not to mention its famous driver—the big black sedan soon became the most recognizable vehicle in Independence, a distinction that made Truman proud. As he tootled around town, running errands with Bess or just taking it out for a spin, passing motorists would honk and wave, bringing that famous toothy smile to the ex-president's face.

Harry cared for the New Yorker the same way he cared for all his cars: with a meticulousness that bordered on the compulsive. He had the oil changed every thousand miles. He had it washed and vacuumed every few days. He habitually inspected the tires, measuring the tread and air pressure. He religiously recorded every gasoline purchase on a small card he kept inside the glove compartment, so he could calculate fuel mileage.

"He was very particular about his cars," was how Margaret put it.

In early May, buried in the avalanche of mail that Truman received was a letter that especially caught his attention. It was an invitation from the Reserve Officers Association to address the group's convention in Philadelphia on June 26. Founded after World War I, the organization not only represented the interests of officers in the military reserves, it also advocated "the development and execution of a military policy for the United States that will provide adequate national security." Truman, a former reserve officer himself, had helped found the association. Attending the convention would give him a chance to catch up with some old friends. It would also give him a chance to speak his mind.

Since leaving the White House, Truman had remained conspicuously mum when it came to the new administration in Washington. "I'm not going to do or say anything to embarrass the man in the White House," he told one interviewer. "I know exactly what he's up against." Privately, though, he was seething. Before leaving office, Truman had proposed a defense budget of forty-one billion dollars. Eisenhower had proposed slashing that by 12 percent—about five billion dollars. The Republicans believed the reduction was necessary to offset proposed tax cuts. Besides, their thinking went, who needs a big army when you've got nuclear weapons? Many Republicans believed atomic bombs alone were enough to deter the Soviets. Eisenhower himself noted that three aircraft with nuclear weapons could "practically duplicate the destructive power of all the 2,700 planes we unleashed in the great breakout from the Normandy beachhead."

To Truman the cuts were reckless and irresponsible. He believed America needed to project strength with muscular armed forces, not just bombs. Truman was sure the Soviets would regard Eisenhower's cuts as a sign of weakness and would seek to expand their influence even further. The Republicans, Truman believed, were sacrificing national security—for tax cuts.

Harry Truman was tired of holding his tongue. It was time he spoke his mind. What better place than the Reserve Officers convention? Truman accepted the invitation. It would be his first major speech since leaving the White House.

And he was determined to drive to Philadelphia to deliver it. He'd been wanting to give his new Chrysler "a real tryout" anyway. He would make a vacation out of it. First he and Bess would drive to Washington—just to visit friends, he insisted. Then they would go up to Philadelphia for his speech, then on to New York to visit Margaret and do a little sightseeing. Then they would drive back to Independence, just the two of them, like they used to do back in the old days when he was in the Senate.

Harry was even convinced he and Bess would "enjoy the pleasures of traveling incognito" on the trip, even though theirs were two of the most recognizable faces in the country. To help preserve their anonymity, he would closely guard their schedule and route.

Bess had her doubts. Unlike Harry, she was not under the illusion that they could drive around the country just like any other retired couple. She also knew it would be a physically demanding trip, especially for Harry, who always did all the driving when they traveled in the car together. Yes, back when Harry was in the Senate, they had driven between Independence and Washington all the time. But, as she surely reminded him, that was a long time ago. They hadn't taken a long car trip together since 1944, when they drove home from the Democratic convention in Chicago—the one at which Harry was nominated for vice president. That was nearly nine years ago.

"Nobody worried much then," Harry countered, "and we made it all right." Why not now?

Bess knew she was fighting a losing battle. She consented to the trip under one condition: Harry must drive no faster than fifty-five miles per hour. She always thought Harry drove too fast.

Harry agreed to Bess's speed limit. The trip was on, and over the next several days he planned it as meticulously as if he were returning to Potsdam. Maps were spread out on the dining room table. The route was planned, the mileage calculated. "I took out the road map and figured the distance—exactly 1,050 miles from my garage door to the door of the Senate garage," he wrote. "I decided on the best places to stop over on the way, as I always used to do." He couldn't have been happier. "I like to take trips—any kind of trip," he wrote. "They are about the only recreation I have besides reading."

The trip would not only give Harry a chance to satisfy his wanderlust. It was also part of his effort to make the transition, as he put it, from Mr. President to Mr. Citizen. Truman saw no reason why he shouldn't go back to being "just anybody again." "Cincinnatus knew when and how to lay down his great powers," Truman wrote of the Roman general. "After he had saved the Republic he went back to his plow and became the good private citizen of his country." But since his return to Independence, he'd found it difficult to escape his fame. Old friends were reluctant to call on him. Even Harry himself was having trouble adjusting, trouble becoming a "normal guy." Stanley Fike, an aide to Missouri Senator Stuart Symington, remembered visiting the Trumans in their home shortly after they returned to Independence. "The president started to walk in front of a lady and Mrs. Truman said, 'Harry, just a minute, let the lady go first.' Of course, when he was president he always went first, this was the protocol. She was calling him back and reminding him that now he was a private citizen."

"Up to this time, I had not had much luck at living like the plain ordinary citizen I had hoped to become on leaving the White House," Harry wrote. "I thought that this holiday would give me a chance to do so at last."

When Harry's friends learned what he was up to, they were flabbergasted. "They organized a regular filibuster," Harry remembered, "trying to talk me out of the trip." But Harry could not be dissuaded. "I am kind of stubborn," he explained, "and since no one could give me what I thought was a sensible reason why we should not go, we went."

When Secret Service Director U. E. Baughman heard about the trip, a chill must have gone down his spine. It was one thing for the ex-president to drive himself to work. It was quite another for him to drive halfway across the country and back.

On September 13, 1899, a sixty-nine-year-old real estate agent named Henry Bliss stepped from a streetcar at 74th Street and Central Park West in New York City and was promptly flattened by an electric-powered taxicab. Bliss suffered massive head and chest injuries and died the next morning, becoming the first person killed in a motor vehicle accident in the United States.

Twenty-five more people would die in motor vehicle accidents before the end of 1899, and the number grew exponentially in the following years: 1,174 in 1909, 10,896 in 1919, 29,592 in 1929. In 1953, the one-millionth traffic fatality was recorded. That year, 36,190 people were killed in motor vehicle accidents in the United States. The fatality rate—the number of deaths per 100 million vehicle miles traveled—was 6.647. That was half the rate in 1937, but still considerably higher than today's rate of less than 1.5.

Driving was dangerous because the cars were big but the safety features were not. For all its newfangled gadgets, Harry's new forty-three-hundred-pound Chrysler didn't even have seat belts. Major American automakers believed consumers would never pay for something so frivolous and wouldn't equip their cars with seat belts until 1955, when Ford began offering them as an option on some models. That innovation was the brainchild of a young Ford executive named Robert McNamara—the future secretary of defense.

There were other factors involved as well: poor roads, lax enforcement of motor laws, a virtual lack of vehicle inspections, few if any driver education programs, the absence of speed limits on some roads. The problem was not unrecognized. Newspapers were filled with gruesome photographs depicting the aftermaths of violent collisions. As president, Truman himself had railed against "what amounts to murder on the road." But the federal government was slow to respond. The predecessor of the National Highway Traffic Safety Administration would not be created until 1966. A year later, automakers were finally required by law to install seat belts as standard equipment.

So perhaps the greatest danger the Trumans would face on their trip would be the simple act of driving. It made U. E. Baughman wish the Secret Service could protect ex-presidents. But Congress wasn't even willing to give them a pension, much less bodyguards. All Baughman could do was the same thing Harry's friends would do: hope for the best.

3

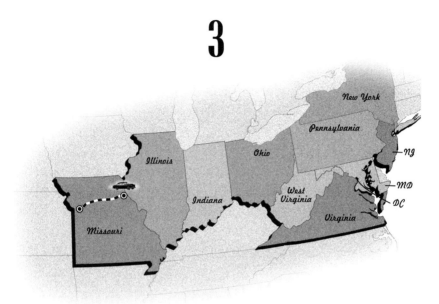

New York

Pennsylvania

Illinois

Ohio

Indiana

West
Virginia

Virginia

Missouri

NJ

MD

DC

Hannibal, Missouri,
June 19, 1953

On Friday, June 19, 1953, Harry skipped his morning constitutional and devoted himself to packing. He and Bess planned to hit the road that morning—and they would not travel light. Harry would fill the New Yorker with eleven suitcases before he was finished, the luggage spilling out of the trunk and onto the backseat. Most people hate packing, but Harry Truman, true to his obsessive nature, relished the task. "He prided himself on being an expert packer," his daughter, Margaret, remembered, "and he was."

Around 7:15, Harry and Bess climbed into the big black car. Harry slowly backed it through the narrow gate at the end of the driveway and onto Van Horn Road (soon to be renamed Truman Road). He had already scraped some chrome off the car backing through the gate, a process he likened to "the camel and the needle's eye." They drove the half-block up Van Horn, turned right onto Delaware Street, went about a mile, then turned right onto U.S. Highway 24. This they would follow 166 miles east to Monroe City, where they would pick up Highway 36.

A crude early version of air-conditioning was an option on the New Yorker in 1953, but Harry's didn't have it. (He never much saw the need for AC.) Missouri was in the grips of a heat wave, and the mercury would top 100 in much of the state that day. In Kansas City it hit 102. So the Trumans rode with the windows rolled all the way down, Harry with both hands on the wheel, Bess resting her elbow on the open window frame. They were, as usual, impeccably dressed: Harry wore a white suit, Bess a rayon print dress. Harry did make one small concession to the heat, however: he drove in his shirtsleeves, his jacket hanging from a hook above the left rear window.

As Independence faded in his rearview mirror, Harry Truman might have been the happiest man in Missouri, if not all forty-eight states. He loved to drive. Back when he was a county judge, he'd driven thousands of

Photo by the U.S. Navy, courtesy of the Harry S. Truman Library

As president, Harry occasionally drove his own limousine. Here he takes the wheel during a vacation in Key West in 1946.

miles touring county courthouses from Colorado to New York before the construction of the new courthouse in Independence. When he ran for the Senate in 1934, he campaigned by car, crisscrossing the Show-Me State in his shiny new Plymouth. He enjoyed it so much, he said he felt like he was on vacation. As a senator, he drove thousands of miles investigating fraud and waste on military bases throughout the South and Midwest and, of course, he regularly drove between Independence and Washington. He always preferred the freedom of the road to the plush confines of a Pullman car. Even when he was president, he would occasionally take the wheel of his limo, much to the consternation of his Secret Service agents.

Driving not only satisfied his need to keep moving; it also helped him gauge the country's mood. "You have to get around and listen to what people are saying," he said.

He fancied himself an excellent driver, naturally, but in reality, riding shotgun with Harry Truman could be a hair-raising adventure. As his longtime friend Mize Peters once told an interviewer, rather diplomatically, "I have driven with him when I was a little uneasy."

By far his biggest vice was speed. Bess was right: Harry drove too fast.

On July 6, 1947, Truman drove a White House limousine back to Washington from an engagement in Charlottesville, Virginia. His passengers included Treasury Secretary John W. Snyder and Admiral William Leahy. Reporters clocked Truman at speeds approaching sixty-five miles per hour on country roads where the posted speed limit was fifty. When the *Richmond Times-Dispatch* reported the transgression, Truman responded with one of his legendary "longhand spasms." "The pace was set by a capable, efficient State Policeman, in a State Police car," he wrote in an angry letter to the paper. "I could not have exceeded the Virginia speed law if I had desired to do so—which I did not." He never sent the letter.

There is no evidence that he was ever charged with a traffic violation, but Harry Truman's driving record was not perfect. On Sunday, March 27, 1938, he was driving home from Washington with Bess and Margaret when he blew through a stop sign at a busy intersection in Hagerstown,

Maryland. Another car plowed into them. Truman's car—a brand-new Plymouth—rolled several times and was totaled. Nobody in either car was seriously injured. "It was almost a miracle that we escaped alive," Margaret remembered. Truman claimed the stop sign was obscured by a parked car. No citations were issued, but a judge ordered Truman to pay the other driver ninety dollars for damages. In his later years, Harry's escapades behind the wheel would become the stuff of legend in Independence. As the *Kansas City Star* once put it, Truman navigated the corridors of power more gracefully than the streets of his hometown. Mostly he was involved in fender benders. Usually he offered the other driver cash to pay for repairs—reportedly so Bess wouldn't find out. (At least one driver refused the money, preferring to preserve his dent as a unique kind of presidential souvenir.) "I'd hear the fellows down at the filling station talk about Mr. Truman out driving around," remembered Sue Gentry, associate editor of the *Independence Examiner*. "They'd say, 'You'd better watch him—he's getting a little wild out there.'"

Bess, of course, had made Harry promise that he would drive no faster than fifty-five miles per hour, even though the speed limit on many highways at the time was sixty or sixty-five—and in some places there were no limits at all. (In Missouri, for example, drivers were merely required to maintain a "reasonable and prudent" speed.) But, owing to his lead foot, Harry found it almost impossible to keep that promise. Just a few miles outside Independence, Bess turned to him and said, "What does the speedometer say?"

"Fifty-five," Harry answered.

"Do you think I'm losing my eyesight? Slow down!"

Harry obeyed, and soon everything else on the road was passing the decelerated Trumans. "Not only that," Harry remembered, "but since we were going so slowly, they had a chance to look us over. Pretty soon the shouted greetings started: 'Hi, Harry!' 'Where you going, Harry?' 'Hey! Wasn't that Harry Truman?'"

"Well," Harry said to Bess, a bit of I-told-you-so in his voice, "there goes our incognito—and I don't mean a part of the car."

Harry and Bess on a trip in 1957. The Trumans were one of those lucky couples who travel well together, though Bess always thought Harry drove too fast.

About an hour after leaving Independence, they crossed the Missouri River near the town of Waverly. When Harry had first proposed the trip, Bess had had her doubts. But now that they were on the road, those doubts melted away in the withering heat. On the bridge over the Missouri, Bess turned to Harry. "Isn't it good to be on our own again," she said, "doing as we please as we did in the old Senate days?"

"I said that I thought it was grand," Harry remembered, "and that I hoped we'd do as we pleased from that time on."

Driving across Missouri on Highway 24 today, one is struck by how little, not how much, things seem to have changed since 1953—at least in appearance. Once the clutches of Kansas City's suburban sprawl are escaped a few miles east of Independence, the two-lane road practically turns into a time machine. You can drive it all the way to Moberly—150 miles, over halfway across the state—without encountering a single fast-food restaurant, big-box store, or chain motel. There are no traffic lights either, just a handful of four-way stops at the bigger crossroads. Rolling hay and soybean fields are interrupted by a succession of small towns where American flags flutter from nearly every house. Except for the cell phone towers, satellite dishes, and pro-life billboards, Harry Truman would have no trouble recognizing the place today.

In one important respect, however, Missouri is much different today than it was in 1953. The Missouri that Harry Truman knew was segregated. Although it never joined the Confederacy, Missouri was a slave state and, in its racial attitudes anyway, very much a Southern state. Schools were segregated by law. All other public facilities—buses, hotels, restaurants, theaters, playgrounds—were segregated by "public consensus." A state law banned marriages "between white persons and negroes or white persons and Mongolians."

Indeed, it would have been all but impossible for African Americans to take a road trip like the one Harry and Bess were taking. In the early 1950s, Senator Lyndon Johnson asked his maid's husband, Gene Williams, to drive his pet beagle from Texas to Washington. Williams explained to Johnson the perils involved in such a trip. "We drive for hours and hours," he said. "We get hungry. But there's no place on the road we can stop and go in and eat. . . . We keep goin' 'til night comes . . . it takes another hour or so to find a place to sleep. You see, what I'm saying is that a colored man's got enough trouble getting across the South on his own, without having a dog along."

Harry Truman was born into a family with Confederate sympathies less than twenty years after the Civil War ended. (His mother refused to sleep in the Lincoln bedroom when she visited the White House.) He was raised in a rigidly segregated society. It was probably inevitable that he would carry his own prejudices. He was known to use the word *nigger* casually. Yet, as president, he proved to be heroically enlightened on racial matters.

He integrated the armed forces. He was the first president to address the National Association for the Advancement of Colored People (NAACP). His support of civil rights infuriated white Southern Democrats, many of whom defected to the Republican Party.

The civil rights movement was at a turning point in 1953. On June 8, the United States Supreme Court ordered new arguments in the case of *Brown v. Board of Education of Topeka.* Original arguments had been heard the previous December, but the justices were having trouble reaching a decision. Chief Justice Fred Vinson was reluctant to end school segregation. "We can't close our eyes to the seriousness of the problem," he told his colleagues on the court. "We face the complete abolition of the public school system." Three other justices were leaning the same way as Vinson. That meant the court would overturn segregation—but only by a vote of five to four. Justice Felix Frankfurter, who was in the majority, knew a ruling by such a narrow margin would be difficult to enforce. He wanted it to be unanimous. To give himself more time to sway his colleagues, Frankfurter requested the new arguments. They were scheduled for the following December. But fate, perhaps, intervened. In September, Chief Justice Vinson dropped dead of a heart attack. "This is the first indication I have ever had that there is a God," said Frankfurter. Eisenhower replaced Vinson with Earl Warren, a liberal Republican. ("He's a Democrat and doesn't know it," Truman once said of Warren.) When it finally issued its ruling on May 17, 1954, the Supreme Court ended segregation by a vote of nine to zero.

Meanwhile, at the very moment the Trumans were speeding across Missouri, a less celebrated but still pivotal chapter in the civil rights saga was being written two states to the south. African Americans were boycotting the buses in Baton Rouge. By law, blacks and whites were required to sit in different sections on buses in Louisiana. When African American leaders in Baton Rouge complained to the city council that black people were often forced to stand on buses with empty seats in the white section, the council passed an ordinance allowing blacks to fill buses from the back to the front and whites from the front to the back, on a first-come, first-served basis. The bus drivers—all white, of course—didn't like the ordinance, because, they claimed, it "created incidents" in which "Negroes seated in the front seats of buses refused to move to make room for white passengers." On June 15, the drivers went on strike. They ended the strike three days later, when Louisiana Attorney General Fred LeBlanc issued an opinion saying the ordinance conflicted with state law and was invalid. LeBlanc's ruling angered African Americans in Baton Rouge, and that night a black organization in the city called the United Defense League (UDL) issued a statement urging blacks to boycott the buses.

The boycott began the next day, June 19, 1953 (the day Harry and Bess left Independence). The UDL organized alternate transportation for blacks, deploying a fleet of 150 vehicles "ranging from 20-year-old jalopies to spanking new Cadillacs," according to the *Baton Rouge State-Times*. Practically every black-owned car in the city displayed a small handmade sign in the window reading FREE RIDE. Black churches collected over six thousand dollars in donations to pay for gasoline and other expenses. Compliance with the boycott was nearly total. A local reporter who rode buses for three hours on the first day of the boycott saw just three black passengers.

On the night of June 20, a cross was burned on the lawn of Mt. Zion Baptist Church, a prominent African American church whose minister, T. J. Jemison, was the president of the UDL. A cross was also burned on the lawn of Jemison's home.

The privately owned bus company, meanwhile, was reporting daily losses of more than fifteen hundred dollars. "A continuation of this loss will ultimately mean that we will have to cease operations," the company's manager warned.

Behind the scenes, African American leaders, city officials, and the bus company were negotiating an end to the boycott. On June 24, the city council passed a new ordinance. It was a compromise of sorts: The first two seats on buses were reserved for whites, the last two for blacks. The remaining seats would be filled by blacks from the back and whites from the front.

At a rally attended by more than eight thousand black citizens that night, T. J. Jemison reluctantly announced that the UDL was calling off the boycott. He said the organization had accepted the new ordinance "under strong protest." "I'm not going to tell you you have to ride the buses," Jemison said. "And when I say put your cars up, I don't mean lock them up and throw away the keys. I want you to keep them handy."

The Baton Rouge bus boycott received scant attention in the mainstream media, but black newspapers covered it extensively. That's probably how a young African American minister named Martin Luther King Jr. heard about it. At the time King was newly married and studying for his doctorate in Boston. He would later call T. J. Jemison to discuss the tactics used in Baton Rouge—tactics that King himself would employ in Montgomery, Alabama, in 1955.

Harry and Bess Truman enjoyed discussing current events, so it is all but certain that, as they cruised along Highway 24 on that hot summer morning in 1953, their conversation turned at some point to the day's biggest news story: Julius and Ethel Rosenberg were scheduled to be executed later that day at Sing Sing, the maximum-security prison in upstate New York.

Three years and three days earlier—on June 16, 1950—Julius Rosenberg, an electrical engineer from New York City, had been arrested and charged with espionage. His wife, Ethel, was arrested a short time later. The couple was accused of giving nuclear secrets to the Soviet Union. That they had communist sympathies is undeniable—after all, they met in New York's Young Communist League—but the evidence against them was hardly overwhelming. At their trial the prosecution's star witness was Ethel's brother, David Greenglass, who had worked on the Manhattan Project. Greenglass had already confessed to spying for the Soviets and agreed to testify against his sister and her husband in exchange for a lighter sentence. On the witness stand Greenglass said he had passed secrets to the Rosenbergs, who in turn handed them over to the KGB. Greenglass would recant his testimony more than forty years later, saying he'd lied to protect his wife and children. He served just ten years in prison and now lives in New York under an assumed name. (In 2008, Morton Sobell, a friend of the Rosenbergs who was also convicted of espionage, told the *New York Times* that Julius Rosenberg was indeed a spy but that Ethel was not, though she knew what her husband was doing.)

A jury convicted the Rosenbergs on March 29, 1951. A week later, Judge Irving Kaufman sentenced them to die in the electric chair. The punishment struck many as unduly harsh, especially in light of David Greenglass's comparatively light sentence and the fact that the couple had two small children who would be orphaned by the executions. In late 1952, after their appeals had been exhausted, the Rosenbergs petitioned Harry Truman for clemency. Truman was not unsympathetic. "I've never really believed in capital punishment," he said. Earlier that year he had commuted the death sentence of a Puerto Rican nationalist who had attempted to assassinate him in 1950. But Truman was also sensitive to charges that he was "soft on communism." He had conspicuously avoided commenting on the Rosenberg case all along, and he had no desire to get mixed up in it at this late date in his presidency. So, this time at least, Harry Truman passed the buck. Rather feebly, he claimed the file was simply too thick to read before he vacated the White House. He left it up to his successor to determine the fate of the Rosenbergs. Dwight Eisenhower would announce his decision that afternoon. Without his intervention, the Rosenbergs would be dead by sundown—in deference to their faith, the executions had been scheduled to take place before the beginning of the Jewish Sabbath.

Around eleven-thirty, the Trumans reached Monroe City, Missouri, where they picked up Highway 36 and continued east toward Hannibal. This stretch of 36 is still a two-lane road—but not for long. The Missouri Department of Transportation is currently expanding the highway. Around the town of Ely, about halfway between Monroe City and Hannibal, I encountered backhoes, bulldozers, and graders readying the earth for three layers of macadam.

When the hundred-million-dollar project is finished, Highway 36 will be a four-lane road all the way across the state, from St. Joseph to Hannibal—the first four-lane, east–west highway in northern Missouri. It will draw vehicles from Interstate 70, which connects St. Louis and Kansas City, and undoubtedly change the character of this part of the state, as national chains move in to take advantage of the increased traffic. Critics decry such "progress," but Harry Truman would love it. In fact, if he saw this road being built today, he'd pull over and watch, because roads were in his blood.

His father, John Truman, was a part-time road overseer, responsible for maintaining the roads in the southern part of Washington Township, Missouri. It was while attempting to move a large boulder from a road one day that John Truman suffered the hernia that ultimately ended his life.

While serving in France during World War I, Harry Truman was deeply impressed by that country's roads. "The French know how to build roads and also how to keep them up," he wrote in a letter to Bess. "They are just like a billiard table."

In 1922, Truman made road improvements the central theme of his first campaign for Jackson County judge. He won, and oversaw the most ambitious road-building program ever undertaken in the county. His approach was "hands on." He personally inspected roads and bridges in the county, and studied various building techniques. He even became a member of the American Road Builders Association. His knowledge deeply impressed Tom Veatch, who oversaw road construction in the county. "He was unusually well informed on the whole subject," remembered Veatch. "He was a 'road scholar'—not a 'Rhodes scholar,' but a 'road scholar.' He really knew roads."

The roads were built on time and under budget.

In 1926, Truman became the president of the National Old Trails Road Association, a group that promoted the construction of a transcontinental road from Baltimore to Los Angeles, mainly along the route of historic trails, including the National Road and the Santa Fe Trail. Two years later, the group decided to erect identical statues honoring pioneer women in each of the twelve states through which the hypothetical road passed. It was a project close to Truman's heart. Both his grandmothers had made the arduous trek from Kentucky to western Missouri in the 1840s. Said Truman of the female pioneers, "They were just as brave or braver than their men because, in many cases, they went with sad hearts and trembling bodies. They went, however, and endured every hardship that befalls a pioneer." Known as the "Madonna of the Trail," each statue stood ten feet tall and weighed five tons. It depicted a bonneted woman holding a baby in her left arm and a rifle in her right hand, a child clinging to her skirt. Truman traveled the country scouting out locations for the statues. "This is almost like campaigning for President," he wrote Bess from Kansas, "except that the people are making promises to me instead of the other way around." The twelve statues were dedicated in 1928 and 1929. Truman attended several of the dedication ceremonies. Even after he became president of the United States, Truman's name was still listed as president of the National Old Trails Road Association on the group's letterhead.

A few months after he left the White House, Harry spotted a crew working on a road near his home in Independence one day. He went down to take a look.

"A shovel (automatic) and a drag line were working as well as some laboring men digging in the old fashioned way," he wrote in his diary. "The boss or the contractor was looking on and I asked him if he didn't need a good straw boss. He took a look at me and then watched the work a while and then took another look and broke out in a broad smile and said, 'Oh yes! You *are* out of a job, aren't you.'"

When he woke up on Friday, June 19, 1953, Sylvester "Bud" Toben had no idea he would meet a former president of the United States that day. He only knew that it was going to be hot out—very hot—which meant business would be brisk at Bud's Golden Cream, his soft-serve ice-cream stand at the junction of Highways 36 and 61 on the western edge of Hannibal. Bud served five-cent cones in three flavors: vanilla, chocolate, and the flavor of the day (usually strawberry). His specialty was a giant banana split called the Pig's Dinner, which he sold for sixty-nine cents. If you finished it, Bud gave you a little yellow and red button that said, "I made a pig of myself at Bud's." It was, quite literally, a nickel-and-dime operation, but Toben excelled at it. The stand opened every year on March 19—St. Joseph's Day; Bud was a good Catholic—and closed on Christmas Eve. After Thanksgiving Toben sold Christmas trees, too.

To help him out at the stand that hot June day, Toben enlisted the aid of his daughter, Toni. Toni spent much of her summers "waiting on trade" at one of the stand's two windows, watching cars pull in and out of the tiny parking lot all day. As a result, she knew more about automobiles than the average twelve-year-old girl. So she was suitably impressed when, a little after noon, a shiny black car with chrome-wire wheels pulled up to the stand. "That Chrysler was beautiful," Toni remembered. "That's what impressed me when it pulled in, because there were very few people who had a Chrysler like that."

When the driver emerged from the car, Toni immediately recognized him as Harry Truman.

Harry went around to the other side of the car and opened the door for Bess. The couple then began walking to Osborne's Café, a diner next door to Bud's. Toni knew her father didn't like Osborne's customers using his lot.

"Dad," the twelve-year-old shouted, "Harry Truman's out in front. Do you want me to have him move his car?" ~~Bud Toben didn't make him move his car.~~

He thought she was mistaken, of course, but when Bud looked for himself, he saw that it was indeed Harry Truman.

Bud told Toni to call her sister, nineteen-year-old Mary—and to tell her to bring a camera.

Bud went outside and introduced himself to the Trumans. The two men talked for a few minutes about the weather, with Harry claiming,

"I've seen it hotter." Truman was a master of small talk. He could chat with anyone about anything. It was a gift, and, according to journalist Charles Robbins, it was part of his "humanness." "[H]e went out of his way to treat others not as 'bodies' or digits but as fellow human beings," Robbins wrote.

Mary arrived with her little Kodak Brownie camera. She asked Harry if she could take a picture of him. Truman struck a deal with her: he told her she could take a picture after he and Bess finished lunch—but only if she promised not to tell anybody else they were in town. Mary agreed, and the Trumans went into Osborne's.

Bud Toben didn't make them move their car.

Inside the diner, Harry and Bess seated themselves. Amid the din of the lunchtime rush, with waitresses harried and dishes clanging, nobody gave them a second glance. They were, by all appearances, a perfectly ordinary,

Harry standing next to his New Yorker in the parking lot of Bud's Golden Cream in Hannibal, Missouri, June 19, 1953.

middle-aged couple. They ordered fruit plates and iced tea and enjoyed their lunch in complete anonymity. "We thought we were getting by big as an unknown traveling couple," Harry wrote. But, just as they got up to pay their bill, a voice shouted from across the room: "Why, there's Judge Truman!" An old Marion County judge had recognized Harry Truman—not as a former president, but from his days on the Jackson County bench thirty years earlier. "The incog[nito] was off," Truman wrote, "and then every waitress and all the customers had to shake hands and have autographs."

"They seemed to be having a good time," John Osborne, the owner of the diner, told a local newspaper. "They were taking their time." Eventually the couple escaped to the parking lot in front of Bud's Golden Cream, where Mary Toben waited with her camera. She snapped a picture of the ex-president and her father engaged in more small talk, Truman in his white suit, Bud Toben in a white T-shirt and dungarees.

After he finished chatting with Toben, Truman slid behind the wheel of the Chrysler and, with a wave, he and Bess pulled away from Bud's Golden Cream. They continued east on Highway 36, which ran right through the middle of Hannibal.

If the Trumans visited Hannibal today, they'd get lost. Highway 36 has been rerouted north around the town. A Dairy Queen opened just up the street from Bud's in the early 1970s, and Toben finally closed his stand in 1974. He took out an ad in the local paper to mark the occasion. "We will discontinue operations . . . after 25 short, successful seasons," it read. "These have been, indeed, most enjoyable years for us. . . . Our Christmas Tree Services will be taken over by the Optimist Club."

A KFC now stands where Bud's once stood.

Osborne's Café went out of business around the same time as Bud's. It's been replaced by an Italian restaurant called Cassano's.

Passing through Hannibal in 1953, at the corner of Third and Hill, Harry and Bess would have seen on their right a simple, white, two-story house—a house that still stands there today. It was the boyhood home of perhaps the only Missourian more famous than Harry Truman himself: Samuel Langhorne Clemens, better known as Mark Twain.

He never went to college, but Harry Truman was as well read as any president. "From the time I was ten years old," he wrote, "I had spent all my idle hours reading." His reading list is impressive, to say the least: Plutarch, Dickens, George Eliot, William Makepeace Thackeray, every Shakespeare play and sonnet, the Koran. But his favorite author, his "patron saint" of literature, was Mark Twain. One of Truman's prized possessions was a twenty-five-volume set of Twain's works, which he bought for twenty-five dollars in 1910—the year Truman turned twenty-six and the year Twain died at seventy-four. As president, Truman kept a framed copy of his favorite Twain quote on his desk in the Oval Office: "Always do right! This will gratify some people and astonish the rest." In Twain's books, however, Truman heard no echoes of his own youth in Missouri. Frail and bespectacled as a child, he never identified with Huck Finn or Tom Sawyer. "I wasn't in that class," he told an interviewer once. "I was kind of a sissy growing up."

As he drove by Twain's house that day, Harry probably contemplated the author's role in another president's life. It was Twain who helped Ulysses S. Grant, penniless and near death from cancer of the throat, complete his memoirs. It has been suggested that Twain even ghostwrote some of the memoirs, which were a critical and commercial triumph. Truman's own memoirs—three hundred thousand words—were due to be delivered to Doubleday in two years, on June 30, 1955. Harry planned to start working on them in earnest as soon as he got back home. The task weighed heavy on his mind. By his own admission, he was no writer.

How he must have wished old Sam Clemens were still around to help him.

Shortly after they passed Twain's boyhood home, the Trumans crossed the Mississippi—*the* river, as Harry called it—and entered Illinois. They kept cruising eastbound on Highway 36, their black Chrysler slicing through waves of green cornfields at precisely fifty-five miles per hour. It was about one o'clock now, and the heat was positively stifling. A few miles east of the town of Jacksonville, they crossed the ninetieth meridian—one-quarter of the way around the world, as a road sign notes today.

Around here, in the middle of nowhere, the car radio crackled with the news: President Eisenhower had denied Julius and Ethel Rosenberg's appeal for clemency. "The execution of two human beings is a grave matter," Ike announced. "But even graver is the thought of the millions of dead whose deaths may be directly attributable to what these spies have done." The Rosenberg children, ten-year-old Michael and six-year-old Robert, were staying with friends of their parents at the time. Michael was watching his favorite baseball team, the Yankees, play the Tigers on TV when the game was interrupted by a bulletin announcing Eisenhower's decision. "That was their last chance," the youngster whispered.

4

Decatur, Illinois,
June 19–20, 1953

About two hours after leaving Hannibal, the Trumans passed through Springfield, the capital of Illinois and the home of Abraham Lincoln. Harry saw a lot of himself in Old Abe, who was one of only two Republican presidents he admired. (Teddy Roosevelt was the other.) "Lincoln," Harry wrote, "set an example that a man who has the ability can be president of the United States no matter what his background is."

Harry and Bess drove past the soaring, silver-domed statehouse, where statues of Lincoln and Stephen A. Douglas grace the grounds. The statues were financed by the state legislature through the same appropriation in 1913 and dedicated on the same day in 1918. The Lincoln statue cost fifty thousand dollars—twice as much as the Douglas statue. Of course, Lincoln was at least a foot taller than Douglas, who was known as the "Little Giant."

In 1858, Douglas defeated Lincoln for a seat in the U.S. Senate. Two years later, Douglas, running as the Northern Democratic candidate for president, faced Lincoln again. (Southern Democrats ran their own candidate, John C. Breckinridge.) Douglas received nearly 1.4 million votes in that contest but lost, of course. Staunchly pro-Union, he became an unlikely ally of Lincoln's after the election. Douglas attended Lincoln's inauguration, and stunned the audience when he took Lincoln's hat and "held it like an attendant" while Lincoln delivered his inaugural address. (Hats have clearly played an important but underappreciated role in presidential inaugurations.)

Even if he'd won the election, Douglas's presidency would have been inconsequential. He contracted typhoid fever and died on June 3, 1861— less than three months after Lincoln took office. He was forty-eight.

In all probability, it was not Stephen A. Douglas but rather a different failed Democratic presidential candidate who was on Harry Truman's mind as he drove through Springfield that day. Less than a year earlier, Democrats had nominated Illinois Governor Adlai Stevenson for president. It was a choice that Truman supported. "You are a brave man," he wrote Stevenson shortly after the convention. "If it is worth anything, you have my wholehearted support and cooperation."

But almost from the moment he was nominated, Stevenson did everything he could to distance himself from Truman, whose popularity was at rock bottom. Stevenson replaced Truman's head of the Democratic National Committee, Frank McKinney, with his own man, and he moved the party's headquarters from Washington to Springfield, where he lived in the governor's mansion. He wanted to "disown any connection with the Truman administration," according to Matthew Connelly, one of Truman's aides. "Stevenson actually was running against Truman. He did not want to get involved with any aspect of the Truman administration."

Naturally, this irritated Truman. In another longhand spasm, a letter he wrote to Stevenson but never sent, Truman said he had "come to the conclusion that you are embarrassed by having the President of the United

States in your corner." In another unsent letter to Stevenson, Truman wrote, "Cowfever could not have treated me any more shabbily than you have."

Still, Truman was nothing if not a loyal Democrat, and he campaigned hard for Stevenson, even harder, some said, than he'd campaigned for himself four years earlier. It was another exhausting whistle-stop campaign, with Truman crisscrossing the country in the *Ferdinand Magellan*. (Stevenson campaigned by airplane.) "He . . . put everything he had into trying to help Stevenson," said Matthew Connelly. But it was for naught. Eisenhower carried thirty-nine of the forty-eight states. He even won Illinois and Missouri.

Springfield held no special place in Harry Truman's heart.

The Trumans didn't stop in Springfield, but I did. I wanted to visit the Abraham Lincoln Presidential Library and Museum, a ninety-million-dollar complex in downtown Springfield that opened in 2005. Unlike most other presidential libraries, it is not run by the National Archives. Instead, the state of Illinois runs it.

With Harry's library, the museum component was practically an afterthought. The original design included just two main exhibit rooms. When it was proposed that one of the rooms be dedicated to telling the story of Truman's life, the former president vetoed the idea. As Wayne Grover, the head of the National Archives, explained at the time, "Mr. Truman . . . would be offended by anything that looked too much like an advertisement for him." In fact, the museum would not include a comprehensive exhibit on Truman's life until the late 1990s.

The Lincoln Library, on the other hand, suffers no shortage of exhibits dedicated to its namesake. The museum, which was designed by HOK, the same architectural firm that designs "retro" ballparks like Baltimore's Camden Yards, has been described as "cutting edge" and "state of the art." It features life-size replicas of Lincoln's boyhood home (a log cabin, of course), his law office in Springfield (which is kind of superfluous, since the real thing is just a few blocks away), his White House cabinet room, his box at Ford's Theater, even his funeral cortege. Each of these replicas is inhabited by mannequins that are very lifelike (except when deathlike is more appropriate) and a little creepy. Gathered around the table in the cabinet room were Lincoln, seven members of his cabinet—and one real live human being dressed in period costume. He gave me quite a start when he said hello.

The museum unabashedly attempts to be hip. The 1860 election is covered by a videotaped MSNBC news report in a room made to look like a modern TV control room. Of course, it's all very interactive as well. One wall is completely covered with Civil War–era photographs. The corresponding captions can only be retrieved by touching a computer screen.

The museum does have some cool stuff: a signed copy of the Thirteenth Amendment, a ticket to Lincoln's second inaugural, a schoolbook containing the earliest known example of his handwriting, a photograph of Fido, the family dog in Springfield. But on the whole it seemed too flashy, designed less to educate or entertain than to simply keep visitors from being bored.

Personally, I like my museums the same way I like my martinis: very dry. Apparently I'm not alone. Historian John Y. Simon has dismissed the Lincoln Museum as "Six Flags over Lincoln" or "Lincolnland." It's a far cry from the "research center" that Harry Truman envisioned for his own library. Yet it has proved immensely popular. The museum welcomed its one millionth visitor in 2007, less than two years after it opened, and (it claims) faster than any other presidential museum. Take that, Harry!

Around five o'clock the Trumans pulled into a Shell station on the outskirts of Decatur, Illinois. Harry asked the attendant to fill the tank. Truman had stopped at this particular station many times back when he was in the Senate. "The old man"—the attendant—"kept looking at me as he filled up the gas tank," Truman recalled. "Finally he asked me if I was Senator Truman. I admitted the charge."

Harry paid the attendant. Then Bess carefully recorded the purchase on the small card Harry kept in the glove compartment to track the car's mileage. It would become something of a ritual on the trip, a small ceremony observed at every service station.

Harry's interest in fuel efficiency was largely financial. Like most Americans, he was concerned about skyrocketing gas prices. Why, just that day, Standard Oil had hiked prices a penny a gallon—to 27.1 cents. The company blamed the increase on rising crude oil prices, which were approaching three dollars a barrel. On Capitol Hill, though, some lawmakers accused the oil companies of collusion and price gouging. The House Commerce Committee had launched an investigation.

Before pulling away from the station, Truman asked the attendant to recommend a good motel in town. "We'd never stayed at one," Truman later explained, "and we wanted to try it out and see if we liked it." It would also save them a little money. A night in a motel only cost about five bucks.

The attendant recommended the Parkview Motel and gave Harry directions. Then, as soon as the Trumans were gone, he called the local newspapers.

The Parkview was quiet when Harry and Bess pulled up. The clerk didn't even recognize them when they checked in. But within minutes the motel's parking lot swarmed with reporters, photographers, and curious locals. Harry, who had "expected to enjoy the pleasures of traveling incognito," was dismayed by the carnivalesque atmosphere. It was just what his friends had warned him would happen.

When Decatur Police Chief Glenn Kerwin learned the former president and first lady were traveling by themselves—without even a single bodyguard—he was aghast. What if something happened to them while they were in his jurisdiction? Kerwin immediately dispatched two officers, Francis Hartnett and Horace Hoff, to the Parkview. The Trumans, Kerwin ordered, were to be shadowed around the clock until they left the city. "I don't need any protection," Harry pleaded when Hartnett and Hoff

Harry unloading luggage from his car outside the Parkview Motel, Decatur, Illinois, June 19, 1953. Harry rejected the suggestion that he be photographed reclined in an easy chair with Bess placing a pillow under his head.

showed up at his motel door. But orders were orders. The former commander in chief was outranked by Chief Kerwin. The cops stayed.

Harry signed a few autographs in the parking lot and sent a note to a child who was ill at the motel. He agreed to be photographed for the papers, as long as the pictures wouldn't appear until the next day—after he and Bess had left town. One photographer suggested the Trumans pose in their room, with Bess placing a pillow under Harry's head while he reclined in an easy chair. Harry vetoed that idea, offering to be photographed taking luggage out of the trunk of his Chrysler instead. Then he asked everybody to back off. He and Bess were exhausted from the long drive in the heat, he explained. They had traveled 350 miles in temperatures exceeding 100 degrees. Now they were going to lie down and take a nap.

By the 1920s it was possible for the first time to drive an automobile long distances over paved roads. But if you did, you had to be prepared to rough it. Hotels were concentrated in city centers, usually around train terminals. Outside urban areas just about the only accommodations available to travelers were squalid campgrounds or flophouses. Then, in 1925, an architect named Arthur Heinman opened what he called a "mo-tel"—a motor hotel—along Highway 101 in San Luis Obispo, California, about halfway between Los Angeles and San Francisco. Heinman's motel was the first in the world. It consisted of a series of two-room bungalows with attached garages that rented for $1.25 a night. The concept proved nearly as popular as the automobile itself, and soon motels of all shapes and sizes were springing up along roadsides from coast to coast. Even the Depression couldn't stem the tide. In 1933, according to *The Architectural Record*, the construction of motels was "the single growing and highly active division of the building industry." By 1940 there were twenty thousand motels in the United States. Nearly all were family-owned, with spectacular neon signs and quirky names like the Linger Longer, the It'll Do, the Close-Inn, and the Aut-O-Tel. To attract guests, some incorporated kitschy elements of popular culture into their design, such as giant replicas of teepees or spaceships. No two motels were exactly alike.

It wasn't just weary travelers who frequented motels. Their remoteness and the relative anonymity they afforded made them perfect for illicit assignations. Bonnie and Clyde hid out in motels. So did John Dillinger. In 1940, FBI director J. Edgar Hoover denounced motels as "camps of crime . . . a new home of disease, bribery, corruption, crookedness, rape, white slavery, thievery, and murder." But the negative publicity didn't hurt business. Motels continued to proliferate after World War II. By 1960 there were sixty thousand. But by then the era of the independent, family-owned motel was already fading.

In the summer of 1951, a Memphis businessman named Kemmons Wilson, his wife, and their five children took a family vacation to Washington. Along the way they stayed in motels, most of which Wilson found grossly inadequate—or just plain gross. Many were dirty. None had air-conditioning. And all imposed a surcharge of two dollars per child, a practice that, for obvious reasons, Wilson resented. "My six-dollar room became a sixteen-dollar room," he remembered. "I told my wife that wasn't fair. I didn't take many vacations, but as I took this one, I realized how many families there were taking vacations and how they needed a nice place they could stay." The motel business, Wilson determined, was "the greatest untouched industry in America."

As soon as he got back to Memphis, Wilson hired an architect to design a new kind of motel. Every room would have air-conditioning, a television set, and a telephone. There would be a swimming pool, vending machines, and free ice. And children under twelve could stay in their parents' room for free.

Wilson didn't know what to call his new motel, so his architect suggested the name of a popular Bing Crosby movie: *Holiday Inn*. (Wilson would eventually be required to pay royalties to Irving Berlin, the composer of the movie's title song.)

In 1952, the year after Kemmons Wilson's disappointing family vacation, the first Holiday Inn opened along a busy stretch of Highway 70 outside Memphis. The gaudy, fifty-three-foot green and yellow sign out front was designed by Wilson himself.

Wilson's goal was to build four hundred Holiday Inns scattered across the country, all exactly alike, none more than a day's drive from another. Within twenty years there were more than one thousand. Clustered around them were countless other motel chains, not to mention fast-food restaurants, all piggybacking on Wilson's phenomenal success.

In 1972 Kemmons Wilson was on the cover of *Time* magazine. "Wilson," said *Time*, "has transformed the motel from the old wayside fleabag into the most popular home away from home."

And so it came to pass that idiosyncratic, independently owned motels were replaced by sterile corporate cookie cutters where, in Kemmons Wilson's opinion, the best surprise is no surprise. In 1962 less than 2 percent of all motels were affiliated with a national chain. Today more than 70 percent are.

The Parkview, the motel where the Trumans stayed in Decatur, is still around. Only now it's a prison. The Illinois Department of Corrections bought the motel in the late 1970s and converted it into a correctional facility for work-release inmates. Officially known as the Decatur Adult Transition Center, or ATC, it houses more than a hundred convicted felons, all male, completing the last three to twenty-four months of their sentences. Security, compared to, say, a maximum-security prison, is light. The "residents" (as they are known in DOC parlance) are permitted to leave the facility during the day to work or attend adult education classes.

Tucked behind a thick stand of pine trees on the corner of 22nd and Pershing, the Decatur ATC still looks like a motel, a long, straight, single-story building—the classic "I" shape—with a reception area in the middle. A tired traveler today could be forgiven for mistaking it for a working motel—until reading the sign on the door to the office:

> ALL PERSONS, VEHICLES AND OTHER PROPERTY
> ENTERING OR LEAVING THIS FACILITY AND ITS
> GROUNDS ARE SUBJECT TO SEARCH AT ANY TIME.
> BY ENTERING PRISON PROPERTY YOU WILL BE
> DEEMED TO CONSENT TO SEARCH. BRINGING
> CONTRABAND INTO A PENAL INSTITUTION IS A FELONY.

Like a Holiday Inn, the best surprise here is no surprise. And they most definitely will leave the light on for you.

I wanted to take some pictures of the building but thought it wise to get permission first. I went inside and explained to the guard at the front desk that I was writing a book about a road trip that Harry and Bess Truman took in the summer of 1953 and I . . .

He cut me off with a wave of his hand. "You'll need to talk to the warden," he said. He took my driver's license and had me sign a logbook. I was given a badge (but was spared the search). Then I was escorted to the warden's office, which was an old motel room, complete with a full bathroom. The burly warden was sitting behind a desk, holding a cell phone to one ear and a landline handset to the other. He looked harried. On his desk was a copy of *Law Enforcement Journal* ("Don't Be Afraid to Pull the Trigger," "Tasers Getting a Bad Rap").

I took a seat and put my homemade business card on the desk in front of him. After he hung up the phones, he asked me what I wanted. No introductions, no pleasantries. He wasn't exactly gruff, but he was all business. I gave him a very condensed version of my spiel: Trumans took a road trip, stayed here when it used to be a motel, can I take pictures? He evinced no interest in the story whatsoever. He just picked up the phone (landline) and called a DOC flack in Springfield. This led to another phone call, and another, before he finally got an answer: yes, I could take pictures, but only of the outside of the building, and I couldn't photograph any inmates or staff—no pictures of people. I said that was fine with me, thanked him for his time, and hightailed it out of his office.

I went back to the front desk to drop off my badge. The guard who'd been there earlier was gone. In his place was a young woman with dark curly hair and a wide red-lipped smile. She laughed when I told her why I was there. When I said it was ironic that an inmate now slept in the same room that Harry and Bess Truman once slept in, she corrected me: "No, *three* inmates do!" Like many American prisons, this one is overcrowded: it is about 25 percent over capacity.

The warden joined us, suddenly looking much more relaxed. He chatted a bit about the facility, the goal of which, he explained, is to help inmates "successfully reintegrate into the community." Besides working or going to school, they are required to attend substance abuse treatment programs if necessary. A lot of people in Decatur were concerned when the ATC opened in 1979. But the facility has proven to be a good neighbor. Inmates set up and take down the stages at the city's annual street festival. They pick up trash along the streets. They participate in Operation Green Thumb, a gardening program. They raise money for the Muscular

Dystrophy Association and help out at the city's annual Christmas party. They prepare and serve a Thanksgiving dinner for the needy.

Since they are so close to their freedom, the inmates at the Decatur ATC have a strong incentive to behave, yet a quarter of them are returned to higher-security prisons for disciplinary reasons. Still, this is one of the safest prisons in Illinois, if not the country. In 2003, for example, there were no assaults reported at the facility.

It would have been nice to rest my head where the Trumans rested theirs in Decatur, but, absent the commission of a felony, that wasn't feasible, so I found the next closest motel. It was less than a mile up 22nd Street. It was called the Tri-Manor.

Opened in the early 1950s, the Tri-Manor is a vestige of the golden days of motels. On its roof is a giant red neon sign that reads, simply, MOTEL. But the sign doesn't work. At night not a single letter is lighted. The Tri-Manor has seen better days, much like Decatur itself, a city named after a War of 1812 hero who was mortally wounded in a duel. As he lay dying, Stephen Decatur is said to have cried out, "I did not know that any man could suffer such pain!" His namesake city could say much the same thing about itself.

When the Trumans came here in 1953, Decatur was a thriving agricultural center, the self-proclaimed "Soybean Capital of the World," home of the food-processing giants Archer Daniels Midland and A. E. Staley. The city also had a broad manufacturing base. General Electric made television sets here, and a host of smaller companies produced everything from pumps and valves to potato chips. In 1954 Caterpillar opened a heavy-equipment factory on the edge of town, and, nine years later, Firestone began making tires here.

But time was not kind to Decatur. The global economy changed. Free-trade agreements were signed. Companies began to cut jobs, close, or move. Labor strife ensued. At one point in 1994, more than 6 percent of the city's workforce was either on strike or locked out as the result of separate disputes at Bridgestone/Firestone, Caterpillar, and Staley. Later that year, ADM was implicated in a global price-fixing scandal. In 1996 two tornadoes hit the city within twenty-four hours. In 2001 Bridgestone/Firestone announced it was closing its Decatur plant.

"People who live in small towns, or even medium-sized ones, tend to be pleasantly surprised when they venture out of state and encounter big-city dwellers who can summon salient facts about the travelers' home towns," Mark Singer wrote in a *New Yorker* profile of the city in 2000. "Residents of Decatur, Illinois, though, have learned not to get all that thrilled."

When the Trumans were here, Decatur was a Norman Rockwell town. Now it feels more like Norman Bates. Which brings me back to my motel.

When I checked into the Tri-Manor, the manager, a short, plump woman with a large scab on her face, told me it was a good thing I hadn't come two years earlier. "Back then it was all druggies and hos," she said. Camps of crime, indeed. "But," she hastened to reassure me, "we've cleaned up since then."

My room at the Tri-Manor was anything but manorial. It reeked of stale cigarette smoke. The door had no deadbolt or chain, just a simple lock in the knob. It didn't shut tightly either. This I discovered in the middle of the night, when the wind blew it open, scaring me senseless. The bathroom door had a large hole at the bottom, apparently from a kick. The furnishings were worn, and the walls were bare and thin. I wouldn't have wanted to shine a black light on the bedspread for all the money in the world. And the color on my TV was off: all the people were purple. At $37.85 a night, the room seemed radically overpriced.

But there was also something appealing about it, in that it was refreshingly un-corporate. This was how motel rooms might have looked before Kemmons Wilson took the element of surprise out of the roadside lodging business. This was how Harry and Bess's room might have looked.

But something tells me the Tri-Manor won't be welcoming any ex-presidents any time soon.

While the Trumans napped at the Parkview Motel in the early evening hours of June 19, 1953, Julius and Ethel Rosenberg were executed at

Sing Sing. Julius went first. He was strapped into the electric chair at 7:04 Eastern time. The current was applied, and, for fifteen seconds, 2,450 volts of electricity passed through his body. At 7:06 he was pronounced dead. Just five minutes later, Ethel was led into the death chamber. She hadn't been told of her husband's execution, but she must have known: the unmistakable stench of his charred flesh was still heavy in the air.

Ethel did not die as easily as Julius. She was a short woman, and the chair, known as Old Sparky, was built for an average-sized man. The helmet and straps were too large for her, so the electrodes, apparently, made poor contact with her body. It took three applications of current over five minutes to kill her. Witnesses reported seeing smoke rising from her head. At 7:16 she was finally pronounced dead. Fifteen minutes later, the last rays of the setting sun disappeared behind the horizon at Sing Sing, signaling the beginning of the Sabbath. The Rosenbergs remain the only American civilians ever executed for espionage. For fear of being ostracized, no close relatives were willing to take in Michael and Robert Rosenberg. After a stint in an orphanage, the children were adopted by Abel and Anne Meeropol. Abel Meeropol was a liberal activist and songwriter who, under the pseudonym Lewis Allen, wrote "Strange Fruit," the classic anti-lynching anthem made famous by Billie Holiday.

About forty-five minutes after Ethel Rosenberg was pronounced dead, Harry and Bess Truman emerged from their motel room, appearing, according to one account, "much refreshed." The reporters camped outside his door asked the former president to comment on the executions. His reply was enigmatic: "My actions in the Rosenberg case speak for themselves." In fact, Harry Truman had taken no actions in the case.

In any event, it was time for dinner. Harry and Bess drove to Grove's, a popular diner in a long, low-slung building on the north side of Decatur. A police car led the way, and several cars filled with reporters and gawkers followed the Trumans, forming an impromptu motorcade. It was not the kind of inconspicuous outing that Harry had hoped for.

The diner fell silent when the Trumans entered. Every eye in the place followed them as they were seated at a table with their unwanted body-guards, Francis Hartnett and Horace Hoff. Harry ordered roast beef, pota-toes, and salad. Bess ordered the same thing. They ate under the constant gaze of their fellow diners, which seemed to make Bess, at least, uncom-fortable. "Mrs. Truman spoke in low tones to her husband during their meal," reported the appropriately named Harold Stalker in the *Decatur Herald*. "[She] glanced around occasionally when she noticed that they were attracting attention in the café." They didn't stay for dessert. The bill came to $1.72. Harry also picked up the tab for the two cops. As Truman walked back to his car, Stalker attempted to interview him but was cut off. "There's nothing to be said of importance anyway right now," Truman snapped, clearly growing a little weary of the constant attention in Decatur.

Grove's is gone, but another restaurant now stands in its place—a McDonald's. Nothing distinguishes it from the other thirty thousand McDonald's in the world. I stopped in for a cup of coffee, taking a seat in a booth with my copy of that day's *Decatur Herald & Review* ("Decatur Man Breaks Record for Weight Lifted at His Age"). In the booth behind me sat a woman roughly the same age Bess was when she and Harry came to this very spot more than fifty years earlier. The woman was sitting alone, talk-ing on a cell phone—not in the low tones of Bess, but very loudly—about a doctor's appointment she'd had that morning. "They found another lump below my thyroid," she announced, oblivious to her fellow diners. "But he don't think it's cancer 'cause it's not hard."

It made me wonder what Harry Truman would think of cell phones. A nineteenth-century man stuck in the twentieth, Harry was a bit of a Luddite. He didn't like using the telephone. He wrote letters instead. And he wrote them in longhand, with a distinctive slashing script. Even the typewriter was a technology he could not bring himself to adopt.

The cell phone would not be suited to Harry's personality. He was preternaturally affable and thrived on human interaction. He liked being around people. The human race, he once said, was an "excellent outfit." Whether playing poker with his cronies or riding in the car with Bess, conversation—face to face—was his raison d'etre. A cell phone isolates its user from those around him. That's why people on cell phones are comfortable discussing, for example, the explicit details of a doctor's appointment in a roomful of total strangers. They feel like they're alone.

I think it's safe to assume that Harry Truman would detest cell phones.

(On a subsequent visit to Decatur, I noticed that the McDonald's had been torn down and was being replaced by another McDonald's, presumably bigger and better than the old one.)

After dinner, the Trumans returned to the Parkview and went to bed.

Later that night, Floyd Zerfowski, a thirty-three-year-old Decatur police officer, reported for work at eleven o'clock as usual. But when he got to the station, he received an unusual assignment: he was to spend the night protecting Harry and Bess Truman. He and another officer, Ray Rex, were sent to the Parkview to relieve Francis Hartnett and Horace Hoff.

It was a boring assignment.

"We got out there and they were already in bed." Zerfowski said of the pointless vigil. "We sat out in front of his room all night long. We found some lawn chairs and we sat out there and watched his motel door. It was sort of amusing. That was an easy job!"

Of the four cops assigned to Harry Truman's unwanted security detail in Decatur, Zerfowski is the last survivor. Now in his late eighties, he lives alone in a tidy ranch house in a forty-year-old subdivision on the edge of town. His only companion is a police scanner, which he listens to all day. Thin and balding, he wears oversized eyeglasses that make him look a little owlish. In preparation for my visit, he had pulled out an old scrapbook filled with yellowed newspaper clippings documenting his law enforcement career.

Zerfowski joined the Decatur Police Department in 1949. Assigned to the graveyard shift, he walked different beats all over the city. "Whenever somebody was off, I usually worked their beat," he explained. "I got to know Decatur pretty well." Zerfowski said there wasn't much crime in Decatur back then, but in his rookie year he was forced to fire his gun for the only time in his career. He interrupted a burglary in progress at a union hall. The burglar attacked him with a pipe. Floyd got off two shots, one of which pierced the burglar's heart, killing him instantly. An inquest ruled the shooting justified.

Floyd retired from the police force in 1970 and went to work as a maintenance man for the Decatur school district so he could qualify for Social Security. He retired for good in 1986. His wife died suddenly of a brain aneurism just a year later.

After all those years of walking a beat, Floyd found it impossible to stop walking in retirement. Some days he would put in as many as fifteen miles inside the Northgate Mall, becoming a familiar and popular fixture among shoppers and workers there. When I first spoke with him in late 2006, however, he was recovering from a broken hip and feared his mall-walking days were over. "Now I just go there and drink coffee," he said a little sadly at the time. But when I visited him a year later, he was feeling much better, and was back up to a mile a day at the mall. "I plan on living to be a hundred," he told me.

The Trumans came out of their room at seven the next morning. Harry presented Floyd and his partner mechanical pencils bearing his name and picture—his usual token of appreciation. "Here's a little gift to remember me by," he told them. (Zerfowski saved his pencil and proudly showed it to me when I visited him.)

Then, once again accompanied by their unwanted entourage of cops and reporters, Harry and Bess went back to Grove's for breakfast. "When he looked up and I saw who it was I almost dropped dead," said their waitress, Helen Werve. "He was very pleasant and said everybody he had met on the way had been very nice." Bess, she remembered, "had her hair all fixed real pretty." Harry ordered scrambled eggs and sausage, Bess a plain omelet. Once again, Harry picked up the tab for his two bodyguards. The total bill came to $3.85. He left a thirty-cent tip and autographed Werve's checkbook. "Truman 10-Per Cent Tipper" read a headline in that afternoon's *Decatur Review*.

Harry and Bess returned to the Parkview to pack their car. Around eight o'clock, they checked out. Floyd Zerfowski and Ray Rex escorted the couple to the Decatur city limits, at which point Chief Kerwin must have breathed a huge sigh of relief. Harry and Bess got back on Highway 36, which they would take to Indianapolis.

That day, a wire-service photograph of Harry unpacking the trunk of his car at the Parkview appeared in hundreds of newspapers nationwide. The caption explained that the Trumans were "motoring leisurely east-ward." For the first time, Americans learned just what their former president was up to. He was doing exactly what many of them did every summer. He was taking a road trip.

5

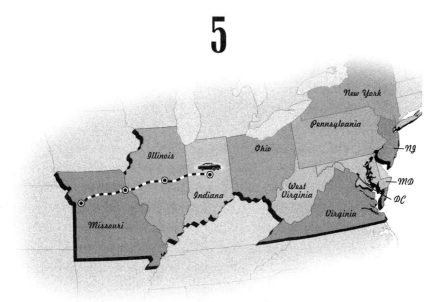

Indianapolis, Indiana,
June 20, 1953

East of Decatur, Highway 36 passes through some serious farmland, land that is far too valuable to be covered with structures. It is striking just how few houses there are. The soil is dark, almost black, too fertile to waste on livestock, so there are no animals here, either. Driving across east-central Illinois in late June is like sailing across an ocean of soybeans and corn. The landscape is flat and utterly treeless. The road is impossibly straight. If my car (well, my dad's car, actually) had been properly aligned, I could have put it on cruise control and taken a nap.

If anything, this place looks even more rural than it did when Harry and Bess passed through in 1953. Back then there were more than 164,000 farms in Illinois. Today there are half that number, though the amount of land being farmed is nearly the same. Chalk it up to technology. Modern machinery has made farming unthinkably productive. GPS guidance systems on tractors prevent overlap when plowing, planting, and harvesting, dramatically increasing efficiency. In 1990 one farm could feed 129 people. Today, one farm can feed 144. When farmers retire, their operations can easily be taken over by their neighbors. And, since they are retiring in droves—the average age of a farmer in Illinois is fifty-five—farms are consolidating rapidly.

With the possible exception of Jimmy Carter, Harry Truman was the last real farmer in the White House. In 1906, when he was twenty-two, Harry quit his job as a bank clerk in Kansas City and moved back to his family's farm in Grandview because his father needed the help. Rising at five o'clock every morning, he worked twelve to fourteen hours a day. It was backbreaking labor. On six hundred acres, the Trumans grew wheat, corn, and potatoes and raised cattle, sheep, and hogs. Harry later said he "did everything there was to do" on the farm: "Plowed, sowed, reaped, milked cows, fed hogs, doctored horses, bailed [sic] hay." With two plows attached to a team of four horses, he'd work maybe five acres in ten hours. "Riding one of these plows all day, day after day" he later wrote, "gives one time to think. I've settled all the ills of mankind in one way or another while riding along seeing that each animal pulled his part of the load."

Harry didn't leave the farm until he went off to war in 1917 at the age of thirty-three.

About thirty-five miles east of Decatur, Highway 36 passes the town of Bourbon. Now that must have brought a smile to Harry's face. And a knowing look and maybe a sideways glance from Bess.

Around noon on Saturday, June 20, Harry guided the New Yorker into the driveway behind a grand Tudor home on Meridian Street in a fashionable neighborhood on the north side of Indianapolis. The Trumans were stopping for lunch at the home of Frank McKinney, Harry's good friend and the former Democratic National Committee chairman.

Claire McKinney (now Claire McKinney Clark), the McKinneys' daughter, said the former first couple's arrival merited neither fanfare nor ceremony.

"My folks were normal, humble people and they didn't get over-awed about things," Clark said. "These were their friends coming to visit and it really wasn't a big deal. We didn't get lots of instructions on how to behave or what to do. Yes, he was the ex-president, but it wasn't a big, big deal. And the fact that it wasn't is a pretty good indication of what my parents were like." And what their relationship with the Trumans was like.

Frank McKinney's was a classic rags-to-riches story. Born to a German mother and an Irish father in a working-class (and solidly Democratic) neighborhood in south Indianapolis, McKinney quit school at fourteen to take a job as a messenger at Peoples State Bank. Five years later he was a teller. By the time he was thirty, he was the president.

McKinney's rise in the Democratic Party was nearly as meteoric. In 1928, at twenty-four, he was appointed party treasurer in Indianapolis. Seven years later he was elected Marion County Treasurer, the only elected office he would ever hold. In 1940 he began working his way up the ranks of the DNC, beginning as vice chairman of the finance committee, until, in October 1951, Truman, who had met McKinney during the 1948 campaign, asked him to be national party chairman.

It was not an enviable offer. McKinney would be succeeding Bill Boyle, a friend of Truman's from Kansas City who had been accused of receiving kickbacks for arranging government loans to businesses. (A Senate committee later cleared Boyle of any wrongdoing.) Meanwhile, the Truman administration was dogged by a scandal involving tax collectors accepting bribes, and the Democratic Party, which had split apart in 1948, was still not fully healed.

McKinney accepted the post, though he "had to be persuaded to take it," Truman recalled. Although Boyle had been paid thirty-five thousand dollars annually, McKinney refused a salary, and he promised to rid the government of corrupt workers. "The only way to deal with termites is to

Harry and Bess with the McKinney family in front of the McKinney home in Indianapolis, June 20, 1953. From left: Bess, Frank McKinney, Frank McKinney Jr., Harry, Margaret McKinney, Claire McKinney.

keep a sharp watch for them and get rid of them whenever they show up," he declared. He persuaded Truman to propose legislation making tax collectors civil service employees rather than political appointees. (Congress passed the bill.) McKinney also oversaw the party's 1952 convention in Chicago, which was deemed a rousing success, if only because none of the delegates walked out as they had four years earlier. His reward, of course, was to get sacked by the nominee, Adlai Stevenson, who replaced McKinney after the convention with a friend and fellow Illini named Stephen Mitchell. "[Truman] always thought that Governor Stevenson made a mistake to replace him," remembered Charles Murphy, a special counsel to the president. "And I think his view [was], that there was enough difference so if it had not happened Stevenson would have won the election."

It's doubtful the firing of Frank McKinney cost Stevenson the election. Matthew Connelly, another Truman aide, said there wasn't a Democrat alive who could have beaten Eisenhower in 1952. But McKinney's work as DNC chairman clearly impressed Truman, and, despite a twenty-year difference in their ages, the two men grew quite close. They had much in common. Neither had attended college. Both were self-made, plain speaking, overachieving men from the Midwest, amateur historians who were accustomed to being underestimated.

After freshening up, the Trumans joined McKinney, his wife, Margaret, and their children, nineteen-year-old Claire and fourteen-year-old Frank Jr., at the family's dining room table for a leisurely lunch: chilled melon balls, breast of chicken on ham, asparagus almondine, stuffed oranges, hot rolls and black currant preserves, and, for dessert, a McKinney family favorite, strawberry angel pie. Thelma Machael, the "women's editor" of the *Indianapolis News*, reported that the Trumans "charmed the McKinneys' daughter Claire and son Frank Jr. with their easy banter at the luncheon table, when Truman deferred to his wife as 'the Boss.'"

"With friendly ease and professional aplomb," Machael wrote, "the McKinneys hosted the luncheon visit in a manner as unflurried as if they were entertaining a group of their children's friends."

After lunch, the party retired to the porch to relax. The temperature hit one hundred degrees in Indianapolis that day, a new record for the date, but Harry Truman could stand the heat anywhere, not just in the kitchen. Dressed in a dark blue gabardine suit with a light blue shirt and polka dot bow tie, he betrayed not a hint of discomfort. Neither, for that matter, did Bess, who, Thelma Machael reported in remarkable detail, "wore a silk print jacket dress with a minute turquoise and purple design scattered over the black silk, relieved with a touch of white at the throat and mid arm."

A handful of newspaper reporters and photographers who'd caught wind of the visit were waiting out on the sidewalk. Truman, who had practically invented the modern presidential press conference, couldn't resist inviting them up to the porch.

"Well-fed, and beaming with good humor," *Time* magazine reported, "Harry Truman met the press, felt the cloth of a reporter's cord suit and allowed as how he had one just like it." He didn't want to say anything about Eisenhower—he was saving that for his speech in Philadelphia. He also didn't want to comment on the ongoing Korean cease-fire negotiations. But he answered a host of other questions with his usual mix of candor and humor.

Was he optimistic or pessimistic about world affairs in general? a reporter asked.

"I always have been optimistic that the peace of the world can be reached and maintained," answered Truman.

"In our time?"

"I am not a prophet."

Asked about rumors that his friend McKinney might be returned to his post as Democratic Party chairman, Truman enthusiastically endorsed the idea. "Frank's the best chairman the party ever had," he said, a not-so-subtle swipe at the incumbent, Stephen Mitchell (not to mention Adlai Stevenson). "Of course," he added, seeming to catch himself, "the present chairman was duly elected and all that."

Would he support Stevenson if he ran again in 1956? Truman said he was for "no candidate" at the moment, but "when the time comes, I'll make my sentiments known." But he promised to campaign for any candidate the Democrats nominated. "The Democratic Party has been very good to me," he said. "It has done all for me it could do for any one man. I am very grateful."

Would he consider running for office himself again? Truman's ambiguous answer seemed to leave the door open. He said he was busy with other things at the moment, but he was still interested in politics, of course.

What about Margaret? Will she run for office? "She's over twenty-one," he said, smiling, "and can do what she wants to." (Privately, he joked that Margaret couldn't run for Congress because "she'd never be able to get up early enough in the morning.")

Truman just seemed to be getting warmed up when McKinney cut him off. "If you're going to get across Ohio today," McKinney said, "you'd better be on the way." Truman concurred, ending the press conference.

Bess also granted an interview on the porch that day. That was exceptionally rare, because she guarded her privacy fiercely. When she became first lady, she steadfastly refused to grant interviews or hold press conferences. When in the fall of 1947 she finally consented to answer questions from reporters, the questions had to be submitted in writing—and her answers were hardly revealing:

> *Did she think there would ever be a woman President of the United States?*
> No.
> *Would she want to be President?*
> No.
> *Would she want Margaret ever to be First Lady?*
> No.
> *If she had a son, would she try to bring him up to be President?*
> No.
> *Did any of the demands of her role as First Lady ever give her stage fright?*
> No comment.
> *What would you like to do and have your husband do when he is no longer president?*
> Return to Independence.

Since she declined to engage the press, the public never really got to know Bess Truman. Her image was that of a dowdy, slightly dour housewife. Nothing could have been further from the truth. "She was full of charm," remembered journalist Charles Robbins, "with a repressed girlish mischievousness and a dry wit that quickly let the air out of pretense and righted departures from common sense."

That she submitted to questions on the McKinneys' porch in Indianapolis was, as Thelma Machael put it in the *Indianapolis News*, indicative of "the deep enjoyment of her present semiprivate life."

"Her gestures are restrained," Machael wrote of Bess on the porch that afternoon, "her laughter soft and sincere and her carriage erect."

The ex-president, Bess reported, was easy to cook for—except for just one thing: "I don't dare serve onions in any form." His favorite meal? Steak with buttered baked potatoes. "Goodness, that man can't put enough butter on baked potatoes!"

She revealed that Harry had a favorite chair back home in Independence, an old wingback that "creaks and groans when he sits in it; the springs sag, and he won't let me have it reupholstered—he likes it just as it is."

Of their road trip Bess said she was acting as chief "navigator, map checker, and road sign watcher. . . . He's driving very conservatively on the trip," she added, approvingly.

Around two o'clock the Trumans said good-bye to the McKinneys—but they would return on their way home. Harry and Bess climbed back into the Chrysler. They picked up Highway 40 in downtown Indianapolis and continued east.

About an hour later, near the town of Greenfield, the Trumans were pulled over by an Indiana state trooper. The state police had set up a roadblock on Highway 40 to hand out traffic-safety pamphlets to motorists. It was part of a program to reduce traffic fatalities and to familiarize out-of-state drivers with Indiana's motor laws. (At the time, traffic regulations varied widely from state to state. Even road markings were not yet fully standardized.)

The Trumans had passed through the roadblock unnoticed, but as they were pulling away, a state trooper named R. H. Reeves recognized them.

Harry was done in by his fastidiousness. "It"—his car—"was so clean that my attention was attracted to it," Reeves said.

Reeves shouted for Truman to pull over. He did, and got out of the car. "What're you selling here?" he asked the trooper. Reeves explained the traffic-safety program and asked the former president to pose for a picture to promote it.

"I'm running about two hours late, but I'll take time for that," Harry said. "I certainly endorse your program." While Bess sat and waited inside the sweltering Chrysler, Harry spent about twenty minutes at the road-block, standing in his shirtsleeves, chatting and signing autographs. Then they were off again. It was nearly four o'clock.

There are no recorded sightings of the Trumans for the next seven hours. In the interim they drove clear across Ohio. Presumably they stopped for dinner. Maybe it was in Columbus. But there are no newspaper reports of their stopping there or in any of the other major towns along their route. Perhaps they finally did manage to travel incognito, at least for a few hours. It's not impossible. It was a busy Saturday night on Highway 40. One imagines Harry and Bess enjoying dinner in blessed solitude, just two ordinary Americans at last.

6

Wheeling, West Virginia, June 20–21, 1953

*T*he road trip is a quintessentially American activity. From the earliest days of the republic, Americans have felt compelled to explore their homeland, in search of everything from gold to good vibes.

Meriwether Lewis and William Clark embarked on the first great American road trip. Lewis left Pittsburgh on August 31, 1803, picked up Clark somewhere along the Ohio River, and set out for the Pacific Northwest—accompanied by a crew of more than thirty, including Clark's slave York. The journey would take more than two years. Fourteen miles was considered a good day's progress. Occasionally they got lucky and stumbled upon an ancient path worn by Indians, buffalo, deer, or elk. Mostly, though, they were on their own. "We had to cut Roads, through thickets of balsam fir timber, for our horses to pass through," Joseph Whitehouse, a member of the expedition, wrote in his journal on September 3, 1805.

In 1806, Thomas Jefferson signed a bill authorizing the federal government to spend thirty thousand dollars to build a road on an old pack trail through the Allegheny Mountains. Running from Cumberland, Maryland, to Wheeling, Virginia (later West Virginia), the road would connect the Potomac and Ohio rivers and effectively link the eastern seaboard and the rapidly growing Midwest. It was the first expenditure of federal funds on a public works project in American history, and it was not without controversy. Critics said the federal government had no business building roads, that there was nothing in the Constitution that even allowed it. In the end, the bill passed by a narrow margin. Completed in 1818, the National Road, as it came to be known, was a remarkable example of nineteenth-century engineering: thirty feet wide, paved with several layers of crushed stone, ditched, and drained. It proved enormously popular—too popular, in fact. Traffic was so heavy that the road quickly deteriorated. In 1822, Congress passed a measure authorizing the collection of tolls on the road to fund repairs. But President Monroe vetoed the bill, saying the collection of tolls would be an unconstitutional exercise of federal power. "It was one thing to make appropriations for public improvements," wrote one historian, "but an entirely different thing to assume jurisdiction and sovereignty over the land whereon those improvements were made." This is a lynchpin of federal highway policy to this day: while the federal government helps fund their construction, interstates and U.S. highways are owned and operated by the states.

Monroe's veto stifled the nation's nascent road-building movement—but it could not quell its wanderlust. Between 1846 and 1866, a "freighter" named Solomon Young ran at least a dozen wagon trains from Missouri to Utah and California. A typical train consisted of forty to eighty wagons, each requiring a team of twelve oxen and two drivers. The merchandise it carried could be worth thirty thousand dollars or more. Once, Young was gone for two years. His wife and children didn't know if he would return. The work was dangerous but lucrative. By 1860 Solomon Young was worth fifty thousand dollars, though he soon lost his fortune in the

Civil War. As an old man, Young's tales of his travels would spellbind his grandson Harry Truman.

Outside major cities, where streets might be paved with stone or brick, nineteenth-century roads were little more than rutted dirt paths that turned into quagmires when it rained. In 1896 a popular magazine even gave readers helpful tips on what to do when a horse got stuck in the mud. ("Steady and support the horse's head, and excite and encourage him, with hand and voice, to rise.")

It wasn't until a new mode of transportation emerged that the so-called "good roads movement" finally took hold in the United States. That new mode was . . . the bicycle. The invention of the "safety bicycle"—the kind we know today, with equal-sized wheels and pneumatic tires—spurred a bicycle craze in the 1880s. Bicyclists successfully lobbied state and local governments to impose taxes for the construction of paved roads. (Motorists should keep this in mind the next time they get stuck behind a bicycle in traffic.) In 1893 Massachusetts became the first state to organize a highway department, and by 1905 thirteen other states had started one.

But it was the automobile, of course, that turned that trickle of road building into a torrent.

In the late spring and early summer of 1903, a doctor named Horatio Nelson Jackson became the first person to cross the country in an automobile. Talk about a road trip. To win a fifty-dollar bet, Jackson and his chauffeur, Sewell K. Crocker, drove a twenty-horsepower Winton touring car from San Francisco to New York in just sixty-three days, in spite of miserable weather and horrendous roads. At one point, the intrepid motorists ran out of spare tires and were forced to wind rope around the wheels to keep going. (Exactly fifty years later, when Harry and Bess made their trip in considerably more favorable conditions, Dr. Jackson was eighty-one and comfortably retired in Vermont.)

Jackson's journey inspired a frenzy of cross-country motoring. In 1904, a caravan of seventy cars set out from the East Coast for the World's Fair in St. Louis. "The logistics for such an expedition at this time were formidable," wrote a Federal Highway Administration historian.

> There were no through routes, no reliable road maps, no way of knowing the condition of the roads in advance, no road signs or route markers. Between major cities, getting repairs for a breakdown, or even fuel, was an uncertain business.

Incredibly, fifty-eight of the autos managed to make it to the fair, and their arrival triggered tumultuous celebrations. America's love affair with the automobile had begun. The St. Louis caravan showed that cars were mechanically capable of making long trips. The only thing holding them back was the woeful condition of the nation's roads.

In 1915 Harry Truman took what was probably his first long automobile trip. He, his mother, and his uncle Harrison piled into his Stafford and drove to Monegaw Springs, a resort along the Osage River in western Missouri about eighty miles south of Grandview. Typical of the times, it was an arduous journey, which he described in a letter to Bess:

> We got within a half mile [of the springs] and ran over a stump. I spilled Uncle Harry over the front seat and threw Mamma over my own head. Neither of them were hurt, except Uncle Harry renewed his profane vocabulary. I backed Lizzie off the stump and ran her into town with a badly bent axle. Mamma and I started for home at 6:00 A.M. on Monday. Got within seventy-five miles of it and it began to rain. Had the nicest slipping time you ever saw. What with a crooked axle and a bent steering wheel I could hardly stay in the road. Five miles south of Harrisonville Lizzie took a header for the ditch and got there, smashing a left front wheel into kindling. I phoned to Ferson and he sent me his front wheel. The accident happened within a half mile of a R. R. station, Lone Ture by name. Mamma and I sat there from

1:30 until 8:00 P.M. waiting for the wheel. It arrived all right and I couldn't get it on. Then it began to rain in real earnest. I got soaked. A good farmer came and took us up to his house and we stayed all night. Next morning he hitched his team to Lizzie and pulled her out of the ditch.

Harry and Mamma finally made it back to Grandview at 3:00 P.M. on Tuesday. The eighty-mile trek from the springs had required thirty-three hours and incalculable patience.

Despite such deplorable conditions, the popularity of the automobile only grew. In 1900 there were eight thousand in the United States. By 1915 there were nearly 2.5 million, and they just kept getting better, faster, and cheaper. By 1917 Henry Ford was selling his Model T for six hundred dollars.

Traffic engineers scrambled to come up with a road surface that could withstand the deluge of horseless carriages. They experimented with roasted clay, oil-earth mixtures, slag from blast furnaces, wooden planks—even steel. But none was deemed practical enough. Then they tried asphalt, a petroleum product that liquefies at temperatures above three hundred degrees Fahrenheit but hardens when it cools. It worked nicely.

After World War I, the federal government began financing state road-building programs in earnest. Asphalt roads began spreading like tentacles across the country, and by 1925 it was possible to drive from San Francisco to New York—the journey that had taken Horatio Nelson Jackson sixty-three days—in less than a hundred hours. In 1926 federal and state transportation officials organized this patchwork as numbered U.S. Highways, with east–west roads given even numbers from north to south, and north–south roads given odd numbers from east to west (hence Highway 1 runs from Fort Kent, Maine, to Key West, Florida). The system originally comprised nearly ninety-seven thousand miles of roads, 3.3 percent of the total mileage at the time.

The numbering system ended the era of named roads. The National Road became Route 40, the Lincoln Highway Route 30, the Dixie Highway Route 25. The passing of the named roads was not unlamented. Ernest McGaffey of the Automobile Club of Southern California complained that the new system substituted "arithmetic for history, mathematics for romance." But the numbered highways made it much easier to navigate the rapidly expanding road system, and some, like Route 66, even managed to evoke a romance of their own.

During the Great Depression the road trip took on a new meaning as millions of Americans took to the road in search of a better life—or at least a job. "European immigrants moved inland from coastal ports along roads," wrote Karl Raitz in *A Guide to the National Road*.

> African American migrants moved out of the South to Northern cities, many following bus routes; others drove farm vehicles and well-used cars along the road net. Great Plains Dust Bowl migrants moved to the California cornucopia in a similar manner. Appalachian migrants, too, moved out of the mountains by following the roads leading north to hoped-for industrial jobs.

During World War II, the road trip was put on hold. Only travel deemed essential to the war effort was permitted. To conserve rubber and fuel, the speed limit was reduced to thirty-five miles per hour nationwide, and tires and gasoline were rationed. A mere 139 new cars were manufactured in 1943, and those, of course, were strictly rationed as well.

After the war, the pent-up demand for automobiles exploded. Production leaped from 69,532 vehicles in 1945 to 2.1 million in 1946, 3.5 million in 1947, and 3.9 million in 1948. (Postwar production would peak at more than seven million in 1955.) It was the golden age of the American automobile.

The country's roads had been badly neglected during the war. Truman recognized the problem. "In recent years," he said in 1948, "our highway construction has not kept pace with the growth in traffic. . . . By any reasonable standard our highways are inadequate for today's demands." But construction materials were scarce, and the demand for housing far exceeded the demand for new highways. Not until 1956 would the Federal-Aid Highway Act be signed—by Dwight Eisenhower—creating the interstate highway system and ushering in the golden age of the American road trip.

Now you can drive from San Francisco to New York in less than forty-eight hours.

Considering Harry Truman's love of roads, it must have bugged him that Eisenhower, not he, came to be known as the father of the interstate highway system.

Around eleven o'clock on the night of Saturday, June 20, the Trumans reached Wheeling, in West Virginia's northern panhandle between Ohio and Pennsylvania. Just outside of town, Harry noticed a crumbling statue of Henry Clay in a park. "Wheeling, for some reason, used to be devoted to Henry Clay," he later observed, though he confessed he hadn't the foggiest idea why. That's surprising, since the statue (long since removed) was erected to honor Clay for his role in extending the National Road westward from Wheeling.

Harry pulled up in front of the McLure House, a hotel in downtown Wheeling. At the front desk, he very much surprised the night clerk, who recognized him immediately and called the manager. "The manager came up and asked why we had not let him know we were coming," Truman said. "I told them that if I had, the street in front of the hotel would be so full that we would have a hard time getting through. He agreed that I was right."

The Trumans checked into a room on the fifth floor and called their daughter, Margaret, who was to meet them in Washington the next day. Margaret had apparently been fielding lots of calls from reporters trying to catch up with her mother and father on the road. America was asking, "Where's Harry?"

Harry told Margaret that reporters could meet him around four the next afternoon at the Gulf station in Frederick, Maryland. It was where he always filled up before driving into Washington.

When it opened in 1852, the McLure House was the largest and grandest hotel in western Virginia. It had an open courtyard with water troughs and hitching posts for horses. The registration desk was on the second floor, since the open lobby on the first floor was a muddy mess. There was a separate entrance for women, marked LADIES, that was wider than the other entrances, to accommodate the cumbersome hoop skirts that were fashionable at the time.

Over the years, nearly every future, current, or former president who passed through Wheeling spent the night at the McLure House: Grant, Garfield, Arthur, Benjamin Harrison, McKinley, Taft, Theodore Roosevelt, and Wilson. Harry Truman himself had stayed at the McLure before, back when he was a senator.

The McLure was also the site of one of the most notorious political speeches in American history. On February 9, 1950, an obscure senator from Wisconsin, Joseph McCarthy, addressed a meeting of the Ohio County Republican Women's Club. It was not an event that portended history. McCarthy's speech, delivered that night in the hotel's Colonnade Room, contained the usual ad hominem attacks on the Truman administration. Much time was also spent discussing agricultural policy. But it was a single sentence that McCarthy uttered—practically a throwaway line—that immortalized the speech.

"While I cannot take the time to name all of the men in the State Department who have been named as members of the Communist Party and members of a spy ring," McCarthy said, "I have here in my hand a list of 205 that were known to the Secretary of State as being members of the Communist Party and who, nevertheless, are still working and shaping the policy in the State Department."

Frank Desmond, the reporter covering the event for the *Wheeling Intelligencer*, included that sentence in his story, though not very prominently: the story jumps from page one to page six in the middle of it. Nonetheless, the Associated Press, cannibalizing Desmond's story, included the sentence in its own dispatch, which went over the wire that night and appeared in hundreds of papers across the country the next morning.

Challenged to produce the list at a press conference in Denver the next day, McCarthy said he would be happy to—but it happened to be in his other suit, which he'd left on the plane. McCarthy, of course, had no such list. He never did substantiate the charge. But the witch hunt that was engulfing the nation had a champion, and, soon, a name: McCarthyism.

That the McLure was the scene of his hated political enemy's defining moment concerned Harry Truman not a wit. He wasn't superstitious. He was just tired. He and Bess had driven three hundred miles from Indianapolis. After chatting on the phone with Margaret, they went to bed.

The McLure House was remodeled, rather disastrously, in the early 1980s. The original red brick exterior was covered with mud-colored concrete panels. A drop ceiling was installed in the lobby, cleverly concealing its vaulted rococo grandeur and rendering it claustrophobic. Harry wouldn't recognize the place today.

When I stayed at the McLure, I noticed there was a banquet room directly across the hall from my room. It was the Colonnade Room, the very room in which McCarthyism was birthed. The room was locked, but I could see inside through a window in the door. It was dimly lit. White tablecloths covered large round tables, awaiting the next wedding reception. To think of all the misery that ensued from what was said, almost offhandedly, in that room more than a half-century earlier, how many lives were ruined. Was it outweighed by the joy of all the marriages that had been celebrated in there since then? I witnessed an execution once, by lethal injection, at the state penitentiary in Potosi, Missouri. Looking into the

Colonnade Room, I had the same feeling I'd had when the cheap Venetian blinds were raised on the window looking into the execution chamber. I was profoundly disquieted. And every time I looked out the peephole in the door of my room, all I could see was the Colonnade Room.

Apart from a large and incongruous group of Russian businessmen in the lobby, I didn't see any other guests at the McLure the night I stayed there. The place felt a bit sad and ghostly. The water coming out of my bathroom faucet was brown when I first turned it on, a sign that I was the room's first occupant in a long time.

The next morning I enjoyed a "complimentary continental breakfast" in the Beans 2 Brew Café, the hotel's coffee shop. This consisted of a pre-packaged cinnamon bun and a cup of coffee. Behind the counter was a chatty woman whose every self-amusing sentence ended with a loud, harsh laugh that would mutate into a hacking smoker's cough. "Would you like me to warm your bun? Ha, ha, ha, hack, hack, cough, cough." I was afraid she might expel something. I passed on the whole bun-warming thing.

Harry came down to the lobby around eight o'clock the next morning. Dent Williams, a *Wheeling Intelligencer* reporter, cornered him. As he had in Indianapolis, Truman sidestepped questions about Eisenhower and Korea, "because any comment I would make would be a half-baked comment, and Lord knows, I've had too many of those half-baked comments."

But Truman, who had apparently researched local issues in the communities along the route of his trip before leaving Independence, couldn't resist taking a jab at the Republican-controlled Congress for cutting funding for a floodwall in Wheeling. "Wheeling needs a floodwall badly," he said, "and I'm sorry to learn that construction funds were stricken from the federal budget."

He talked about how well the Chrysler was running, how hot it had been in the Midwest, how happy he and Bess were to be on the road again. His only regret, he said, was that he couldn't travel incognito. "I've found that it's impossible to travel cross-country unnoticed," he told Williams.

As if on cue, Williams overheard a hotel guest tell his young son, "That's Mr. Truman over there."

The interview was interrupted when the desk clerk told Harry he had a phone call. The call was transferred to a lobby telephone. After a few minutes, Harry hung up the receiver and returned, smiling, to Williams. "Another nut caught up with me," the former president said, laughing.

At eight-thirty Bess came down, and the former first couple had breakfast in the hotel's coffee shop, probably the precursor to the Beans 2 Brew Café.

After breakfast, the Trumans checked out of the McLure. Before paying, though, Harry checked the bill very carefully. If there was one thing he couldn't stand, it was being overcharged. In 1941—when he was in his second term as a U.S. senator, mind you—he wrote Bess from a Memphis hotel. "Had breakfast in the coffee shop downstairs and they charged me fifty-five centers for tomato juice, a little dab of oatmeal and milk and toast. I don't mind losing one hundred dollars on a hoss race or a poker game with friends, but I do hate to pay fifty-five centers for a quarter breakfast."

From Wheeling, the Trumans continued east on Highway 40, following the path of the old National Road through the rugged Allegheny Mountains of southwestern Pennsylvania and western Maryland. Near Farmington, Pennsylvania, they passed Fort Necessity, where, during the French and Indian War in 1754, George Washington, then a twenty-two-year-old lieutenant colonel in the British army, suffered one of the worst defeats in his military career, surrendering the fort to French forces. (Incidentally, Washington had been sent to the area to build a road.)

Just past the town of Addison, Pennsylvania, they dipped south into Maryland. Charles Mason and Jeremiah Dixon surveyed the border between Pennsylvania and Maryland in the 1760s. Until then, both colonies claimed the land between the thirty-ninth and fortieth parallels, and in the 1730s they'd even gone to war over it. Mason and Dixon split the difference—their line is about halfway between the two parallels. The Mason-Dixon Line has become the symbolic division between North and South in the United States, though no state that bordered it ever seceded from the Union.

Truman later said he was "impressed with the way the highway over the mountains had been improved from the old blacktop hairpin curves" that he had driven as a senator. If that's the case, I can't imagine what traversing the Alleghenies on Highway 40 was like back when Harry was in the Senate, because even today it can be downright scary. The road is twisty, with transmission-killing, ear-popping climbs and hair-raising, brake-burning descents. The car I was driving (my father's) had just turned a hundred thousand miles back in Ohio, and I felt sorry for having to make it work so hard. It was a far cry from my drive across Illinois, where I could have nodded off at the wheel safely.

I am told there are spectacular views of verdant, tree-covered mountains unfolding under azure skies, but I barely caught a glimpse of any of that, focused as I was on not hurtling off the side of a mountain. It surprised me how precarious the drive was, but U.S. highways are not built to the same standards as interstates, where the maximum grades are generally 6 percent and the minimum design speeds are seventy-five miles per hour in rural areas and fifty-five in mountainous and urban areas.

Near Grantsville, Maryland, I reached the highest point on the old National Road, and the highest point on all of Highway 40 east of the Mississippi: Negro Mountain, elevation 2,827 feet. Local legend has it that the mountain was named after Nemesis, an African American who died fighting for the British in the French and Indian War and was buried on the mountain. The June 10, 1756, *Maryland Gazette* mentions a "free Negro who was . . . killed" in a "smart skirmish" with local Indians. (On the same page are "ran away" ads, listing the names and detailed physical descriptions of escaped slaves.) But little else is known about Nemesis.

Rosita Youngblood, a state lawmaker from Philadelphia, wants to change the name of the mountain, which extends into Pennsylvania. Youngblood told the *Philadelphia Daily News* her granddaughter discovered the name while working on a seventh-grade class project. "My granddaughter said, 'Grandmom, is this true?' I said, 'There's no such thing as Negro Mountain.' Then I learned it was true." Youngblood has introduced a resolution in the Pennsylvania House calling for the formation of a commission to study the issue. "If they decide to call it Nemesis Mountain," she said, "I'd be happy with that."

Youngblood's crusade baffles lawmakers from rural Somerset County, Pennsylvania, where part of the mountain is located. "I never knew 'negro' was a bad word until she mentioned it," said State Representative Bob Bastian.

7

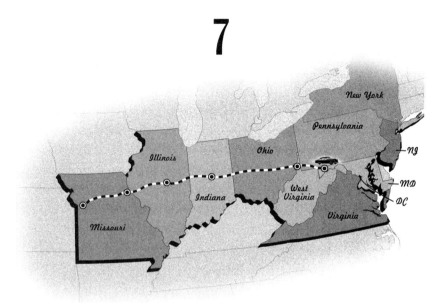

Frostburg, Maryland,
June 21, 1953

*A*round twelve-thirty the Trumans pulled into Frostburg, a small coal-mining town on the eastern slope of Big Savage Mountain in far western Maryland. Looking for a place to eat, Harry had just turned onto a side street when he saw a man in a suit waving him down. Bemused, he stopped the car. The man was Martin Rothstein, the town doctor. Doc—as everybody in Frostburg called him—approached the Chrysler. He recognized the former president immediately.

"I'm sorry, Mr. Truman," Doc said a little sheepishly. "But you're going the wrong way."

"What do you mean?" Truman said.

"This is a one-way street," Doc explained, "and you're going the wrong way."

Bess leaned across the front seat to the driver's side window.

"He never listens to me," she said to Rothstein. "I thought he was making a wrong turn."

Truman thanked Doc and asked him if there was any place in town open for lunch.

"Yeah," Doc answered, "there's one right around the corner. The Princess." It was Doc's favorite restaurant. He ate there all the time.

Truman was familiar with the Princess. He'd stopped there a couple times when he was a senator making the trip between Independence and Washington. It was owned by George Pappas, a Greek immigrant who'd come to the United States in 1907 with fourteen dollars in his pocket. Pappas opened the Princess in 1939. Originally it was a confectionery, but over the years he began serving soups and sandwiches, and by 1950 he had turned it into a full-service restaurant.

Harry and Bess sat in a booth near the front and ordered the Sunday supper special: roast chicken with stuffing, lima beans, mashed potatoes, coleslaw, rice pudding, and coffee—for seventy cents.

George Pappas Jr., the owner's son, was working the grill that day, and when the Trumans' waitress, Grace Felker, brought their order back to the kitchen, she told Pappas, "That looks like Harry Truman out there."

"I looked out," Pappas remembered, "and I said, 'It sure does.' And it was. It was old Harry."

While the younger Pappas prepared the Trumans' meals, telephones all over Frostburg began ringing. At the time, the town had no direct-dial service, so all calls had to be routed through an operator. It didn't take long for the word to get out. Howard Ward, the Frostburg correspondent for the *Cumberland* (Maryland) *Evening Times*, was at home changing out of his Sunday best when he got a call from a friend telling him that the former president and first lady were in town.

"Yeah, right," said Ward, thinking it was a prank. But after he hung up, his curiosity got the best of him. He put his suit back on and headed for the Princess.

"Townspeople started to drop in for a Coke," Ward reported in the next day's paper, "and one bystander estimated the restaurant did a bigger soft drink business in the time the Trumans were there than in any other similar period."

The Trumans did not enjoy a quiet repast. Children badgered Harry for his autograph. The adults weren't much better behaved, constantly interrupting the couple's lunch to shake hands.

"Through it all," Ward reported, "they remained gracious and were not annoyed."

"We lunched at Frostburg," Truman later recounted, "at the Princess Restaurant, which is run by an old Greek who is a damn good Democrat. I had been there before, but in those days they didn't make such a fuss over me. I was just a senator then."

George Pappas died in 1963. George Pappas Jr. took over the restaurant and ran it until 1981, when his own son, George W. Pappas, took over. George Jr., a spry eighty-six, still puts in occasional shifts in the kitchen.

"My boy does a good job" running the restaurant, George Jr. told me when I visited the Princess. "My dad would be proud of him."

George Jr. served eighteen months as a mess sergeant in the South Pacific during World War II. He said it was an honor for him to have served his former commander in chief lunch.

"He was a good old fellow," he said of Truman. "Good president too." Like many of his generation, George Jr. gave Truman credit for ending the war.

"That was really a tough decision, for that man to drop that bomb on all them people."

The Princess Restaurant still looks much as it did when Harry and Bess ate there in 1953. Along one wall is a soda fountain, with a long counter and fixed, round stools. Along the opposite wall are a dozen booths, each with a small, coin-operated jukebox, one song for ten cents, three for a quarter.

Photo by author

George W. Pappas in the Truman booth at the Princess Diner, Frostburg, Maryland, 2008.

A plaque above the booth in which the Trumans sat commemorates their visit:

MR. & MRS. HARRY S. TRUMAN

ATE DINNER IN THIS BOOTH

FATHER'S DAY

SUNDAY, JUNE 21, 1953

The booth is not original. It was replaced during a remodeling about fifteen years ago. George W. Pappas kept the old one in his garage for several years, until his wife suggested that the space might be better utilized by a motor vehicle. George called the local historical society to see if it was interested in this unique piece of local history, but, alas, it didn't have any room for the booth either. So, reluctantly, George put it out with the trash one day.

George sat down to talk with me in the remodeled Truman booth. A lifetime of diner food clearly had not affected him adversely. He was fifty-seven but looked at least a dozen years younger. He spoke with the accent common to this part of Maryland. "Power" becomes "pyre." "The Princess" is "the prince's."

George is the middle of three children. Neither his older sister nor his younger brother ever evinced much interest in the restaurant business, but George was fascinated by it from the start. When he was in the first grade he would come into the Princess every morning at five, just to "hang out" until it was time to go to school at eight. He went to work at the restaurant full time in 1969. His father paid him the minimum wage: $1.30 an hour.

I asked George if he was a "damn good Democrat" like Truman said his grandfather was. He laughed in a way that indicated he was not.

"Granddad and I talked about a lot of things, but we never talked about politics," he told me. George said he thought taxes were too high, and that the government made it too hard to run a small business like the Princess. He complained, for example, that his soda fountain license cost more than his restaurant license (twenty-five dollars vs. ten dollars), even though his might be the last soda fountain in Allegany County.

Besides, George explained, most of his friends are Republicans, and if he wanted to vote for them in a primary election, he had to be a Republican too, since Maryland's primaries are closed. (In 2008 the McCain-Palin ticket carried the county with 62 percent of the vote.)

Of all the small mom-and-pop businesses that the Trumans are known to have patronized on their trip, the Princess Restaurant on Main Street in Frostburg is the only one I found that has survived, more or less intact, in the same family. "Granddad was a hard worker and a thinker," said George. "In 1949 he decided to stop selling beer to attract the 'church crowd.' Beer was a nuisance anyway. Business went up immediately." George says his father was no less diligent. "They were both hard workers and they'd give you a good meal for a good price."

When the Trumans came to Frostburg in 1953, Main Street positively bustled with businesses, including Durst Furniture, Prichard's Hardware, Maurice's Department Store, Hohing's Men's and Boys' Store, a G. C. Murphy's five and dime, a Rexall, an Acme, and an A&P. Besides the Princess there were a dozen other places to get a meal, ranging from drugstore soda fountains to white tablecloth restaurants: Al's, Bob's, Boney's, the Duchess, Finzel's, Peck's. On Friday nights, coal miners from all over the county would bring their families to Main Street for dinner and a movie, to do a little shopping, or just to hang out. It could get a little raucous sometimes. It was what they did for entertainment.

Today, all those businesses are gone. Except for the Princess.

George took me outside. Standing in front of the restaurant, he pointed to a vacant building across the street.

"That used to be the five and dime," he said.

"And that"—he pointed to another vacant building down the street—"used to be the furniture store." There were at least five vacant storefronts on a three-block stretch of Main Street.

What happened? Lots of things. Highway 40 was rerouted around the town, siphoning traffic from Main Street. Then Interstate 68 was built, siphoning even more. A mall opened down the road in LaVale, followed by a Wal-Mart Supercenter and other big-box stores.

But there were less obvious factors. Technological advances made it easier to mine coal from the surface, which is cheaper than underground mining—and requires far fewer workers. Before Frostburg knew it, Friday nights on Main Street were a lot less boisterous.

Furthermore, many of the businesses on Main Street were family-owned, and, as George W. Pappas well knew, it can be hard to keep a family-owned business in the family. He gestured toward the vacant building where Prichard's, the hardware store, used to be. "The grandkids, they went up to Penn State. They didn't want to come back. Why bother? It all came down to dollars and cents. When they found out Wal-Mart was coming, that was the icing on the cake. Why bang your head against the wall trying to compete with Wal-Mart? They didn't want to go through that." Prichard's closed in the late 1990s.

George has four children. He would like to see one of them take over the Princess someday, but he's not holding his breath. His son graduated with a degree in culinary arts from Johnson & Wales University in Providence, Rhode Island. "But," said George, "he's talking about moving to South Carolina with his girlfriend."

Nonetheless, George has faith in the future of the Princess. In fact, he's planning on enlarging it. When I visited, he'd just received the permits he needed to nearly double the size of the restaurant's kitchen.

"I'm loyal to Main Street," he said. "You have to be passionate about it."

While in Frostburg, I had dinner at the Princess—in the Truman booth, of course. I ordered the same meal Harry and Bess had. It was delicious, although the roast chicken dinner that Harry and Bess enjoyed for seventy cents now costs $9.50—still, not a bad deal.

While they were trying to enjoy their lunch at the Princess, a local Democratic Party activist named Bill Byrnes approached the Trumans and introduced himself. (Byrnes would later win election to the Maryland House of Delegates.) He asked the ex-president if he would be willing to visit his elderly mother, Elizabeth Byrnes, who had recently broken her hip in a fall and was bedridden.

"My mother has been a Democrat for ninety-two years and she's pretty sick," Byrnes told Truman. "Will you please come over to the house and cheer her up?"

"Who could say no to that kind of an invitation?" Truman recalled.

So, after lunch—George Pappas "refused to take our money for the meal," Truman remembered—the Trumans followed Byrnes out to his mother's house in Eckhart Mines, about two miles from Frostburg.

"She was bedfast and quite feeble," Truman said. "My arrival was a surprise to her. She looked me over and then said, 'Mr. Truman, you're better looking than I thought you were.'"

"We had a nice chat," Truman continued. "That little detour to Eckhart, Maryland, may not sound like much, but it was the high point of our whole motor trip."

As Truman left, Mrs. Byrnes whispered to him, "May God bless you, Mr. President."

Harry and Bess had planned on spending just a few minutes at Mrs. Byrnes's house, but they ended up staying half an hour, chatting with neighbors on the porch. It was two o'clock before they finally got back on the road.

A few miles east of Frostburg, the Trumans passed through the Cumberland Narrows, a thousand-foot-deep gorge carved into the Allegheny Mountains by Wills Creek. It was through this narrow gap that the National Road was threaded, linking the East and the Midwest. This irregular bit of topography was God's gift to Manifest Destiny.

The Gulf station at the corner of West Patrick and North Jefferson in Frederick, Maryland, looked more like a rocket ship than a filling station. Behind the two pumps was a tall, slim deco building with soaring arched windows and a steeple on top. Behind that was a garage with two bays. Opened around 1940, it was said to be the most modern and innovative service station in Frederick County. The restrooms were sparkling. It even had an electric water cooler, the first in town.

The Gulf station was also the neighborhood candy store, where children bought gumballs, popsicles, jawbreakers, and Hershey bars after school. And it was a political clubhouse of sorts.

The station manager, Carroll Kehne, was a devout Democrat. His grease monkey, Albert Kefauver, was a rabid Republican. The two men discussed politics constantly, always amicably, often with customers and local raconteurs. "People who know me politically call me Mr. Democrat," Kehne recalled in his later years. He started a Democratic Club in Frederick because he "saw men running for office bumming money from business-men so they could run." The club helped raise money for local Democratic candidates. Kehne firmly believed that politicians should be "settled" and attend strictly to politics. "You can't do a good job running the government and making important decisions if you're always worrying about your kids or girlfriends or whatever."

Around three-thirty on the afternoon of Sunday, June 21, 1953, a newspaper reporter came into the station and asked Albert Kefauver to help him fix a flat. "Then another newsman came in and I thought he was just going to talk to his buddy," Kefauver remembered. But then another showed up. And another.

One of the reporters asked to use the phone. Carroll Kehne asked him if it was a local call. "No," the reporter said, "I want to call Margaret Truman to see when her father is supposed to get here."

"I didn't believe him at first," Kehne said. "But the next thing I knew, he"—Truman—"was driving up to the pumps in a beautiful new black Chrysler. . . . I didn't know he was coming."

By now a dozen reporters, photographers, and newsreel cameramen were crowded around the pumps. Kehne filled Truman's car with gas and checked the oil while his fifteen-year-old son, Carroll Jr., washed the windows. "When President Truman stepped out of the car," the younger Kehne remembered, "he offered to shake my hand. I stated it was wet, but that didn't faze him. He said, 'That's no problem!'"

"I made up a ticket for his gasoline and made him sign it," the elder Kehne recalled. "But I wouldn't let him pay it. I just wanted to be able to say that I treated President Harry S. Truman to a tank of gasoline."

Harry went inside the station. "The Boss wants a glass of water," he announced, "and I'd love a Coke." Leaning on the counter, he spent about twenty minutes chatting with Kehne and Kefauver while he enjoyed his soft drink. "We was talking about everything in general," Kehne recalled.

"He was the kind of guy who could talk to you about anything, fixing cars or changing oil, or politics." This event, Kehne's son told me, was the highlight of his father's life. "My dad was so very excited, as he truly loved Harry as a president. Being a Democrat made it even more pleasant for him."

At one point, Kehne asked Truman to give Kefauver a hard time for being a Republican. "Na," said Truman. "It's too hot to give anybody hell."

When Truman finished the Coke, Kehne saved the empty bottle.

Back outside, the newspaper photographers and newsreel camera operators asked Harry and Bess to pose with Kehne reading a map. It was

Courtesy of the Historical Society of Frederick County, Maryland

Harry finishes off his Coke at Carroll Kehne's service station in Frederick, Maryland, June 21, 1953, while Kehne (left) and his mechanic Albert Kefauver watch. When Kehne asked Truman to give Kefauver a hard time for being a Republican, Harry said it was "too hot to give anybody hell."

preposterous, of course; Harry knew the way to Washington by heart. But he obliged them, smiling, as he always did.

Years later, in his memoir *Mr. Citizen*, Truman recalled the scene at the Gulf station:

> The press caught up with us at the filling station in Frederick where I had always filled up in times past. I was reminded of the time my mother visited us at the White House. I had wanted her to meet some of these same press correspondents, but I was a little uncertain how she would take to the idea, so I put off saying anything about it until I was leading her from the plane into the midst of them. Then I said: "Mama, these are photographers and reporters. They want to take your picture and talk to you."
>
> "Fiddlesticks," she said. "They don't want to see me. If I had known this would happen, I would have stayed home!"
>
> There on the road in Frederick, I felt the same way she did.

Really? According to the *New York Times*, "Mr. Truman . . . greeted the photographers and reporters at Frederick like long-lost brothers." "You're a sight for sore eyes," he said.

The newsreel footage of the former president at Carroll Kehne's Gulf station would be shown in movie theaters around the world. When it was shown at a theater in Whittier, California—Richard Nixon's hometown—the applause was so loud, according to one attendee, it drowned out the audio.

In 1975 Carroll Kehne closed his service station. He was sixty-five. It was time to retire. Besides, the business was changing. "This is what you call the old, country-type gas station," he told the *Frederick Post* shortly before the closing. "Where people always gather and have good times. But this is one of the last."

"All the new stations are concerned with," he complained, "is just how quick you get in and how quick you get out."

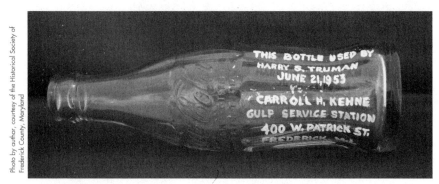

Photo by author, courtesy of the Historical Society of
Frederick County, Maryland

The Coke bottle that Harry Truman drank from at Carroll Kehne's service station in
Frederick, Maryland, on June 20, 1953. After Kehne died, his son donated the bottle
to the Historical Society of Frederick County.

The striking deco service station was torn down shortly after it closed.
In its place stands a transmission shop's nondescript, four-bay garage.

Carroll Kehne died in 1994. Among his belongings, his son found the
Coke bottle that Harry Truman had drunk from all those years before.
Carroll Jr. donated it to the Historical Society of Frederick County, where
it currently resides, lovingly swaddled in acid-free archival paper.

In honor of Harry's pit stop in Frederick, H. I. Phillips composed a poem
for his syndicated newspaper column. It was a spoof on "Barbara Frietchie,"
a John Greenleaf Whittier poem about a Frederick woman who became a
local hero when she allegedly stood up to Confederate troops during the
Civil War.

> Up from the meadows rich with corn,
> Clear in the steaming mid-June morn,
> The gasoline stations of Frederick stand
> And give to Harry a hearty hand.
> Round about them the tourists sweep;
> Clicking and clacking the meters creep;
> Routine and drab is the station's way,
> Oftentimes dull . . . but NOT THIS DAY!

8

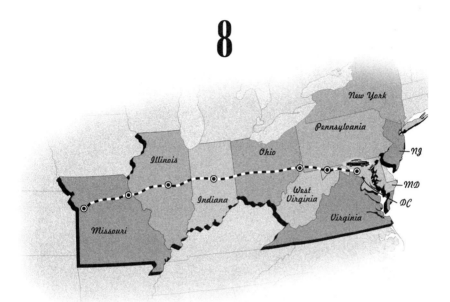

Washington, D.C., June 21–26, 1953

*A*t 5:40 P.M. on Sunday, June 21, Harry and Bess pulled up in front of the Mayflower Hotel on Connecticut Avenue in Washington. A doorman helped Harry on with his double-breasted suit jacket. Harry supervised the unloading of luggage.

Never before had a former president returned to the capital quite like this: driving his own car in his shirtsleeves, as if he were nothing more than a curious tourist—which, Harry insisted with a gleam in his eye, is all he was.

Margaret was waiting for her parents at the hotel. She had come down from New York to stay with them while they were in Washington, acting as a kind of unofficial press secretary, a role she clearly relished.

The Truman family stayed in suite 676, which had been redecorated especially for them. (C. J. "Neal" Mack, the hotel manager, jokingly called

From the Washington Star Collection, D.C. Public Library. Reprinted by permission of the D.C. Public Library. Copyright the Washington Post.

A doorman helps Harry on with his jacket upon his arrival at the Mayflower Hotel, June 21, 1953. Harry liked the Mayflower so much he called it "Washington's second-best address."

it the "ex-presidential suite.") There was a parlor with green walls and white-shaded lamps, a small dining room, two bedrooms, and a kitchen. For this, Mack had agreed to charge the Trumans a "special daily rate" of just fifteen dollars. That was a significant discount: the usual rate was thirty-six dollars.

Shortly after checking in, Truman invited the reporters who'd covered his return to the capital up to his suite.

"You're awfully nice to come up here just to see an old has-been," he said as they filed in. To all questions about politics, Congress, Ike, or Korea, his answer was the same: "No comment." Mostly he just wanted to talk about the drive from Missouri. It was exactly 1,055 miles from his home in Independence to the Mayflower, he reported. With a touch of pride, he added that his new Chrysler was getting sixteen to seventeen miles a gallon.

The trip, he said, was "wonderful," "lovely."

His smile, one reporter noted, was wider than ever.

He said he had no plans to see President Eisenhower. "He's too busy to see every Tom, Dick, and Harry that comes to town," he said, putting special emphasis on the last name.

He said he only came back to Washington to see "old friends" and insisted he would be "keeping away from politics." He was, of course, being disingenuous. Over the next four days Truman presided over a veritable government in exile, meeting with Democratic Party leaders and even calling together his old cabinet. He was back in his element, and he couldn't have been happier. "He was like a kid on holiday," journalist Charles Robbins recalled, "exchanging quips with the newsmen, welcoming his former staff and members of his cabinet, hurrying from one telephone to another to talk to senators, representatives, judges."

And he did it all right under Eisenhower's nose. The White House, Robbins said, "maintained a tomblike silence" while Harry was in town.

At the time, there was a rumor going around Washington that Truman would run for president again in 1956, with Adlai Stevenson as his running mate—or, perhaps, vice versa. Truman insisted he wasn't interested in running for anything, but, judging by the way he behaved on his return to the capital, it was hard to believe him.

No hotel has played a more important role in American politics than the Mayflower. Just two weeks after it opened in 1925, it hosted an inaugural ball for Calvin Coolidge (which the famously reticent president did not attend). Herbert Hoover lived at the hotel between his election and inauguration, as did FDR, who wrote his first inaugural address in suite 776. FBI Director J. Edgar Hoover and his longtime aide Clyde Tolson ate lunch side by side in the hotel's Town & Country Lounge nearly every day for twenty years. Queen Elizabeth and Winston Churchill stayed there. So did the Chinese delegation negotiating détente with the Nixon administration in 1973. Gerald Ford was offered the vice presidency there.

Harry Truman liked the Mayflower. As vice president, he once sat in with the hotel's band. "He played piano with us (The Fairy Waltz, Chopsticks, etc.) and it was very cozy," the Mayflower's bandleader, Sidney Seidenman, wrote in a letter to his son, who was in the army at the time. "He seems a very swell guy. I don't suppose the German Vice Presidential equivalent would go around playing piano with the likes of me, now, would he?" In a 1948 speech at the hotel, Truman declared his candidacy for election to the presidency in his own right. ("I want to say that during the next four years there will be a Democrat in the White House, and you are looking at him!") The following January, he celebrated his inauguration there. That was an especially joyous event for Truman, who had, of course, been unable to celebrate his ascension to the presidency theretofore. The Mayflower, he said, was "Washington's second-best address," a phrase that now appears on T-shirts sold in the hotel's gift shop.

What you won't find in the gift shop is any mention of the hotel's role in some of Washington's most salacious political scandals. If the Mayflower's walls could talk, they would have been subpoenaed—or bought off—a long, long time ago.

Kennedy's alleged mistress, Judith Exner, kept a room at the hotel, and JFK is said to have met Angie Dickinson at the Mayflower for more than drinks. A former girlfriend of Washington Mayor Marion Barry testified that she smoked crack with him at the Mayflower in 1989. (That infamous undercover video, however—"Bitch set me up!"—was shot across town

at the Vista.) Bill Clinton and Monica Lewinsky were famously photographed embracing at a campaign event at the Mayflower in 1996, and,
three years later, Lewinsky was interviewed in the hotel's presidential suite
by House investigators trying to impeach the president.

More recently, on February 13, 2008, New York governor Eliot Spitzer
(aka client 9) met a call girl named "Kristen" in room 871. That tryst
would cost Spitzer forty-three hundred dollars and his political career.

On Monday morning, Bess and Margaret went out to do some shopping while Harry and a group of his old advisors convened in his suite to
put the finishing touches on the speech he would deliver in Philadelphia
later that week. The first draft had been prepared by David Lloyd, his
White House speechwriter. "It was a lively exegetical session," remembered
Charles Robbins, who was there. "He would read a line or two aloud, then
pause for comment. From the ensuing argument, the laughter and byplay,
there slowly emerged a different speech." Harry replaced all the fifty-cent
words with much cheaper ones. "The final product," wrote Robbins, "was
pretty much all his."

At noon, Truman went to the Capitol for lunch with Democratic
members of Missouri's congressional delegation. He went by limousine.
The Packard Motor Car Company had offered him the use of a brand-
new eighty-five-hundred-dollar limo while he was in Washington. (The
company also provided a "smartly uniformed" chauffeur.) The limousine
was identical to two that the company had recently delivered to the White
House for President Eisenhower's use.

"We shipped this car down from Detroit for the use of Mr. Truman
as a courtesy," explained Donald C. Jeffrey, Packard's manager of government sales. "We don't play sides." Truman, who was probably a little tired
of driving anyway, gladly took the company up on its offer. His Chrysler
would spend the rest of the week in the Mayflower garage.

At lunch, Truman told his fellow Missouri Democrats that their party
was "on the comeback trail." He said farmers back home were organizing

"Never Again" clubs, promising to never again vote Republican. "We gave them three-hundred-dollar cows," he said, "now they've got thirty-dollar Eisenhower calves."

Walking back to the limousine after lunch, Truman was mobbed outside the Capitol by tourists who had come to see the sights, never expecting to see one in the flesh. They crowded close around him, jostling for position, begging for an autograph or a handshake or a snapshot. As was his policy, he patiently obliged every request. Once, when asked how he coped with such onslaughts, Truman laughed and said he tried to put himself in other people's shoes and imagine how he would feel "if some supposed bigshot high-hatted me."

Occasionally, however, his patience was tested. At a college basketball tournament in Kansas City, about three hundred autograph seekers rushed his box when he and Bess were introduced over the public address system. Even after it was announced that he would give no autographs while the game was in progress, "the more rugged members of the crowd" continued to pester him with their requests. "We never saw the finish of the game," he remembered. "Our host lost his nerve and smuggled us out with five minutes left to go."

On the way back to the Mayflower in his limousine, Truman spotted his good friend and erstwhile secretary of state, the debonair Dean Acheson, walking alone along 17th Street NW. Truman had his driver honk the horn repeatedly, but Acheson, lost in thought, paid no attention. Finally the limo pulled up alongside him. Truman stuck his head out the window. "You're the hardest pickup I ever encountered," he said. For five minutes the former president and his former secretary of state chatted casually on a Washington sidewalk, just like old friends, which they were. Acheson asked Truman about the drive from Independence. "Had a governor on the seat with me," Harry said, referring to Bess as a speed-regulation device. "Had it up to seventy a few times, but she'd always pull me in."

That night the Trumans attended a cookout at Clark Clifford's house. Clifford had been Harry's White House counsel and would go on to advise three more Democratic presidents, becoming the ultimate Washington insider. He and his wife, Marny, lived in an antebellum farmhouse on Rockville Pike in Bethesda, Maryland.

It was a typical American barbecue in every way—save for the guest list. Besides the former president and first lady, Chief Justice Fred Vinson and his wife were among the twenty-two high-powered attendees.

Cocktails preceded dinner. Clifford, wearing an apron, cooked the steaks himself on a charcoal grill on the patio. The guests ate at tables set up in the Cliffords' sprawling backyard. It was, Bess Truman later wrote, the happiest evening she and Harry had spent in a long, long time.

At the cookout, Harry renewed his acquaintance with the Cliffords' thirteen-year-old daughter, Randi. Her father had taken Randi to the White House many times when he worked there, and Harry had befriended her. When she was eight, Randi sent the president a photograph of her in her Brownie uniform. Truman wrote her back, thanking her for the picture. "He was wonderful to me," Randi remembered.

Some thirty years later, on a vacation with her own family in the early 1980s, Randi visited the Truman Library. The former president's desk was on display. On it she saw an old photograph of a smiling buck-toothed little girl in a Brownie uniform.

It was the photograph she'd sent the president.

Clark and Marny Clifford died in 1998 and 2000, respectively, and the family sold the house on Rockville Pike to a young couple named Tim and Kristen. I mailed them a copy of an old newspaper clipping about the Truman cookout and asked if I—a perfect stranger—could visit their home. I was happily surprised when they said yes.

Like Harry and Bess, I visited the home on a steamy early summer evening. Unlike Harry and Bess, I took the subway. The home is a short walk from the Medical Center stop on the Washington Metro's Red Line. What was once a rural farmhouse has been completely engulfed by suburbia. To reach it, I had to negotiate a bewildering maze of intentionally winding (and sidewalk-free) streets in postwar subdivisions. Many were the drive-ways with portable basketball hoops.

When I arrived, Kristen gave me a tour of the house while Tim finished cleaning up after dinner and while their three young children, accompanied by a friend, wreaked playful havoc. Joining us on the tour was Kristen's father, Doug, a gregarious George Kennedy look-alike who has researched the history of the house. He'd come over specially to see me.

As Doug explained, the old wooden house is an excellent example of the Georgian revival style, a classic "two over two," with two rooms on the first floor divided by a center hallway and staircase, and two rooms on the second. Later additions were built on either side of the house, doubling its size.

After the tour, Kristen went off to help Tim while Doug and I took seats at the dining room table. Doug showed me a sixteen-page history of the house he'd written. He also produced a thick three-ring binder filled with photographs and photocopied tax and census records, each carefully inserted inside a protective plastic sleeve. It was heartening to see him taking the history of his daughter and son-in-law's home so seriously. It was also nice of him to have done so much research for me, bless his heart.

Doug's sleuthing revealed that the house was built in 1854 by a farmer named Samuel Perry. At the time, Perry owned 444 acres along Rockville Pike, already a well-trod route connecting the capital and Rockville, Maryland. Perry and his son-in-law also owned a dozen slaves, who lived in a small stone cottage on the property.

Doug also discovered that Harry Truman was not the first president to visit the home—nor the last. In 1910, when the house was owned by an adventurer named Leigh Hunt, his friend Teddy Roosevelt stopped by. Like Harry, TR embarked on a long trip shortly after leaving the White House, though Teddy's was slightly more adventurous: he went on an African safari. Upon his return he delivered to Hunt two souvenirs he'd picked up on his travels, stuffed and mounted lion and hippopotamus heads, which Hunt hung over the mantle in the living room.

Clark and Marny Clifford bought the house in 1950, and over the next half-century they would entertain a parade of future, current, or former presidents: Truman, Kennedy, Johnson, and the elder Bush. On the day he left office, Johnson came over for lunch. So, in all, at least five presidents have visited the house, which must be some kind of record for a private home in Bethesda, anyway.

Tim and Kristen have done a lot of remodeling since they bought the house (including the removal of Clark Clifford's thirty-two-line switch-board in the basement). They said they haven't seen any ghosts, no visions of Harry in his summer suit, enjoying a bourbon in the backyard, though they did discover a bust of Clifford in a closet. (Kristen said she contacted the Clifford family but was told she could keep it since "everybody in the family who wanted a bust of him already had one.") They've had many cookouts in the big backyard, but, so far, anyway, none has been attended by a president. In fact, when I asked Kristen who their most famous house-guest had been, she thought for a moment and said, "You."

On Tuesday, June 23, Harry woke up early and took his usual morning walk—his first in Washington without Secret Service agents in more than eight years. At his usual brisk pace, he covered two miles in thirty minutes, walking along Connecticut Avenue and K Street. He never came within three blocks of the White House. Along the way, he was greeted by passersby, cabbies, truck drivers, and motorists: "Hello, Harry," "Hello, Mr. President," "Glad to see you back."

Back at the hotel, Truman spent the day welcoming a string of visitors to his suite. One of his callers was the Iranian ambassador to the United States, Allah-Yar Saleh, who presented the former president with a Persian rug. The timing of the meeting is curious, for at that very moment the CIA was plotting to overthrow Saleh's boss, Iranian Prime Minister Mohammed Mossadegh, and return the shah to the Peacock Throne. The motive, of course, was oil. In 1951, Mossadegh announced plans to nationalize the country's oilfields. This infuriated the British, who controlled Iran's oil through the Anglo-Iranian Oil Company (later known as British Petroleum, or BP). The British asked the Truman administration to help them remove Mossadegh. Truman, who was up to his eyeballs in Korea at the time, wasn't interested—but his successor was. On April 4, 1953, Eisenhower's director of central intelligence, Allen W. Dulles, signed off on an operation, code-named Ajax, to "bring about the fall of Mossadegh." The agent in charge of the operation was Kermit Roosevelt—Theodore's grandson. Iranians working for the agency and posing as communists harassed religious leaders to turn public opinion against Mossadegh. The CIA recruited an Iranian general to lead a coup. On August 19, 1953, demonstrators paid by the CIA attacked Mossadegh's house. The resulting clashes killed three hundred people. Mossadegh fled, the general was installed as prime minister, and the shah returned to the throne. The British thanked the Americans by opening Iran to U.S. oil companies.

The CIA considered the coup a shining success and, in the ensuing years, it would inspire similar efforts to overthrow anti-American regimes in Guatemala and Cuba, with decidedly mixed results.

Mohammed Mossadegh was arrested and, after a show trial, sentenced to death. The shah commuted the sentence to three years' imprisonment and house arrest for life. Allah-Yar Saleh, Mossadegh's ambassador to the United States, returned to Iran and led the moderate opposition to the shah's pro-Western government. The coup set the stage for the Islamic Revolution in 1979, not to mention generations of anti-American sentiment in Iran.

To Truman, the coup came to symbolize a larger problem: how the CIA, which he had organized in 1947, had been "diverted from its original assignment" of merely collecting intelligence. "It has become an operational and at times a policy-making arm of the government," he wrote in 1963. "This has led to trouble and may have compounded our difficulties in several explosive areas. I never had any thought that when I set up the CIA that it would be injected into peacetime cloak and dagger operations."

The shah, for his part, would curry Truman's favor for years, sending him Christmas cards every year and get-well cards when he got sick.

While Harry welcomed callers to his suite, Bess and Margaret attended a tea at the Women's National Democratic Club. Bess wore a blue lace dress and a matching straw hat. She looked ten years younger, said one guest. She never looked happier, said another. Margaret, wearing a white silk dress with brown velvet trim, was asked if she and her parents planned to do any sightseeing in Washington. "Why go sightseeing in a place where you have lived nineteen years?" she said. "It hasn't changed that much since January, has it?" She also denied rumors that Harry and Bess would do some house hunting when they visited her the following week in New York. "They are not going to live in New York or Long Island," she said. "They are going back to Missouri—that's home." Margaret also denied reports of a new romantic interest. "No," she sighed. "I am still looking."

Also at the tea was another former first lady, Edith Bolling Wilson, the widow of Woodrow Wilson. It was a rare public appearance for Mrs. Wilson, who was eighty. When someone asked her what first ladies talked about when they got together, she just laughed and shook her head. (Besides Mmes. Truman and Wilson, two other former first ladies were alive at the time, Grace Coolidge and Eleanor Roosevelt.)

That night, Harry "reconvened" his old cabinet for a fancy dinner in a ballroom at the Mayflower. Seated at the head of a horseshoe-shaped table decorated with wildflowers and fruit-filled epergnes, it must have occurred to the former president that he was less well off than any of his subordinates, most of whom had moved on to lucrative careers in the private sector. Dean Acheson, Agriculture Secretary Charles Brannan, Interior Secretary Oscar L. Chapman, and Attorney General James McGranery had all joined high-profile law firms in Washington. Defense Secretary Robert Lovett was a partner at the investment bank Brown Brothers Harriman. Treasury Secretary John W. Snyder was a vice president at the automaker Willys-Overland. Labor Secretary Maurice J. Tobin was a prosperous businessman in Massachusetts.

Dean Acheson gave the toast that night, and it was long remembered by those in attendance as one of the best tributes to Truman—or to anyone, for that matter—they had ever heard. Acheson began by recalling how he'd unexpectedly bumped into his old boss on the street the day before. "At that moment," he said, "I knew how the Korean prisoners felt when the guards opened the stockade gates."

Acheson continued,

> Mr. President, we are reliably informed that among the Mohammedans the faithful turn to the East when they pray. In Washington the faithful turn to the West. And so your return is to us a very real answer to prayer. . . .
>
> President Truman's fundamental purpose and burning passion has been to serve his country and his fellow citizens. This devoted love of the United States has been the only rival which Mrs. Truman has had. . . .
>
> The greatest of all commanders never ask more of their troops than they are willing to give themselves. . . . The president has never asked any of us to do what he would not do. When the time came to fight, he threw everything into it, himself included. And what we all knew was that, however hot the fire was in front, there would never be a shot in the back. Quite the contrary! He stood by us through thick and thin, always eager to attribute successes to us and accept for himself the full responsibility for failure. . . .
>
> It is for reasons such as these that this visit of yours brings us such happiness. These visits of yours must be regular affairs, for we all badly need the refreshment and inspiration that they bring us.
>
> To you, Mr. President, and to your enduring health and happiness, we join in a final toast.

While I was in Washington, another former president returned to the capital—sort of. Jimmy Carter held a book signing at the Books-A-Million in a strip mall in McLean, Virginia, between a wine store and an Advance Auto Parts, and about ten miles west of 1600 Pennsylvania Avenue.

The ex-presidential book signing is a ritual begun by Harry Truman. In a hotel ballroom in Kansas City on November 2, 1955, Harry autographed four thousand copies of his memoirs. According to his publisher, it was the first time an ex-president had "agreed to sit down and sign copies of his book." Not that Harry was crazy about the idea. "I will go along with any party arrangements you make for Doubleday," he wrote one of the publisher's publicists before the event, "but don't get me into any advertising for pens, cakes or anything, because I won't do it."

Jimmy Carter's book signing was scheduled for 7:00 P.M., but when my wife and I showed up at five, about fifty people were already lined up outside the store, which was closed in preparation for the event. A Books-A-Million rep moved up and down the line, making clear the ground rules. Mr. Carter would sign only books—no photographs, no baseballs, no greeting cards. He would sign no more than five books per person, and he would sign only those books that he had authored (he's written about twenty-five). At least one of the books had to be his new one (*A Remarkable Mother*, his paean to the indefatigable Miss Lillian). He would not personalize inscriptions. He would only sign his name. And he would only sign the title page. We were asked to open our books to that page before presenting them for signing.

Around 5:45, the line started to move. The former president, it seemed, was running early. Three Secret Service agents stationed at the front door gave us the once-over with handheld metal detectors and poked through our bags. The line wound through a maze of bookshelves. Before we knew it, we were in the presence of the thirty-ninth president (or thirty-eighth, by Truman's reckoning).

He sat behind a large faux mahogany desk with a red velvet rope in front of it. Black drapes covered the bookshelves behind him. Secret Service agents stood sentry at each side of the desk. He was wearing a white dress shirt with blue stripes. He hunched slightly as he signed title pages in rapid-fire succession: J Carter, J Carter, J Carter, J Carter. When I examined his autograph later, I was impressed by its legibility.

When I reached the desk, I handed my books to a Books-A-Million minion, who handed them to the former president. I stepped to the front of the desk as he began to sign them. It reminded me of the "Soup Nazi" episode of *Seinfeld*. A strict protocol was to be observed, but I wasn't sure what it was. It was so quiet I could hear the sound of the pen scratching across the page as he signed the first book. This was not like bumping into an ex-president outside the Capitol. It felt a little funereal. The very arrangement discouraged interaction. I wasn't even sure we were allowed to address the former president. But I was determined to ask him . . . something. We'd purchased only three books for him to sign. Time was running out. Finally, I blurted out, "Mr. President, did you ever meet Harry Truman?" He stopped signing for a moment and looked up at me. His expression was serious. He seemed to be rummaging through his mental filing cabinets. "No," he said after a moment in his familiar quiet drawl. "I wish I had." He resumed signing but continued talking. "I never met another Democratic president until Bill Clinton. I did meet Richard Nixon

Photo by Allyson Algeo

Former president Jimmy Carter signing a book for the author at a Books-A-Million bookstore in McLean, Virginia. In 1955, Harry Truman was the first ex-president to hold a book signing.

when I was governor. But I was just a peanut farmer before that, so I never met Harry Truman." With that our books were signed. I said, "Thank you, Mr. President." He looked up at me and smiled. He had already started signing the next pile of books.

Our exchange lasted maybe thirty seconds. Which is probably more face time than anybody else got that night. At his previous book signing, I heard he'd signed sixteen hundred books in ninety minutes. That's 3.3 seconds per book—less than seventeen seconds for the maximum of five books.

In this regard, at least, Carter defeats Truman. At his signing in Kansas City, Harry averaged about nine books a minute—a relatively leisurely rate of some seven seconds per book. (Unlike Carter, however, Harry signed his full name—and with "mechanical precision," according to one eyewitness.)

On Wednesday, June 24, Harry went back to the Capitol. In room S-211, a committee room just off the Senate floor, he had lunch with forty-four of the forty-seven Democratic senators then serving, including two first-termers, Lyndon B. Johnson and John F. Kennedy.

Truman regarded both future presidents with some circumspection. He considered Johnson a trifle too ambitious. (Johnson was just twenty-eight when he was elected to the House in 1937. In 1955, at forty-two, he would become the youngest Senate majority leader in history.) Truman also thought Johnson a bit of a suck-up—and not an altogether accomplished one. When Truman's mother died in 1947, then-Congressman Johnson obsequiously wrote the president, saying he would donate a book in memory of the "First Mother" to the Grandview Public Library. Truman wrote back and thanked Johnson, but added, "I regret to advise you that Grandview has no Public Library." Johnson biographer Robert A. Caro said the relationship between the two men "would never be particularly warm," and Margaret Truman said her father "never quite trusted" Johnson.

Toward Kennedy, however, Truman felt something approaching antipathy. Elected to Congress at twenty-nine, Kennedy was no less ambitious than Johnson. But at least Johnson had worked his way up from the hardscrabble Texas Hill Country. Kennedy embodied the kind of elitist sense of entitlement that Truman despised. Furthermore, Truman never cared for Kennedy's father, the haughty and overbearing Joe Kennedy, whom Truman had once threatened to throw out a hotel window for belittling FDR. When the younger Kennedy's religion became an issue in the 1960 presidential campaign, Truman quipped, "It's not the pope I'm afraid of, it's the pop." Truman boycotted the Democratic National Convention in Los Angeles that year, claiming it had been "rigged" in Kennedy's favor. But when Kennedy won the nomination, Truman, ever the dutiful Democrat, campaigned for him.

There is no record of what occurred inside that committee room during lunch that day. Surely Harry gave his standard pep talk. Jack Kennedy was undoubtedly distracted, maybe even a little nervous, for it was his last day as Washington's most eligible bachelor. That night, he would announce his engagement to a twenty-three-year-old George Washington University graduate whose "Inquiring Camera Girl" column ran in the *Washington Times-Herald*. Her name was Jacqueline Lee Bouvier.

Lyndon Johnson, meanwhile, was probably gazing covetously at the ceiling of room S-211, on which was painted a magnificent fresco by the Italian artist Constantino Brumidi. When he became majority leader, Johnson made the room his new office.

After lunch, the Democratic senators invited Harry onto the Senate floor to visit his old desk. Protocol, however, demanded that he call on the president of the Senate first. So Harry walked across the hall to the office of Richard Nixon and paid what might be the most uncomfortable courtesy call in the annals of Congress. Nixon was one of only two politicians Truman is said to have truly hated. (The other was Lloyd Stark, the Missouri governor who unsuccessfully challenged Truman for his Senate seat in the 1940 Democratic primary.) As a representative and later a senator, Nixon was a constant thorn in Truman's side. As a member of the House Un-American Activities Committee, he relentlessly pursued charges that communists had "infiltrated" the Truman administration.

But it was the 1952 presidential campaign that forever turned Truman against Nixon. Throughout that campaign, Nixon, the Republican vice presidential candidate, had excoriated the Truman administration for supposedly coddling communists. Nixon said "real Democrats" should have been "outraged by the Truman-Acheson-Stevenson gang's toleration and

Harry and Vice President Richard Nixon pose outside Nixon's office in the Capitol, June 24, 1953. Nixon was one of the two men in politics Harry truly hated.

defense of communism in high places." Nixon went "down and around over the country and called me a traitor," Truman bitterly recalled. He would never forgive Nixon. Privately he called him a "squirrel head," a "son of a bitch"—or worse.

But in Nixon's Senate office that warm early summer day, the two consummate politicians did what they knew they had to do. They dutifully posed for photographers, arm in arm, smiling broadly, their mutual contempt nicely concealed. (The papers would say the two men had "buried the hatchet," a suggestion that made Truman laugh.)

To much applause, Truman was escorted into the Senate chamber by Lyndon Johnson and Senate Majority Leader William Knowland. Truman immediately walked over to Robert Taft, the Ohio Republican who was one of Truman's fiercest opponents in the Senate. Taft was gravely ill, his body riddled with cancer. Thin and pale, he struggled to his feet with the aid of crutches. The two old foes shared a long, warm handshake. Taft, a perennial presidential candidate, turned to a Republican colleague, Andrew F. Schoeppel of Kansas, and said, "Harry and I have always had the viewpoint that he'd make the best Democratic candidate and I'd make the best Republican candidate for the reason that we each think that the other would be easiest to defeat." A month later, Taft was dead.

Truman then walked over to his old desk in the back row. (At the time it was assigned to Hubert Humphrey, one of the three Democratic senators absent that day.) Truman smiled broadly as the applause continued. When it finally subsided, Nixon invited Truman to say a few words.

"I think I have told you before," Truman said, "that the happiest ten years of my life were spent on the floor of the Senate. I used to sit in this seat; and I had a seat here for the simple reason that, when the going became too rough, there was always a way to get out." Truman motioned toward a nearby door. The chamber erupted in laughter.

"This body," he continued, "of course, has great responsibilities. Its members do not need to be told that by a former senator. But it is up to this body to keep the peace of the world. My ambition has always been to

see peace in the world for all nations; and if that happens, it means peace
and prosperity for our own nation.

"I have had a most wonderful experience in driving across the country
as a chauffeur in an automobile—a privilege which I had not enjoyed for
about eight years. . . . Mrs. Truman watched the speedometer very carefully and we arrived safely.

"I express sincere appreciation for the courtesy which this body has
extended to me. I have enjoyed it very much."

Applause filled the chamber again. Though brief, Truman's remarks
were historic: he was the first ex-president to address the Senate since
Andrew Johnson in 1875. (Johnson, the only former president elected to
the Senate, served less than five months before dying.)

As he departed the chamber, again escorted by Johnson and Knowland,
an impromptu receiving line formed. Truman moved along the gauntlet,
shaking hands. All the senators he greeted warmly—save two. William
Jenner, an Indiana Republican, and John Marshall Butler, a Maryland
Republican, received handshakes that, the *New York Times* noted, were
"quick and perfunctory." Both were allies of Joseph McCarthy.

McCarthy himself was conspicuously—and, some said, prudently—
absent.

His private meetings with lawmakers not only gave Harry a chance to
catch up on politics. They also gave him a chance to lobby—discreetly,
to be sure—for a pension. The issue was not new. After Ulysses S. Grant's
financial problems came to light in 1880, his friends launched a campaign
to raise $250,000 in private contributions for a trust fund, the interest from
which would be paid to "the surviving ex-President whose Incumbency is
most distant in point of time." Grant, naturally, would be the first recipi-
ent. The campaign ended when Grant indicated he would not accept the
pension.

After he left the White House, Grover Cleveland was asked if the best
way to deal with ex-presidents wasn't to "take them out to a five-acre lot

and shoot them." "Five acres seems needlessly large," Cleveland replied, "and, in the second place, an ex-president has already suffered enough."

In late November 1912, Andrew Carnegie offered to pay future ex-presidents twenty-five thousand dollars a year so they could "spend their latter days free from pecuniary cares in devoting the intimate knowledge they have gained of public affairs to the good of the country." By limiting the pensions to "future" ex-presidents, Carnegie pointedly snubbed his old trust-busting nemesis Teddy Roosevelt, the only living ex at the time. Roosevelt was too rich to care. "In any event," he said upon learning of Carnegie's offer, "[my] interest isn't in pensions for ex-Presidents, but in pensions for the small man who doesn't have a chance to save, and who, when he becomes superannuated, faces the direst poverty." The sole immediate beneficiary of Carnegie's offer would have been his good friend William Howard Taft, who had recently lost his bid for a second term (largely because Roosevelt had run as a third-party candidate). Taft had hinted at his upcoming need in a speech shortly after the election. "I consider that the President of the United States is well paid," he said, ". . . unless it is the policy of Congress to enable him in his four years to save enough money to live in adequate dignity and comfort thereafter. . . ."

Carnegie's proposal was widely condemned as "undemocratic." "The idea of ex-Presidents being dependent on private bounty is distasteful to many of Mr. Taft's associates and friends," the *New York Times* reported. Taft was forced to disavow the offer, and Carnegie withdrew it. (Taft, as it happened, found a good post-presidential job in 1921, when Warren Harding appointed him chief justice.)

Members of Congress, meanwhile, exhibited an aversion to presidential pensions that bordered on hostility. (They were more generous with presidential widows. At least twelve had been allocated pensions, usually around five thousand dollars a year. They were also more generous with themselves. A congressional pension plan was begun in 1946—too late for Harry, though.)

In 1912, shortly after Carnegie made his pension offer, Albert S. Burleson, a Democratic congressman from Texas, proposed that ex-presidents be made permanent, nonvoting members of the House of Representatives at an annual salary of $17,500. The proposal went nowhere.

In 1948 none other than Senator Robert Taft, son of William, proposed a "substantial" pension—perhaps twenty-five thousand dollars a year—which would allow former presidents "to live in a dignified manner." He also said exes should be made nonvoting members of the Senate. But, again, Congress did nothing.

In an editorial published shortly before Truman left office, the *New York Times* spoke out in favor of pensions for ex-presidents. "A president nowadays is likely to be a worn-out man when he lays down his office," the paper wrote. "He shouldn't have to embark on making a living even in a comfortable and dignified way."

To Harry Truman, a pension was a matter of principle. Members of Congress got pensions. So did federal judges, and generals and admirals. Yet he got nothing—and he had been commander in chief for nearly eight years! "If you were a rich man before becoming President you went home to your estates," he wrote in September 1953, "[and] if your means were modest you did the best you could to earn a living. . . . You were just a private citizen. Ideally, this fits in with our notions of the equality of man. Practically, though, it presents a few problems."

Even if he didn't get a pension, Truman argued, the government should at least help him pay his expenses. Truman estimated the cost of maintaining his office in Kansas City at more than thirty-six hundred dollars a month. The government, he believed, should pick up 70 percent of that cost, the remainder being "what I would ordinarily have been out on my own hook if I hadn't tried to meet the responsibilities of being a former President."

Still, Congress wouldn't budge.

In contrast to the bitter denunciations he had sometimes suffered in the editorial pages during his presidency, the newspaper coverage of Truman's return to Washington was mostly fawning.

A cartoon on the front page of the *Washington Star* depicted Harry as a tourist, a travel guide in his back pocket and camera in hand, standing on the sidewalk, peering at the White House through the iron gate. It greatly amused Truman, who once described the White House as a "prison." "I'd much rather be on the outside looking in than on the inside looking out," he joked.

"The friendly quality that was so much a part of the Truman family during their years in Senate life and later in the White House was still with them during their recent visit here," said an editorial in the *Star* (which had endorsed Dewey in 1948). "It was good to have them back. They looked fine, and it's nice to know they're happy and enjoying life. One hopes that they'll make a habit of dropping into town from time to time. Old friends are always welcome."

Not everybody was so welcoming. Harry's old enemies on the right couldn't abide his carefree return to Washington. "Harry S. can stroll blithely around the nation's capital, without a care in the world, secretly hugging himself with glee," wrote the newspaper columnist George Dixon, who noted that Truman had run up a budget deficit of better than six billion dollars in the final year of his administration. "He did the dancing, but Dwight D. has to pay the piper."

But Harry didn't give a damn what George Dixon or any of his ilk thought. He had the time of his life on his first trip back to the capital. "As soon as we arrived in Washington," Harry wrote, "the calendar seemed to have been turned back a year. . . . It seemed like a dream to relive such an experience. For one solid week, the illusion of those other days in Washington was maintained perfectly. The suite we stayed in at the Mayflower could have been the White House; many of the visitors were the same. Everything seemed just as it used to be—the taxi drivers shouting hello along the line of my morning walks, the dinners at night with the men and women I had worked with for years, the conferences, the tension, the excitement, the feeling of things happening and going to happen—all the same. I was deeply moved by the spontaneous expression of good will shown me."

9

Philadelphia, Pennsylvania, June 26–27, 1953

*O*n the afternoon of Friday, June 26, Harry took the train to Philadelphia. He rode in a private railcar loaned to him by the Pennsylvania Railroad, another "favor" that the former president gladly accepted. Bess and Margaret, meanwhile, drove ahead to New York City in the Chrysler. Harry would meet them there after his speech.

Philadelphia played a pivotal role in Truman's political career. It was the site of the 1948 Democratic National Convention, where Truman roused languid delegates in a sweltering auditorium with a characteristically pugnacious acceptance speech: ". . . I will win this election and make these Republicans like it—don't you forget that!" It was the opening salvo of the whistle-stop campaign.

Five years later, almost to the day, Truman was returning to Philadelphia to deliver the first major speech of his post-presidency.

At 4:12 P.M. his train pulled into 30th Street Station, where he was greeted by a delegation of city officials as well as a contingent from the Reserve Officers Association. Dressed in a blue summer suit and a Panama hat, the former president looked relaxed and jovial. He was driven to the Warwick Hotel, where he took a nap. Then he was driven several blocks to the Bellevue-Stratford Hotel, the site of the Reserve Officers Association's twenty-seventh annual convention.

Standing in a receiving line before dinner, Truman, now donning a white dinner jacket and black bow tie, greeted another member of the Reserve Officers Association who, like Truman, was a colonel in the army reserves: J. Strom Thurmond, former governor of South Carolina and erstwhile presidential candidate. Back in 1948, Thurmond had bolted the Democratic Party to protest its civil rights platform. "There's not enough troops in the army to break down segregation and admit the Negro into our homes, our eating places, our swimming pools, and our theaters," he declared. Thurmond, who had secretly fathered an illegitimate child with his African American maid twenty-three years earlier, ran for president as the candidate of the States' Rights Democratic Party (aka the Dixiecrats). In his standard stump speech, Thurmond castigated Truman, whom he described as "mad with the lust for power." What Truman was proposing, he said, was "a program so full of narcotics that the American people are in danger of being lulled to sleep by it. They have named this program 'civil rights.'"

Thurmond carried four Southern states, capturing thirty-nine electoral votes and ending the Democrats' stranglehold on the region. Two years later, Thurmond returned to the Democratic Party and ran unsuccessfully for the Senate on a decidedly anti-Truman platform. And just the preceding fall, he'd endorsed Eisenhower, not Stevenson. (Thurmond would get elected to the Senate as a Democratic write-in candidate in 1954. He would hold the seat the rest of his life. In 1964 he switched parties and became a Republican.)

Truman, understandably, didn't much care for Strom Thurmond, whose disloyalty to the Democratic Party was something that Truman

Harry delivers his first major speech as a former president at the Reserve Officers Association convention in Philadelphia, June 26, 1953. "Do not be misled by the desire for lower taxes into cutting corners on our national security," he warned.

couldn't stomach. But in the receiving line that night, Harry did the same thing he'd done with Ike on Inauguration Day and Nixon two days earlier. He smiled. He shook Thurmond's hand. The flashbulbs popped.

After dinner, Truman was introduced as "a colonel, U.S. Army, retired, and the former President of the United States." He received a two-minute standing ovation.

He stood behind a small lectern that had been placed on the head table. A sign leaning against the front of it read RESERVES ASK ONLY THE RIGHT TO BE READY. The lectern was covered with microphones—the speech would be carried live on radio stations nationwide. Television cameras were there too, and it was dreadfully hot under the klieg lights, though Harry, as usual, never let on. The Bellevue-Stratford's Grand Ballroom was packed with more than a thousand people, most of the men in uniform, the women in gowns. They sat at round tables covered with white tablecloths, or stood in the balcony overlooking the floor.

"He stepped to the microphone like a man who can graciously take applause," wrote Raymond C. Brecht in the *Philadelphia Bulletin*. "Then he took off the gloves."

He began innocuously enough, speaking slowly in that familiar voice, flat, a little high-pitched, the pronunciations still unmistakably Missourian ("entire" he rendered "EN-tire"). He spoke of how he enjoyed reading the morning papers now, "without having to make plans for handling the problems that appear there."

"Occasionally," he said, "the temptation has been very strong to do a little Monday-morning quarterbacking and advise my successor on how he should handle particular situations. But so far I have resisted that temptation, and I think I deserve a little credit for that."

He acknowledged that the Republicans had supported him when "the United States took the lead in defending the Republic of Korea against brutal aggression." He also noted that there had been "more continuity than . . . change" in American foreign policy since the Republicans took over. "This is as it ought to be."

"Unfortunately, however, the elections of last fall have strengthened the irresponsible element in the Republican Party. The grave burden of national leadership has apparently brought no change in the attitude of the reckless and isolationist wing of the Republican Party. . . ."

"Our plans were to build the defense forces we needed as soon as possible, and then to continue these forces at whatever strength was necessary for as long as necessary."

His voice was rising, now, the words coming faster.

"I am sorry to read, however—and I'm sure you are—that a great deal has happened to cut that program down." He was referring to Eisenhower's proposed defense cuts.

He held his hands in the air, as if measuring an imaginary fish. Then he chopped them down to drive home his point.

"There can be no doctrine more dangerous than the notion that we cannot afford to defend ourselves. And no doctrine quite so foolish, either. . . .

"The greatest danger period of the 'cold war' is not necessarily behind us, as some seem to think. We may be in our greatest danger period now, or it may be ahead of us. Nobody on this side of the Iron Curtain knows what is going on in the minds of the men in the Kremlin. . . .

"Big talk does not impress the rulers of the Soviet empire. . . . What impresses them are planes, and divisions, and ships. . . .

"We must be strongly armed, now and as far ahead as we can see. If the Soviets are genuinely interested in real settlements, we must be able to negotiate from strength. If they are tempted to make war, we must be able to deter them by our strength. And if they should attack, we must be able to beat them back, by strength. No matter what way lies ahead, the essential thing is always strength. . . .

"I think that those who talk about our defense program being too big may be letting their pocketbooks obscure their judgment. It is only natural to wish that we didn't have to tax ourselves so much for defense. This is perfectly human. We would all like lower taxes. But I warn you soberly and plainly: Do not be misled by the desire for lower taxes into cutting corners on our national security.

"Increasing the risk of World War III means increasing the risk of atom bombs on our homes. Think about that hard and think about it often. . . .

"The world depends upon us," he said in conclusion. "Let us meet the challenge." It was ten o'clock. The speech had lasted twenty-four minutes. The ovation it received lasted several more.

Truman returned to his seat and watched a performance by a choir from Naval Air Station Pensacola. At ten-thirty he returned to the private railcar at 30th Street Station and spent the night on board before proceeding to New York.

Like Harry, I took a train from Washington to Philadelphia. Unlike Harry, I didn't ride in a private railcar loaned by the Pennsylvania Railroad (which ceased to exist in 1968). Instead, I was a passenger on the rolling stock of the National Railroad Passenger Corporation. In other words, I took Amtrak. Coach class, of course.

It was June 26, 2008—the fifty-fifth anniversary of Harry's speech at the Reserve Officers convention. From 30th Street Station, I took a subway to Center City (as downtown is called in Philadelphia) and walked to the Bellevue-Stratford Hotel, the site of Harry's speech. Opened in 1904, the Bellevue-Stratford is a nineteen-story beaux arts masterpiece. It was Philadelphia's grandest hotel—until it made history of a most unpleasant kind.

In the summer of 1976, the American Legion held a convention at the hotel. More than two hundred people who attended it were stricken with a mysterious pneumonia-like malady. More than thirty eventually died of the illness, which was attributed to a bacterium in the hotel's air-conditioning system. Researchers named the bacterium *Legionellosis*. The illness it causes has come to be known as Legionnaires' disease.

If the best surprise in the lodging business is no surprise, then the worst is probably death. Naturally the outbreak had a deleterious effect on business, and the Bellevue-Stratford was forced to close by the end of that year. Since then it had been bought and sold, opened and closed, and remodeled and renamed many times. In its present incarnation it is known simply as the Bellevue. It is, in essence, an upscale mall. The once-ornate lobby has been subdivided into shops, including a Polo Ralph Lauren and a Tiffany. There's also a Palm restaurant and the requisite Starbucks. The middle floors have been converted into office space. Only the very top floors still offer accommodations, in the form of a boutique hotel managed by the Hyatt chain.

One important aspect of the old Bellevue-Stratford has been preserved, however: the Grand Ballroom on the second floor. This is where Harry delivered his speech to the Reserve Officers Association. The ballroom is still rented out for swanky occasions. On the day I visited, however, it was empty. Stacks of chairs sat on the edge of the dance floor. Round folding tables leaned against the wall.

At the front of the room there was a small stage with an orange back-drop. I walked up to the edge of the stage and turned to face the empty room. I was standing in the very spot where Harry had stood exactly fifty-five years earlier, front and center in his white dinner jacket, under the blazing klieg lights, measuring an imaginary fish, and giving Ike hell.

The Philadelphia speech was vintage Truman, blunt and forceful with a dash of hyperbole ("atom bombs on our homes"), and it energized Democrats. To the *Philadelphia Bulletin* the "smiling man from Missouri" looked like he would be a "big cannon" in the 1954 congressional elections.

Republicans, however, were unmoved. "Mr. Truman is back at the old stand," said Leonard W. Hall, the head of the Republican National Committee, "soft on economy, soft on money and soft on communism. The American people know that . . . President Eisenhower put some mus-cle into American defense and foreign policies." Hall asserted Truman had been "given a well-deserved rest by the American people, and he should take it." Republicans were also quick to point out that Truman himself had slashed defense spending between the end of World War II and the begin-ning of the Korean War.

President Eisenhower had no response. He was spending the weekend at the presidential retreat in the Maryland woods—not far from Frederick, actually. FDR and Truman had called the retreat Shangri-La. Ike had recently renamed it in honor of his grandson: Camp David.

The immediate effect of the speech was negligible. The very next day, the Republican-controlled House Appropriations Committee voted to slash another $1.3 million from the defense budget. "Mr. Truman's influ-ence with the 83rd Republican Congress appeared to be about as great as it was with the 80th," quipped the *Washington Star*.

But the long-term effect of the speech was more profound. By attack-ing his successor so fiercely so soon after leaving the White House, Harry Truman set the tone, not only for his own ex-presidency, but also for the ex-presidents after him. He was the first ex-president to engage in partisan politics in the age of modern mass media. Earlier exes had been politically active, of course. But in the thirty-four years between the death of Teddy Roosevelt and the end of the Truman presidency—a period during which the first commercial radio and television stations went on the air—ex-presidents were mostly seen but not heard.

After TR died in 1919, there were four ex-presidents before Truman: Taft, Wilson, Coolidge, and Hoover. Taft was chief justice and Wilson was infirm, so neither was especially active politically. For a year or so, Coolidge wrote a newspaper column called "Calvin Coolidge Says," in which Silent Cal said almost nothing. The columns were mostly bland essays on conservative business and political principles. He died less than four years after leaving office. (Upon learning of his death, Dorothy Parker quipped, "How can they tell?") As for Hoover, he wrote critically of the Roosevelt administration; his 1934 book *The Challenge to Liberty* compared the New Deal to fascism. But poor Herbert was lost in the political wilderness, and nobody paid much attention to him.

But Harry Truman—people paid attention to Harry Truman. His plainspoken, straightforward style was perfectly suited to the new broadcast media. If not the first television president, he was, at least, the first television ex-president. He turned the ex-presidency into a bully pulpit in its own right, and in doing so transformed it into the institution it has become.

10

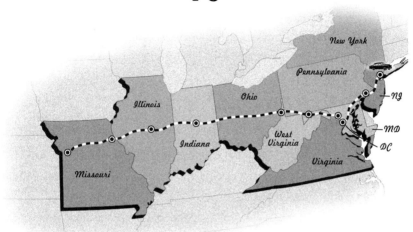

New York, New York,
June 27–July 5, 1953

*H*arry's private railcar, which was attached to the regular Philadelphia Express, arrived at Penn Station in New York around 9:40 on the morning of Saturday, June 27. "I'm having the best time in the world," he told reporters as he stepped onto the platform. From the station he was driven to the Waldorf-Astoria by Ed Hastings, the hotel's vice president.

When he first learned the Trumans were planning to visit New York, Hastings had written Harry, offering the couple accommodations at the Waldorf. Truman, who had spent many nights at the hotel as president, replied that he would "very much like to take advantage of" Hastings's invitation. "I'll need a couple of bedrooms and a parlor," Truman wrote. "Please inform me just what the expense will be for that sort of arrangement."

Hastings immediately wrote back: "For this, your first visit of a few days, the management of the Waldorf-Astoria will be pleased to have you as our guest." If the former president found the accommodations accept-able, "we can then discuss the matter of rates, for future visits."

"It certainly is kind of you to give me such service," Truman answered. "Your suggestion is all right and I more than appreciate it."

Which is how the cash-strapped former leader of the free world was able to afford eight nights at one of the finest—and most expensive—hotels in the world.

After he checked into his suite, Truman went downstairs for a haircut and shoeshine. A clutch of reporters and photographers were waiting for him.

Truman was photographed smiling broadly in the barber's chair, his legs crossed, a white smock covering his blue suit. It was a rare public appearance without his eyeglasses.

The haircut cost $1.50. Truman tipped the barber a buck. The shoe-shine cost fifteen cents. He tipped the bootblack a quarter. Truman's big tips were reported with some incredulity in the next day's papers, as if the former farmer and haberdasher from Missouri was a bumpkin. Truman "shattered a theory," the *New York Daily News* reported, "that tourists were lousy tippers."

As was becoming customary, Harry invited reporters up to his suite for an impromptu press conference—though Harry insisted it was only a "talk."

He said he stood by his speech the night before in Philadelphia. "I've been in politics forty years," he added, "and I'm not out of it yet."

He expressed concern over the health of British Prime Minister Winston Churchill, who had recently suffered a stroke. "I think very highly of Winston Churchill," Truman said. "I hope it is not serious. He's a great man. The world needs him." (Churchill recovered and lived another eleven years.)

Truman said he was "just a plain tourist" in New York. Although he and Bess had visited the city many times before, they had never really gone sightseeing. "I really don't know much about this big city," he confessed.

Their guide would be Margaret, who had moved to the city the previous January to pursue a career in television. He reported that Margaret had driven Bess to New York in his new Chrysler and had liked the car so much that he was worried she might "take it away" from him.

Before sending the reporters away, Truman invited them to join him for his morning constitutional the next day. "If you boys can get up to the Waldorf before 7:00 A.M., you'll be able to see me walking along Park Avenue."

Later that afternoon, Harry took a cab uptown to meet Bess and Margaret at the Carlyle Hotel, where Margaret lived. Like a plain tourist, he would take cabs (though not the subway, it appears) everywhere while he was in New York. One excited cabbie ferrying the Trumans made an illegal turn on purpose, right in front of a traffic cop. "I want a ticket," he said. "A ticket riding President Truman. So my wife'll know." The cop smiled and waved him on. The cabbie was disappointed.

Margaret cooked dinner for her parents in her apartment. At eight-thirty, Harry and Bess took a cab back to the Waldorf. "Margaret's a good cook," Harry reported.

The upper floors of the Waldorf-Astoria are known as the Waldorf Towers, a kind of hotel within a hotel, where rooms—sumptuously appointed apartments, actually—can be rented by the night or leased for long-term occupancy. This is where the Trumans stayed, in suite 32-A, which comprised a kitchen, six bedrooms, five full baths, and a seven-hundred-square-foot living room—quite a bit more than the couple of bedrooms and a parlor that Harry had requested. Cole Porter lived in 33-A, the suite directly above the Trumans. Douglas MacArthur, the intractable general whom Truman had fired two years earlier, resided five floors above, in 37-A. And directly below, in suite 31-A, lived the only other living ex-president, Herbert Hoover.

Harry Truman and Cole Porter apparently did not cross paths at the Waldorf, though, if they had, they would have had something to talk about:

Dean Acheson, Truman's dear friend and former secretary of state, had been Porter's roommate at Harvard Law School. Nor did Truman encounter MacArthur in the hotel's impeccably decorated halls, though the decorous staff surely took measures to prevent such an awkward rendezvous.

If Truman and Hoover met at the Waldorf, the event went unrecorded. Neither former president's daily calendar indicates a meeting with the other, and there was no correspondence between them from mid-1952 to September 1953. It appears the two men, whose relationship was alternately testy and genial, were having a tiff.

Hoover had once been a genuine American hero, a self-made millionaire-turned-humanitarian who organized relief efforts that saved millions from starvation in Europe during and after World War I. In 1928 he was elected president in a landslide, but less than a year after he took office, Wall Street crashed and the Great Depression rose. After he lost the 1932 election to FDR, Hoover, rendered persona non grata in Washington, retired to California. In 1940 he moved into the Waldorf. When one of Roosevelt's aides suggested that Hoover might be best qualified to oversee mobilization efforts on the home front during World War II, FDR dismissed the suggestion out of hand. "I'm not Jesus Christ," he said. "I'm not raising him from the dead."

It was Harry Truman who did that. Shortly after taking office, he invited Hoover to the White House "to talk over the European food situation." Hoover accepted the invitation, and on the morning of May 28, 1945, he met with Truman in the Oval Office. It was the first time Hoover had set foot in the White House in more than twelve years.

Hoover was wary of Truman. After the way he'd been treated by Roosevelt, he said he was inclined to tell the Democrats "to all go to Hell." But when Truman asked him to oversee relief efforts in postwar Europe and Asia, Hoover, ever the humanitarian, could not refuse.

In 1946 Truman appointed Hoover honorary chairman of the new Famine Emergency Committee, but Hoover's role was anything but ceremonial. He traveled the world in an army transport plane, cajoling and begging grain-producing nations to donate some of their precious stocks to starving nations. In Venezuela he slipped in a bathtub, cracking several vertebrae, but refused to curtail his trip. In Argentina he resolved to "eat even Argentine dirt," if that was what it took to get Juan Peron to release the 1.6 million tons of grain that Hoover wanted. Hoover got the grain.

Just as he had after World War I, Herbert Hoover had saved millions from starvation. "Yours was a real service for humanity," Truman wrote him.

On April 30, 1947, Truman undid one of FDR's more egregious slights against Hoover. He signed a bill restoring Boulder Dam's original name: Hoover Dam. The gesture moved Hoover greatly. At a Gridiron Club dinner ten days later, Hoover praised Truman's "high service to our country." Hoover had come to respect and even like Truman, and the feeling was mutual. "With esteem and keen appreciation to a great man," Truman scribbled on Hoover's program that night.

Their budding friendship, however, could not survive electoral politics. In the 1952 presidential campaign, Truman, campaigning for Adlai Stevenson, repeatedly cited Hoover as the embodiment of all that was wrong with the Republican Party: reactionary, ruthless, callous. The Democrats had been running against Hoover since 1932, with much success, and Truman wasn't about to stop now.

To Harry it was only politics, but old Herbert took it personally, and their fragile friendship shattered. It was unfortunate and sad. At the Waldorf, they were so close that if Harry had stomped on the floor, Herbert would have heard him. But both men were stubborn. There would be no rapprochement in New York.

To pundits, the image of Truman, Hoover, and MacArthur sharing the same building was irresistible. H. I. Phillips imagined the three towering figures meeting in a Waldorf elevator:

> Douglas—You two boys should know each other. Herbert, this is Harry Truman, remember?

Herbert—That reminds me I must speak to the management. The tone here isn't what it used to be. (To the General) Putting Mr. Truman up in your suite?

Douglas—Come, come, Herbert. . . . Watch your reputation for sagacity.

Herbert—I'm amazed to see you two boys together.

Harry and Douglas—If you're surprised you can imagine how we feel.

Douglas—We once flew thousands of miles to contact each other, Harry. It's a small world.

Harry—How's the fade-away business?

Douglas—You should know!

At seven o'clock the next morning, June 28, Harry stepped out of the Waldorf for his morning walk. The weather was warm and muggy, but the former president was characteristically dapper in a white summer suit with a double-breasted jacket. He wore a white Panama hat with a navy blue band. A crisp handkerchief peeked perfectly out of his breast pocket. "You all didn't get much sleep," he cheerily said to the dozen drowsy reporters and photographers gathered to document his ambulating.

Flanked by his former White House appointments secretary Matthew Connelly and a Waldorf security guard (provided at the hotel's insistence), Harry headed west on 50th Street to Park Avenue. He turned north onto Park to 51st Street, then turned west onto 51st. It was early on a summer Sunday morning, and midtown Manhattan was as sleepy as it ever gets, but everywhere Harry went he was recognized. At 51st and Madison, a cabbie yelled, "Hiya, Harry!" Truman waved. At 51st and Fifth, a bus driver yelled out, "Hello, Harry!" Truman waved again.

He turned south onto Fifth Avenue, passing St. Patrick's Cathedral, where the early mass was just beginning. He stopped in front of the cathedral to shake hands with a cop who recognized him, and to chat briefly with a churchgoer he happened to bump into. Her name was Marguerite Peyton Thompson. Harry knew her. She was a member of the Democratic National Committee and had seconded his nomination at the 1948 convention in Philadelphia. "I'm just going to church," Thompson said to Truman. "Good woman!" he replied. (Truman himself did not attend church regularly. He once wrote of his Baptist faith, "I'm a member but not a strenuous one.")

At 44th Street, the photographers accompanying him asked Harry to stop and pose for a picture with the Empire State Building in the background. He agreed, but on one condition, a condition that endeared him to New Yorkers. "The one thing I want you to do," he told the photographers, whose spent flashbulbs littered the sidewalk and street, "is to kick those damn bulbs to the curb." Used flashbulbs were a scourge to motorists and pedestrians alike. The scolded photographers sheepishly complied.

From Fifth Avenue he turned east onto 43rd Street to Madison Avenue, then headed back uptown on Madison. He walked briskly as usual, and by now some in the press pack were panting.

On Madison, just north of 43rd, Matthew Connelly spotted a quarter lying heads up in the street. He picked it up and handed it to his old boss. "Here's a little luck for you," Connelly said. Truman took the quarter. He held it up and studied the raised image of one of his predecessors for a moment. He slipped it into his pocket. "That goes in my collection," he said, promising never to spend it.

A few blocks later, a beefy cabbie named Marcus Straisant recognized the former president. He hastily parked his cab and rushed toward him. "How are ya?" Straisant asked excitedly, thrusting his hand toward the former president. "How's your family? You got a lot of friends here, they'd all vote for you anytime."

Truman was startled by the cabbie's effusiveness. He took a step back, smiling. "You embarrass me," he said.

From Madison he turned east onto 48th Street, then north on Park Avenue back to the hotel. It was 7:22. In all he covered some twenty-

Courtesy of AP/Wide World Photos

Harry shakes hands with New York cabbie Harry Lefkowitz while another cabbie, Marcus Straisant, looks on, June 28, 1953.

one blocks in twenty-four minutes. The *New York Times* calculated that he covered a north–south block in eighty-seven steps. He dismissed the press corps. "Roll call at the same time tomorrow," he said. "I expect all you men to muster here."

At one o'clock that afternoon, Margaret picked up her parents at the Waldorf in her new four-door Lincoln sedan. With Margaret behind the wheel, Harry in the passenger's seat, and Bess in back, they drove to the River Club at 447 East 52nd Street, where they had lunch with Mr. and Mrs. Daniel Longwell. Mr. Longwell was the executive editor of *Life* magazine, which held the serial rights to Truman's memoirs. After the meal, though, Truman insisted, not very believably, that he and Longwell had not discussed the memoirs. "We talked about ex-presidents, ex-secretaries of state, and sealing wax and shoes," he said with a laugh.

Margaret dropped off her parents back at the Waldorf at 3:45. Bess stuck her head back into the car to say good-bye to her daughter. "Come on, Ma." Harry chided Bess. "You're blocking traffic."

Harry and Bess stayed in that night. Maybe they ordered room service for dinner. In any event, they celebrated their wedding anniversary quietly.

Exactly thirty-four years before, on June 28, 1919, Harry S. Truman and Elizabeth Virginia Wallace had been married at Trinity Episcopal Church in Independence. They'd met as children in Sunday school but didn't marry until he was thirty-five and she was thirty-four. Their courtship was complicated by the fact that Bess's mother, Madge Wallace, didn't think Harry was good enough for her daughter—an opinion she retained, to some degree, even after Harry became president.

Harry had just returned from military service in France the month before the wedding. One of his army buddies wrote Harry, "I hope you have the same success in this new war as you had in the old." But their marriage was no war. As Harry and Bess grew older their love seems only to have deepened. "You are still on that pedestal where I placed you that day in Sunday school in 1890," he wrote her on their twenty-ninth anniversary in 1948. "What an old fool I am."

It's unlikely a more loving couple than Harry and Bess Truman ever occupied the White House.

When a Washington newspaper described Bess as "dumpy," Harry countered that she looked exactly how a woman her age ought to look. While they were in New York, Harry's friend Leonard Lyons, a *New York Post* columnist, offered to arrange a private screening of the new Marilyn Monroe movie *Gentlemen Prefer Blondes*. Harry declined. "Real gentlemen," he told Lyons, "prefer gray hair."

Theirs was an "ideal marriage," according to Stanley Fike, a family friend. "Never been any question in my mind or in the mind of anyone I

have ever known, but that there was only one woman in Harry Truman's
life and that was Bess Truman, Bess Wallace Truman."

Since Bess never cared for the spotlight, it's not surprising she and
Harry celebrated their anniversary in privacy.

Besides, when you're in a suite at the Waldorf Towers, why bother going
out?

I had neither the connections nor the cash to spend a week at the Waldorf,
where a cheap room nowadays runs about five hundred dollars a night.
So I e-mailed the public relations firm that handles media requests for the
hotel. I told them about the book and asked if it would be possible for me
to get a reduced rate. The response, in so many words: "Nice try."

Nonetheless, in the interest of research, I was determined to stay at the
Waldorf, and with minimal prodding, my wife, Allyson, agreed that yes, it
might be nice. I booked a room online for two nights, careful to mention
the book again. When we checked in, we were pleasantly surprised to be
upgraded to a room in the Waldorf Towers—where Harry and Bess stayed.

At the Waldorf, I interviewed James Blauvelt, the hotel's executive director of catering—and unofficial historian. When he's not overseeing ban-
quets in the Grand Ballroom, where Carnegie Hall and the Metropolitan
Opera hold fundraisers with ticket prices beginning at a thousand dollars
and tables costing a million, Blauvelt manages the hotel's archives. He is
well suited to both tasks. Punctilious, erudite, and jovial, his words are
well enunciated, and he speaks in complete paragraphs. He looks like the
kind of guy who goes to a lot of cocktail parties—and kills at every one.
Blauvelt's father was a globe-trotting pharmaceutical executive, so he practically grew up in hotels. He studied hotel management in college and has
been working at the Waldorf for nearly thirty years. He became the hotel's
unofficial historian by accident. About twenty years ago, he found the
archives in cardboard boxes, abandoned in a storage area. Blauvelt couldn't
help but organize them, and soon he found himself the de facto go-to guy
for questions about the Waldorf's history.

Blauvelt gave me the abridged version of that history. The hotel was the result of a feud between two Astor cousins, William Waldorf Astor and John Jacob Astor IV, who had built competing hotels next to each other on Fifth Avenue in the 1890s. Eventually the two hotels merged, though the feud apparently continued. The cousins couldn't agree on whose name should go first in the merged hotel's name, so, as Blauvelt emphasized, officially it is spelled with an equal sign, not a hyphen: Waldorf=Astoria.

In 1929 the original Waldorf was demolished to make way for the Empire State Building. Legend has it that the financing for the new Waldorf was secured the day before the stock market crashed. However, as Blauvelt explained, the Depression had a silver lining. "It turned out that labor was so inexpensive and abundant that they were able to lavish great detail and quality into the construction of the building." There was no rush to finish the building either, since business wasn't expected to be brisk anyway.

When it finally opened on October 1, 1931, the Waldorf was the largest and most luxurious hotel in the United States, if not the world. Each of its two thousand rooms had a private bathroom. It had twenty-four-hour room service, and a pneumatic-tube system for delivering messages to rooms. It even had its own radio station. President Hoover, a future tenant, spoke at the grand opening. "The erection of this great structure," he said, "has been a contribution to the maintenance of employment, and an exhibition of courage and confidence to the whole nation."

As expected, however, business was bad, and the Waldorf barely survived the Depression.

If the Trumans were to come back today, Blauvelt told me, they would have no trouble recognizing the place. Not that it hasn't changed a lot since 1953. Major "renovations" in the 1960s and '70s that obscured the building's grandeur have been reversed. "It was decided that the building was something of a treasure trove—one of the largest art deco structures in the United States, filled with that detail in its furniture and fixtures, as well as its architectural design. And also a lot of important beaux art elements. So restoration began in 1982 and continues to this day. There's been over four hundred million dollars spent on this constant restoration of the original. So when you look at old photographs of the hotel, it looks remarkably similar to the way it does now."

I asked Blauvelt if the arrangement whereby the Trumans were allowed to stay at the hotel for free was unusual. Resisting the urge to roll his eyes, he patiently explained to me the facts of hotel life. "The publicity that their visit would bring would be important to the hotel as a marketing strategy." But Blauvelt speculated there was another reason the Trumans got comped. "They had probably been very nice guests when he was in office, and that also makes a difference."

I'd noticed a Mexican flag flying over the entrance to the hotel when we checked in. It turned out that Felipe Calderon, the president of Mexico, happened to be staying at the Waldorf as well. This wasn't unusual, Blauvelt explained. "There isn't a day that goes by that there isn't at least one head of state in residence." The hotel even has a diplomatic affairs department. "Heads of state, if they're coming to New York"—here Blauvelt waved his hand in a fait accompli gesture—"they know."

Our stay at the Waldorf was expensive (Sunday brunch, ninety-five dollars per person) but uneventful. Which is exactly how the Waldorf wants it. We never ran into President Calderon. The suite that Harry and Bess stayed in, 32-A, was occupied, but I did manage to sneak a peek at the door. It was white. (In 2008, the suite directly upstairs, where Cole Porter—and, later, Frank Sinatra—once lived, went on the market. The rent was $140,000. Per month. But that includes a washer and dryer. And pets are allowed.)

While in New York, I also went to the River Club, where Harry, Bess, and Margaret had lunch with *Life* editor Daniel Longwell and his wife. It was, and (as I discovered) still is, a very exclusive private club on the east side of midtown Manhattan, in a grand building that overlooks the East River (as well as the FDR Drive, but the FDR Drive Club doesn't have the same ring, I guess). The *New York Times* has described it as "ultra-discreet." The club was founded in 1931. Its early members included Theodore

Roosevelt's son Kermit and department-store heir Marshall Field III. The current membership list is closely guarded, of course, but it's worth noting that the club is located inside the River House, an exclusive co-op whose residents include Henry Kissinger.

Rather naively, I walked in the front door and asked the guard, a gentleman in a green uniform with gold trim, if he had any pamphlets with some information about the club. Maybe an application form. Like it was a Gold's Gym. He looked a little confused. "No," he said. "We don't have nothin' like that." Clearly, the River Club is not hurting for members. Then I asked him if he could tell me a little bit about the club, how old it was, who belonged to it, that sort of thing. "No," he said. "They don't want us to be talkin' about nothin' to nobody." I was under the distinct impression he wanted me to leave. So I did. All I got to see was the lobby, which, truth be told, was quite nice, with lots of plush carpeting and brass fixtures.

Harry was up bright and early again on Monday, June 29, emerging from the hotel for his walk at 6:57. He took a slightly different route than the day before, but the spectacle was the same. Everywhere he went he was met with welcoming cries: "Hi, Harry!" "Try again in three years!" "We miss you, Harry!" It was hard to believe that barely a year earlier he had been the least popular president in American history. Even Truman himself had a hard time believing it. "The whole trip has been heart-warming," he said. "I am amazed at the friendliness, and it makes me think that I haven't spent my life in vain." But the constant attention also gave him a greater appreciation of his life back in Independence, where his presence was regarded with nonchalance. "I couldn't live in New York," he observed, "although I've enjoyed this visit very much. I don't like going around wearing false whiskers and dark glasses."

At noon, Harry, Bess, and Margaret had lunch at the Waldorf with Basil O'Connor, president of the National Foundation for Infantile Paralysis and the head of the Harry S. Truman Library, Inc. O'Connor was spearheading the library's fundraising efforts. After lunch, he announced that four hundred thousand dollars had been raised and another four hundred thousand pledged toward a goal of $1.75 million. The rest of the money, O'Connor told reporters, would be raised in "small sums" from a "substantial number of the American people."

Truman noted that he personally received none of the money raised. He also pointed out that he and his brother and sister were planning to donate up to eighty acres of the family farm in Grandview for the library. "And it's very valuable property; it's a real gift," he added. "I don't mind telling you some of the family are not as happy about it as they should be." Then, referring to his old nemesis, the senator from Wisconsin, he added wryly, "If any of you want to take a look at the property to see if there are any financial advantages to me, you might ask McCarthy to make the investigation."

That night the Trumans had dinner at the 21 Club with a group of friends. Margaret joined them as well, accompanied by her "escort" (as the papers put it), a Marine colonel and former White House aide named Warren Barker.

Opened at 21 West 52nd Street on New Year's Eve 1929, 21 survived repeated raids by Prohibition agents to become one of the most popular and famous restaurants in New York. Sometimes the maître d' had a hard time figuring out where to seat all the movie stars, politicians, sports heroes, and business titans who dined there. He faced a special challenge when, shortly after the Truman party was seated, New York Governor Thomas Dewey arrived. "It was completely coincidental," a 21 spokesman said. The two rivals in the 1948 presidential election were seated on different floors. Each probably didn't even know the other was in the restaurant until reading about it in the papers the next day.

After dinner, Harry and Bess went to see *Wonderful Town*, a musical comedy at the Winter Garden Theater on Broadway. Written by Joseph Fields and Jerome Chodorov, with music by Leonard Bernstein and lyrics by Betty Comden and Adolph Green, *Wonderful Town* is the story of two sisters from Ohio who move to New York City in search of fame and fortune in 1935. Starring Rosalind Russell and Edith Adams (the wife of Ernie Kovacs), and directed by George Abbott, the show opened to rave reviews just four months before the Trumans went to see it. The *New York Times* called it "the most uproarious and original musical carnival we have had since *Guys and Dolls*" and said Russell gave "a convulsing and ingenious performance." The musical would go on to win six Tony Awards, including Best Musical and Best Actress (for Russell).

Margaret, an accomplished singer in her own right, may have suggested her parents see *Wonderful Town*, although Harry, at least, didn't need much convincing. He was a big fan of musical theater. As a young man he often ventured into Kansas City to see shows at the Orpheum and the Grand.

As the Trumans entered the Winter Garden, everyone in the audience of fifteen hundred rose and applauded, and the orchestra struck up "The Star-Spangled Banner." At intermission they cheered again. "I didn't know what to do about it," Truman said. "They cheered as if I were still president. So I pretended I was still president and waved back."

After the closing curtain, the Trumans were ushered backstage, where they were introduced to the stars of the show. Truman told Rosalind Russell he "loved" her performance.

In New York, I had lunch at the 21 Club with an old friend from college. Unfortunately, the meal was preceded by two very large vodka martinis (up, dry, with olives). As a consequence, I don't remember much about 21. I seem to recall football helmets hanging from the ceiling, and at some point I ended up getting into a long, friendly, animated discussion about FDR and Truman with the men's room attendant. The foie gras and steak tartar, which my friend insisted I order, were, to the best of my recollection, eaten. My memories of the subway ride back to Brooklyn, where I was staying with friends at the time, are hazy.

Harry never would have let this happen to himself. Though he was far from a teetotaler, he almost never got drunk. He could nurse a single bourbon for hours, savoring every drop. "I don't think he ever takes over two drinks at a time," his friend Mize Peters once observed. Though there are numerous accounts of his drinking, there are none of his being inebriated, much less half passed out on a New York City subway at three in the afternoon. When I got back to my friends' apartment, I went straight to bed for a "nap," which, come to think of it, is what Harry did most afternoons.

After 559 performances at the Winter Garden Theater, *Wonderful Town* closed on July 3, 1954. Apart from a brief Broadway revival in 2003, the musical has been largely forgotten. That's partly due to the sheer complexity of the songs. Frequent and unusual meter and key changes render *Wonderful Town* too challenging for all but the most accomplished high school and community theater groups. (One song, "Christopher Street," has seventeen key changes.) Absent the rejuvenating energy of summer stock productions, *Wonderful Town* has faded into obscurity. It was too complicated for its own good.

On Wednesday, July 1, Harry took another morning walk. This time his route took him down Park Avenue to 49th Street, where he turned west. Just past Rockefeller Plaza, he noticed a small group of people standing on the sidewalk, looking into a building through a large plate-glass window. Curious, Harry looked inside too, and, seeming a little like Mr. Magoo, he appeared as one of the faces in the background of the *Today* show.

The program had debuted on NBC a little more than a year earlier. Hosted by Dave Garroway, an affable disc jockey from Chicago, *Today* was an experiment in early-morning television, combining news and entertainment, and airing live from coast to coast. The show was broadcast from the "fishbowl," a studio on the ground floor of the RCA Exhibition Hall that was visible from the street. The unusual studio wasn't just a gimmick. It also helped fill the show. When a segment ran short, cameras would pan the crowd standing outside while music played, sometimes for as long as five minutes.

The early reviews of the show were bad, and the ratings weren't much better. Who was home to watch TV at that hour anyway? Children—

and their mothers, of course. After the program introduced a year-old Cameroonian chimpanzee named J. Fred Muggs on January 28, 1953, ratings skyrocketed, though not everyone was amused. The show's newsreader, Jack Fleming, didn't care to deliver the headlines seated next to a chimp (and not a particularly friendly one, by most accounts), so he quit. Fleming was replaced by Frank Blair, who was less offended by the simian; Blair stayed with the program for twenty-two years. *Today*, of course, grew into a colossus. It now generates about a half-billion dollars in revenue annually for NBC. (J. Fred Muggs "retired" from the program in 1958, reportedly after biting Martha Raye on the arm. Believe it or not, in 2008 the chimp was still alive and well, living with a handler in Florida.)

Harry hated the way television turned politicians into "play actors," but he understood, perhaps sooner than most, the power of the medium. "Television is on the threshold of great development," he declared in a speech on August 13, 1943—when most people barely had any idea what television was. "It is true that there are many technical and commercial difficulties that must be overcome. But the day cannot be far off when our homes, schools, offices, and automobiles will be equipped with television sets. We will see news and sporting events while they are actually happening."

Truman's State of the Union address on January 6, 1947, was the first to be televised. Transmitted from the House chamber by coaxial cable, the speech was carried on stations in New York, Philadelphia, and Washington. According to one report, the picture was "for the most part . . . of acceptable clarity." Not that a lot of people were watching. Only about fourteen thousand sets were in use at the time.

Later that year, Truman installed the first television set in the White House, a $1,795 behemoth that he plopped down next to his desk in the Oval Office. In 1949, Truman's inauguration was the first to be televised. By then there were stations in fourteen cities as far west as St. Louis, and as many as ten million viewers watched the ceremony—more than had witnessed all previous inaugurals combined.

Four and a half years later, when Tom Naud, one of the *Today* show's announcers, spotted Harry Truman's bespectacled visage in the window behind Dave Garroway, he grabbed a microphone and ran outside to grab an impromptu interview with the former president. Naud asked Truman how he stayed in shape and how fast he walked. Then Truman had a question for Naud. Pointing through the window into the studio, he asked, "What's that fellow doing with the baby in there?" The baby in question was J. Fred Muggs.

His cameo complete, Truman smiled and waved and went his merry way.

I was determined to appear as one of the faces in the background of the *Today* show too, so early on the morning of Friday, May 2, 2008, I set out from my friends' apartment in Brooklyn for the NBC studios at Rockefeller Center. How hard could it be? All I had to do was stand there.

I had forgotten, however, that *Today* hosts live concerts on Rockefeller Plaza most Fridays. By the time I reached the plaza, it was already teeming—with women of a certain age. They were there to see Neil Diamond.

The crowd was impenetrable. I couldn't get anywhere near the stage, where all the cameras were.

Not only that, I hadn't brought a sign. A sign, it turns out, is nearly a prerequisite for getting your mug on *Today*. The cameras favor people with signs, especially signs that mention the *Today* show. The handmade *Today* show sign is practically a modern form of folk art. A stocky guy next to me was holding a large piece of red cardboard with Magic Marker letters: WHERE IN THE WORLD IS MATT LAUER? (Lauer, one of the program's hosts, periodically disappears to strange and exotic locales, leaving viewers to guess his whereabouts.) I asked him why he'd made it. "To get on TV," he said with a shrug. Why else? Soon he waded fearlessly into the crushing mob, a strategy for which I had neither the inclination nor the physique.

So there I was, stuck in the back of the crowd and signless. Neil played "Song Sung Blue" and "America." The crowd was only growing larger.

When he launched into the obligatory song from the new CD, I finally gave up and headed back to Brooklyn, disappointed.

Back at my friends' apartment, I decided to watch the show, which I had recorded. Mostly I was curious to see what Neil Diamond looked like from less than a block away. Imagine my surprise when I saw myself. Unbeknownst to me, a camera mounted on a robotic crane had panned over the crowd exactly one hour and thirty-one minutes into the program. In a sea of screaming Diamond-heads I could clearly be seen for about a second, standing ramrod straight and stone faced. I looked a bit like a stalker. Or an assassin. Nevertheless, I had, in fact, appeared on the *Today* show.

Later in the show I saw a close-up of a sign: WHERE IN THE WORLD IS MATT LAUER? The camera pulled back. The stocky guy who'd been standing next to me had had his wish fulfilled too.

After his morning walk on Friday, July 3, Harry visited the new United Nations headquarters on First Avenue. Truman played a crucial role in the creation of the UN. On the evening of April 12, 1945, just minutes after he had hastily taken the oath of office in the cabinet room of the White House, an aide asked Truman if the San Francisco conference on the United Nations was going to take place as scheduled in less than two weeks. "I said it most certainly was," Truman remembered. "I said it was what Roosevelt had wanted, and it had to take place if we were going to keep the peace. And that's the first decision I made as President of the United States."

It was at the San Francisco conference that the United Nations charter was ratified. Afterward, a committee formed to find a home for the new organization. European delegates argued for Geneva, the home of the League of Nations, but the Soviets (of all people) pushed for the United States. "The Old World had it once," said Soviet ambassador Andrei Gromyko, "and it is time for the New World to have it." Besides, as Gromyko pointed out, the United States was conveniently located between Asia and Europe. The committee chose the United States—specifically several square miles covering parts of Westchester County, New York, and Fairfield County, Connecticut. The idea was to create an international version of the District of Columbia.

In early 1946, the General Assembly voted to move the UN from London to New York City until its permanent home in the suburbs was ready. In the summer, the Security Council began meeting in a gymnasium on the campus of Hunter College, a women's school in the Bronx. Meanwhile, Westchester and Fairfield were having second thoughts about hosting the organization. "A lot of homeowners . . . got alarmed about the idea of all these foreigners with diplomatic immunity tearing around, running over their children, and having property that couldn't be taxed," recalled Isaac Stokes, an American diplomat posted to the UN at the time. In a referendum, Greenwich residents voted 5,505 to 2,019 against hosting the UN. The General Assembly abandoned the "international D.C." idea and reopened the search for a home. That fall, with classes about to resume at Hunter College, the Security Council was forced to move into an abandoned war factory on Long Island.

With Westchester and Fairfield now out of the running, cities began to furiously compete for the honor (and lucre) of hosting the UN, much as cities compete for the Olympics or the Super Bowl today. Isaac Stokes was the unlucky diplomat assigned to field calls from cities convinced "they had '*the* place' for the United Nations." "I remember Virginia Beach coming in," said Stokes.

> Well, the first thing I said to them was, "You've got to face one fact. There are black members in the U.N." I guess at that point there were only two, Haiti and Ethiopia. But there were some very dark Indians and so on. They obviously had second thoughts after that.

Ultimately four cities were chosen as finalists: Boston, San Francisco, New York, and Philadelphia. The Soviets vetoed Boston because the city's

Roman Catholic Archbishop, Richard J. Cushing, was a vocal critic of their "Godless" regime. European countries opposed San Francisco because it was too far afield. That left Philadelphia and New York, and, for a time, the leading contender was the City of Brotherly Love. "They had done all their homework," remembered Isaac Stokes. "They were prepared to offer practically the entire Fairmount Park . . . to the UN."

Enter William Zeckendorf Sr., a real estate developer who had recently purchased seventeen acres overlooking the East River in midtown Manhattan for nearly ten million dollars. It was a run-down area of slaughterhouses and meatpacking plants that Zeckendorf planned to turn into a business park to rival Rockefeller Center. Then, on the morning of Friday, December 6, 1946, Zeckendorf read an article in the *New York Times* about the likelihood that New York would lose the United Nations. The developer called Mayor William O'Dwyer and told him the UN could have the land he'd purchased "for any price they wish to pay." O'Dwyer summoned Robert Moses, who called Nelson Rockefeller, who called his father, John D. Rockefeller. The elder Rockefeller, who wasn't crazy about Rockefeller Center facing competition from Zeckendorf's development anyway, agreed to give the UN $8.5 million to buy the property. The catch, according to Isaac Stokes, was that Congress had to pass a law allowing him to claim the donation as a tax deduction, since contributions to international organizations were not deductible. The law got passed and Rockefeller gave the money to the UN, which bought the land from Zeckendorf, who took a loss on the deal but rescued the organization from Philadelphia.

President Truman convinced Congress to loan the UN sixty-five million dollars, interest-free, to pay for construction of the organization's headquarters. (The loan was paid off, on time, in 1982.) Truman himself laid the cornerstone on United Nations Day, October 24, 1949, and construction was completed less than a year later. Designed by a multinational team of architects, the centerpiece of the headquarters is the thirty-eight-story aluminum, glass, and marble Secretariat Building, which soars 550 feet above the East River.

When Harry arrived for his tour, Secretary General Dag Hammarskjold greeted him in front of the Secretariat Building. Hammarskjold had just been installed the previous autumn, and the two men had never met. They shook hands for photographers, who begged them for "just one more" shot. "Photographers," Truman warned Hammarskjold, "are tyrants." Eventually the handshake ended and Harry and Dag went up to the secretary general's top-floor office for coffee. Afterward, Truman stopped by the pressroom to chat with UN correspondents (and have another cup of coffee). In the Trusteeship Council chamber, a meeting was adjourned so he could shake hands with the delegates. Next door, in the Economic and Social Council chamber, Hammarskjold proudly pointed out the ceiling, which had been designed by an architect from his native Sweden. Pipes and ducts were left exposed, a symbolic reminder that the work of the United Nations, like the ceiling, would never be finished.

"Acoustically correct!" Truman declared.

With the former president setting a brisk pace, the tour lasted just forty minutes. "I feel top-notch about the whole thing," he said at the end. "I am wishing all the success in the world to the United Nations. That will be my wish as long as I live."

The United Nations hasn't changed much since Harry visited in 1953—and I'm not talking about its seeming inability to solve the world's problems. The buildings look much the same. Security, however, is a different story. A 1953 travel guide says visitors could feel free to "wander around in most of the public lobbies, lounges, and outdoor terraces and grounds." There was no charge for admission. Today everyone must pass through a metal detector. There is absolutely no wandering. And a tour costs $13.50.

My tour group was led by a petite and brilliant woman named Julia. Her knowledge of the UN was absolute. She probably could have recited the member nations in alphabetical order. And she never referred to the UN as "the UN." To Julia it was "the organ-eye-zation." She was most efficient. Her only flaw was that she couldn't decide what to do with her hair.

Between each stop on the tour she'd either tie it up in a scrunchie or take it down again. It was distracting. Yet also enchanting.

We toured the chambers: Security Council, Trusteeship Council, Economic and Social Council. Then we came to a small exhibit on disarmament. It included artifacts recovered from the sites of the two nuclear weapons dropped on Japan in 1945—the Truman bombs. From Hiroshima there were cans and coins and bottles all fused into a charred lump by the heat of the blast. From Nagasaki, a stone statue of St. Agnes that stood less than a kilometer from ground zero, the back mottled and charred. None of this was here when Harry visited, of course. But, implicitly anyway, the exhibit questioned his judgment. The bombings killed more than two hundred thousand people. Truman always claimed he never had any second thoughts about authorizing the use of nuclear weapons against the Japanese. "They never would have surrendered otherwise," he told an interviewer in 1955. "I don't believe in speculating on the mental feeling and as far as the bomb is concerned I ordered its use for a military reason—for no other cause—and it saved the lives of a great many of our soldiers. That is all I had in mind."

"I have never worried about the dropping of the bomb," he wrote in 1964. "It was just a means to end the war and that is what was accomplished."

Julia put her hair up and shepherded us to the General Assembly Hall, where all 192 member-nations have seats. (Actually, each gets six seats, three for delegates and three for alternates.) When Harry visited back in 1953, just sixty nations were represented in the General Assembly. In fact the UN was built to accommodate only as many as seventy, a number that was exceeded in 1955, forcing major renovations. Julia explained that the nations are seated by lottery. Each year, the secretary general randomly selects the name of one country, and the seats are assigned in English alphabetical order beginning with that country. In 2007, Mexico was the lucky Number 1, so it got the best seats in the house, followed by Micronesia. Poor Mauritius—its delegation got the worst seats in the house. Well, not the worst—those are up in the balcony, where we were.

The General Assembly happened to be in session, and the secretary general was delivering a report. I couldn't figure out what it was about, but it sounded dreadfully dull. The hall was less than half full. Some of the delegates appeared to be dozing. It seemed no more exciting than the average city council meeting—and considerably less exciting than one in, say, Philadelphia or Chicago.

And that was it. Julia led us outside, let her hair down again, and delivered a short soliloquy in which she stressed that the UN was not a governmental organ-eye-zation. She ended with a quote from Kofi Anan, who was once asked why God was able to create the world in seven days while it has taken the UN more than sixty years to achieve what it has.

"The good Lord," replied Anan, "had the advantage of working alone."

The next day was the Fourth of July. Harry and Bess celebrated by catching another show, the matinee performance of the play *My Three Angels* at the Morosco Theater on 45th Street. (The theater, where both *Death of a Salesman* and *Cat on a Hot Tin Roof* opened, was demolished in 1982 to make way for a Marriott hotel.) That night they had a quiet dinner at the Waldorf and went to bed early. It had been a whirlwind week. It was time to go home.

11

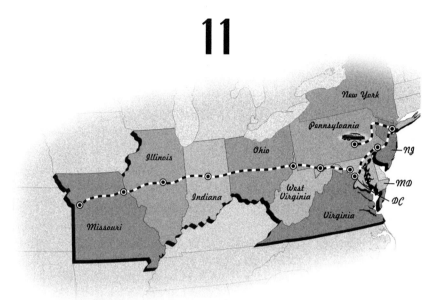

Pennsylvania (or, Abducted), July 5–6, 1953

*T*he Automobile Club of New York predicted a record-breaking one million cars would be on the city's highways over the Fourth of July weekend in 1953. (The auto club also predicted a record-breaking number of highway fatalities, prompting this jolly headline in the *New York World-Telegram and Sun*: "Hundreds to Die as Nation Observes Independence Day.") To get a jump on the holiday traffic, Harry and Bess got up before dawn on Sunday, July 5. Two bellhops helped Harry carry their luggage down to the garage, but Harry loaded it all into the car by himself, despite the bellhops' protestations.

"I'll go back up and get the folks for breakfast," Harry announced after all the bags were stowed to his satisfaction.

A few minutes later, Harry, Bess, and Margaret entered the hotel's Norse Grill.

Courtesy of AP/Wide World Photos

Harry and Bess pulling away from the Waldorf-Astoria in New York, July 5, 1953. Margaret is in the back seat. Harry dropped her off at her apartment before heading for home.

"He ordered a half grapefruit, toast, coffee, and bacon," the *New York Times* solemnly reported. "The women ordered cantaloupe."

After breakfast, the family posed for photographs at the garage entrance, and Harry gave his autograph to two youngsters. When asked which way he planned to drive home, Harry was cagy. "It'll be a zigzag route," was all he would say.

It was seven o'clock now, and Harry was eager to hit the road.

"This has been a happy week," he told the reporters and photographers who'd come to chronicle his departure. He and Bess had had so much fun, he said, "it makes it so we want to come back."

Then he and Bess and Margaret climbed into the big black Chrysler.

"Well, let's go!" he said.

He pulled out of the Waldorf garage and turned right onto 49th Street. At Madison Avenue he turned right again. At 76th Street he parked in front of the Carlyle, where Margaret lived. Bess asked Margaret, probably for the millionth time, if she was sure she didn't want to ride back to Independence with her parents. Yes, said Margaret with a smile. She was much too busy in New York to go home just then.

Bess waited in the car while Harry and Margaret went inside. In the lobby Harry kissed his daughter good-bye.

Emerging from the hotel, Harry asked a passerby, "Say, where is this West Side Highway?" He planned to take the highway to the Holland Tunnel.

"Are you really Mr. Truman?" said the perplexed pedestrian. Truman laughed, admitted he was, and got his directions.

They pulled onto the highway at 57th Street and headed north—the wrong direction. A newspaper photographer named Tom Gallagher who was following the Trumans realized their mistake. He caught up with them at 72nd Street and got them turned around.

It was 7:40 by the time the Trumans arrived at the entrance to the Holland Tunnel, where the toll taker recognized Harry and shook his hand before taking his fifty cents.

Emerging in New Jersey, they took the Pulaski Skyway to Newark, where Harry picked up Highway 22 and headed west, toward Pennsylvania, disappearing into the growing crush of traffic, just another holiday motorist.

Shortly before noon, Harry pulled into a service station on the east side of Harrisburg, Pennsylvania. One of the attendants, Herbert Zearing, was cleaning the windshield when he realized who his customer was. "I kept working because I didn't want to look surprised," said Zearing. Meanwhile, the other attendant, Lester Lingle Jr., filled the car with 11.1 gallons of premium gasoline. The bill came to $3.45. Harry paid with a twenty. Bess, as she had throughout the trip, dutifully logged the purchase.

After filling up, Harry drove through downtown Harrisburg, past the green-domed capitol, where, according to one account, "one middle-aged man pointed excitedly at the Truman car as he gaped after the driving ex-president." He crossed the Susquehanna River, picked up Highway 11, and continued west.

In the town of New Kingstown, just a few miles west of Harrisburg, the Trumans passed a small white building surrounded by a dazzling sea of flowers in full bloom. This caught Bess's eye. "Harry, turn around," she said. "Go back. I want to see that." Harry did as Bess asked. The building was a restaurant called the Country House. They got out to admire the flowers. Then, since they were hungry anyway, they went inside for lunch.

They were seated and ordered two large fruit bowls. At first, nobody recognized them, even after they chatted with several other customers.

But one of the cooks had his suspicions. He went out to the parking lot. When he saw the Missouri plates on the big black Chrysler the couple was driving, his suspicions were confirmed. "The place became very excited after that," said the next day's *Harrisburg Patriot*, "and everybody asked for autographs."

The building that housed the Country House is now the New Kingstown post office. I went inside. It looked exactly like every other small town post office, with a small counter and a wall of PO boxes. There was nothing distinctive about it. It was difficult to imagine it as a restaurant.

A little farther down Highway 11, in the town of Carlisle, I paid Harvey Sunday a visit. Harvey was the owner of the Country House. Today he lives in a retirement home, in a small room with a bed, a desk, and an easy chair. He shared this room with his wife, Helen, until she died on September 11, 2001—"the day that New York got blowed up," as Harvey put it. "She died right there," he told me, pointing to the bed he still slept in every night.

Though nearly ninety and confined to a wheelchair, Harvey's mind was still razor sharp. He looked me right in the eye as he spoke. His green eyes were so piercing that I had to look away occasionally, pretending to fiddle with my tape recorder. Harvey said he and Helen built the Country House in 1950. He was working on his father's farm at the time. "We growed hogs and steers and we growed corn and hay and wheat and barley," Harvey said. "We thought we could work the farm produce into the restaurant."

Harvey and Helen didn't know the first thing about the restaurant business, but they worked hard and learned quickly. "We wanted to make it stand out a little," Harvey said. He added a bell tower to the building, and customers were encouraged to ring the bell. Helen decorated the pine walls with hand-painted trays and ironstone china. She did the landscaping, too, planting the hundreds of flowers that drew the attention of passersby—including a former first lady.

The Country House was a cut above most roadside eateries. In fact, Harvey winced when I called it a diner. It was a restaurant, he gently corrected me. The tablecloths were white. The menu included filet mignon and "choice seafood."

Harvey was washing dishes in the kitchen the day the Trumans unexpectedly showed up at his restaurant. "I finally got to talk to Harry after they were about ready to go," Harvey said. "I didn't want to bother him but I didn't want to miss him either." Harvey remembered Harry telling him he was "very happy" with his meal. Harry wasn't just being nice either. For years afterward, he would recommend the restaurant to friends who were driving through central Pennsylvania. "After that we had a lot more customers from Independence, Missouri, than we had before," Harvey said.

The restaurant was successful; some days upward of a thousand meals were served. It was hard work, but Harvey and Helen enjoyed it. "What we liked about it was the results," Harvey said—the financial results. But they had three kids, too, and it was hard to give them the attention they deserved. "We looked around and realized we weren't spending enough time with the children." So, in 1960, Harvey and Helen sold the restaurant to the Dutch Pantry chain. The Dutch Pantry closed in 1970, and the U.S. Postal Service bought the building a few years later. It was converted into a post office. The bell tower was removed.

After they sold the Country House, Harvey and Helen took over his father's farm full time. They finally retired in the late 1980s. The farm has since been turned into a golf course, a development that does not disturb Harvey in the least. "I think it was a good idea," he told me. "Wish I'd done it myself, but I was too old."

Harvey slowly wheeled himself over to his desk, moving the chair with his feet. He reached for a framed picture and handed it to me. It was a color brochure from the heyday of the Country House, the kind you might have found on a display rack at a highway rest stop. "Authentic Country Dining!" it announced. "Come to the Country House and discover an atmosphere that is both intriguing and inviting." I read the copy out loud. "You'll relax in air-conditioned comfort in one of five handsomely appointed dining rooms." Harvey smiled.

"If it wouldn't've been for the kids not getting enough attention," he said, "we'd've probably still had it."

In Carlisle, the Trumans picked up the Pennsylvania Turnpike. For Harry, a certified road aficionado, this must have been a thrilling experience.

When it opened in 1940, there was nothing like the Pennsylvania Turnpike. Built on the ruins of an abandoned railroad line, it stretched 160 miles from Carlisle west to Irwin, over and, via seven tunnels, through the Allegheny Mountains. The turnpike was an engineering marvel, with two twelve-foot lanes in each direction, separated by what was then a spacious ten-foot median. (For a time it was fashionable to picnic in the grassy median, until the state police deemed the practice foolhardy.) Access was limited to eleven interchanges, and all intersecting roads passed over or under the turnpike, so there were no intersections—and no traffic lights—and no speed limits. Ten service plazas gave motorists a place to fill their tanks (and themselves) without having to leave the cocoon of the road.

It cost seventy million dollars to build. Franklin Roosevelt, sensing its military value, prodded Congress to kick in $29.5 million. The rest of the money came from the sale of bonds, which would be paid off by collecting tolls of roughly a penny per mile for passenger vehicles. (Today the rate is about six cents per mile.)

Critics derided it as a boondoggle and a "road to nowhere," but the turnpike proved a stunning success. Traffic the first year was nearly twice as heavy as projected, and toll revenue exceeded $2.6 million, easily enough to meet expenses. (The accident rate was higher than expected, too, so a speed limit of seventy miles per hour was imposed.)

The Pennsylvania Turnpike wasn't merely a way to get from one place to another; it became a destination in its own right. Tourists came from all over the country to see the self-proclaimed "World's Greatest Highway," and the service plazas did a brisk business in turnpike souvenirs: postcards, glasses, mugs, plates, pennants, ashtrays, and countless other trinkets.

Its success spurred other states to build similar toll roads: Illinois, Maine, Ohio, New Jersey, and New York. By 1957 it was possible to drive from New York to Chicago without even thinking about a traffic light. The feasibility of a nationwide system of limited-access highways was now indisputable.

The tolls on the Pennsylvania Turnpike were supposed to be lifted once the bonds sold to finance construction had been retired. Instead, however, the commission that operated the turnpike used toll revenue to finance new projects, setting in motion a constant need for tolls. By 1956 the turnpike stretched all the way across the state, 360 miles from Ohio to New Jersey, with a 110-mile extension from Philadelphia to Allentown and Scranton. (Apropos of Harry's injunction against memorials to the living, a tunnel on the extension was going to be named after the chairman of the turnpike commission until he was convicted of attempting to defraud the commission of nineteen million dollars.) More recently, the commission has approved plans to expand large sections of the turnpike from four lanes to six.

So-called perpetual tolls troubled some transportation officials, who said the fees would "stifle free transportation and injure the national welfare." In 1950, the trade journal *Engineering News-Record* warned that never-ending tolls were "pernicious."

On the Pennsylvania Turnpike, Harry Truman must have found it extremely difficult to abide by his wife's prohibition against speeding. To his credit, he did—yet he still got in trouble.

Harry was in the left lane, cruising along at fifty-five with a line of cars behind him, when Pennsylvania State Trooper Manley Stampler pulled alongside him and motioned for him to pull over. (At the time, state police cars in Pennsylvania had no emergency lights.)

Harry later claimed the only reason the trooper pulled him over was to "shake hands."

That's not how Manley remembers it.

Now comfortably retired in suburban Phoenix, Manley whiles away the days penning cantankerous letters to the editors of local newspapers. ("It only cost $430 million to send the Phoenix Mars mission to the Red Planet. What a bargain. That money could have been spent to help the Hurricane Katrina victims . . .")

Manley was just seventeen when he dropped out of high school to enlist in the navy in 1945. After his discharge, he joined the Pennsylvania State Police. "It was kind of a romantic thing to do," he told me. He was assigned to the barracks in Bedford, a town of three thousand in the rural south-central part of the state.

Mostly he just patrolled the turnpike, an assignment he enjoyed. On his breaks he would stop at the Howard Johnson's at the Cove Valley service plaza and flirt with a pretty waitress. When he asked her to marry him one day, she said yes.

July 5, 1953, began as a "typical day," Manley remembered. He was pulling an eight-hour shift on the pike. When he saw that big black Chrysler blocking traffic in the left lane, he had no idea who the driver was. He only knew the law was being broken.

When he realized he'd pulled over the former president, Manley was flabbergasted. He hadn't heard about the Trumans' trip. "I just couldn't believe that I had pulled this man over." But he had a job to do. He gave Harry a brief lecture, the same one he delivered to countless other motorists.

"I told him what he had done wrong and he said he didn't realize it—that it wasn't intentional. Then, I told him how dangerous the turnpike is and . . . wouldn't he please be more careful." Truman was smiling, Manley remembered. "He was very nice about it and promised to be more careful." Bess leaned over and said, "Don't worry, Trooper, I'll watch him." With that, Trooper Stampler told the former president and first lady they were free to go. The stop had lasted only about two minutes, though to Manley "it seemed a long time."

To this day there is no doubt in Manley Stampler's mind that Harry Truman was in violation of the law. "This guy was blockin' traffic, so I pulled him over—that's all there was to it." But he let him off with just a warning. "I wasn't going to give him a ticket—he was the president of the United States." Here Manley paused for a moment. "Maybe some other presidents, but not Harry Truman." As for Truman's claim that he only pulled him over to shake hands, Manley laughed. "I don't remember shaking his hand. Didn't ask him for an autograph, either. Wish I had. Might be worth something today."

Back at the barracks at the end of his shift, Manley casually said to his desk sergeant, "You'll never guess who I pulled over today." The sergeant excitedly phoned the *Bedford Gazette*, and the next day the story appeared in newspapers nationwide. The press had a field day. "From the standpoint of the personal safety of one of America's two living ex-presidents," wrote the *Philadelphia Inquirer* in an editorial, "we hope Mr. Truman will exercise greater care in the future. Fortunately Private Stampler was forbearing. He didn't give the ex-president a ticket. But the next time—who knows?"

After Manley Stampler pulled them over, neither wire services nor major newspapers made any mention of the Trumans until they checked into a hotel in Columbus, Ohio, at noon the following day, Monday, July 6. After all the attention their trip had received so far, it was almost as if they had fallen off the face of the earth for nearly a day. The 250-mile trip from Bedford to Columbus should have taken no more than five hours. When they arrived in Columbus, they were vague about their whereabouts the previous night. Harry would only say they'd stopped in a "small town east of Columbus."

What's even more bizarre is that Harry and Bess went missing on the sixth anniversary of a most peculiar event—an event that undoubtedly piqued the curiosity of then-President Truman, who had more than a casual interest in the phenomenon it represented. The event has come to be known as the Roswell Incident.

Although the precise chronology is still much disputed, many researchers believe July 5, 1947, is the date on which a rancher named Mac Brazel discovered some unusual debris on his ranch in southeastern New Mexico. The debris consisted of a metallic, aluminum foil–like substance that couldn't be ripped or burned, and some pieces of wood inscribed with what looked like hieroglyphics. The next day, Brazel drove seventy-five miles to the nearest town, Roswell, and walked into the Chaves County Sheriff's Office with two cardboard boxes filled with some of the debris. Sheriff George Wilcox agreed the stuff looked strange, and he contacted the local air force base.

The next day the air force sent two men to Brazel's ranch to collect the rest of the debris. On July 8, the base issued a press release, which was nicely summarized in the headline of that afternoon's edition of the *Roswell Daily Record*: "RAAF Captures Flying Saucer on Ranch in Roswell Region." The wire services picked up the story.

Unidentified flying objects were very much on Americans' minds that summer. Less than two weeks before Mac Brazel took that strange debris into Roswell, a thirty-two-year-old Idaho businessman and private pilot named Kenneth Arnold had seen something strange in the sky while flying his small plane near Mount Rainier in Washington state. At 2:59 P.M. on Tuesday, June 24, 1947, Arnold saw nine disc-shaped objects moving in formation at a speed he estimated to be in excess of a thousand miles per hour. He said they looked like "flying saucers," a name that stuck. On July 4, several dozen people attending an Independence Day picnic in Twin Falls, Idaho, reported seeing discs "flying in a 'V' formation." That night, a United Airlines pilot and copilot flying a DC-3 out of Boise observed nine flying saucers at an altitude of seventy-one hundred feet over the town of Emmett, Idaho.

The "capture" of the flying saucer near Roswell understandably caused some anxiety. Now aliens were after us! After communists, it seemed there was nothing Americans feared more than little green men.

Not to worry, said the air force. On July 9 it issued a press release saying the debris recovered near Roswell was merely the remains of a crashed weather balloon. (In 1994 the Pentagon would say it was actually a top-secret listening device used to detect nuclear tests in the Soviet Union.) Still, the air force was determined to get to the bottom of the UFO phenomenon, and in the fall of 1947 it launched an investigation that would eventually spawn the famous Project Blue Book.

On July 10, 1947, just two days after the flying saucer was reported captured near Roswell, President Truman was asked at a press conference if he had "seen any flying saucers." "Only in the newspapers," was all Truman said, prompting much laughter from the reporters.

Truman, however, took the matter quite seriously. In 1948, he summoned his air force aide, General Robert B. Landry, to the Oval Office. Landry said the president told him "the collection and evaluation of UFO data . . . warranted more intense study and attention at the highest government level." Truman ordered Landry to consult with the appropriate government agencies and report directly to him quarterly "as to whether or not any UFO incidents . . . could be considered as having any strategic threatening implications at all." This Landry did for more than four years. "Nothing of substance considered credible or threatening to the country was ever received from intelligence," Landry recalled.

Still, the sightings continued. In the summer of 1952, Truman's own house was buzzed by flying saucers. It all began on a steamy Saturday night, July 19. On the top floor of the control tower at Washington National

Airport, an air traffic controller named Joe Zacko saw a mysterious blip on his radar screen. Then he looked out the window and saw a bright light in the sky. He pointed it out to his partner, Howard Cocklin. "If you believe in flying saucers," Zacko said to Cocklin, "that sure could be one."

Suddenly the bright light shot away at an incredible speed. "Did you see *that*?" Cocklin said. "What the hell was *that*?"

Radar screens at two nearby air force bases also picked up unidentified blips that night, and a pilot reported seeing unusual objects in the sky near the capital, "like falling stars without tails." Three days later the *Washington Post* reported on the "eerie visitation"—"perhaps a new type of 'flying saucer,'" the paper helpfully speculated. Soon the sultry capital was swept up in a UFO frenzy. Up to fifty sightings a day were reported. A State Department employee saw a small light in the sky that "floated around in space" and disappeared. A radio station engineer saw mysterious lights near the station's transmission tower.

On the night of July 26—a week after the first sightings—controllers at National reported at least a dozen more unusual blips. This time the air force dispatched two F-94 jets to investigate. The pilots saw strange lights. One tried to give chase but couldn't catch the lights—even though his jet was capable of speeds approaching six hundred miles per hour.

Truman demanded answers, but the Pentagon was hard pressed to deliver them. An air force official said he was "fairly well convinced there is nothing in the phenomenon to indicate that it is a menace to the country," but added that he could not "discount entirely that they are visitations from a foreign country or another planet." "Perhaps it's due to the heavy use of TV during the conventions," a navy official speculated. (The Republican and Democratic national conventions took place around the same time as the sightings.)

Eventually the Pentagon settled on an answer that seemed to satisfy both the president and the public: "temperature inversion." A layer of hot air in the atmosphere had caused radar systems to mistake objects on the ground for objects in the air. "I'm satisfied in my own mind," said General John A.

Samford, the head of air force intelligence, "that the recent sightings here result from heat inversion." Samford went on to reassure the public that a thorough analysis had found "no pattern of anything remotely consistent with any menace to the United States."

Of course, this theory did not explain how the lights had outraced an F-94, but the press, at least, bought it. Perhaps the explanation that the UFOs were the result of all the hot air in the nation's capital was too good to resist. In any event, the papers stopped reporting UFO sightings and the matter was soon forgotten—though, to this day, the sightings have not been fully explained.

So Harry Truman was well acquainted with UFOs. Which is why his seeming disappearance on the very anniversary of the discovery of the Roswell crash is, to put it mildly, a rather interesting coincidence—or is it a coincidence?

Alas, it is. Harry and Bess weren't abducted by aliens—at least not on the night of July 5, 1953. Though it went unreported at the time, the Trumans spent that night in Washington.

But not *that* Washington.

Residents of Washington, Pennsylvania, often distinguish their town from the nation's capital by calling it "Little Washington" (or, in the local accent, "Little Worshington"). Wedged in the southwest corner of the state, the town is the eponymous seat of Washington County. Chartered by the Pennsylvania legislature in 1781, it was the first county in the nation to be named for the Father of Our Country, who was still in his forties at the time and eight years away from becoming president.

Ironically, Washington (the place) ended up giving Washington (the man) nothing but headaches. George Washington owned land in the county, but even as president he was unable to pry the rent from his tenants, so he ended up selling the nettlesome property. Then, in 1794, farmers in Washington County revolted against a new federal tax on whiskey. (Whiskey was a serious cash crop at the time. It's been estimated that one in six farmers in the county operated a still.) The Whiskey Rebellion was the first serious test of the powers of the federal government, and Washington was forced to send more than twelve thousand troops to the area to crush it.

The National Road was routed through the town of Washington, and by the mid-nineteenth century it was a center of agriculture, with crops and livestock being shipped east and west. But it was the discovery of coal and, later, oil, that turned Washington into a bona fide boomtown.

Yet, as the twentieth century began, the town had no proper hotel. "Every night," a local historian lamented, "the tourists were taken into private houses in all sections of the town." In November 1920, frustrated community leaders organized an effort to build a hotel, which would be named after the town's namesake. They formed the George Washington Hotel Company and sold stock at fifty dollars a share. They raised more than six hundred thousand dollars in a month. Local banks loaned the company another six hundred thousand, and construction began at the corner of Main and Cherry the following August.

The ten-story George Washington Hotel opened on Washington's Birthday in 1923 with a special reception for its eight hundred or so stockholders. It was said to be the finest hotel on all the National Road. Each of its 210 guest rooms had a private bath and a telephone, and its ballrooms were as fine as those in any hotel in the country.

It was the George Washington Hotel that Harry and Bess Truman checked into on the night of July 5. It had been a long day. They had driven nearly four hundred miles. As usual, word of the famous couple's arrival quickly spread through town, and soon the lobby was filled. A reporter from the local paper, the *Observer*, called the Trumans' room. Harry answered the phone, but he wasn't in a talkative mood. "We had a very pleasant trip here from New York City," he said, "but we are tired and do not care to grant an interview."

Instead of ordering room service for dinner, the Trumans went down to the hotel's Pioneer Grill, but only after the manager promised they "would not be molested while eating." Still, their meal was interrupted several times by the usual assortment of well-wishers and autograph seekers. After dinner, a photographer for the *Observer* asked them to pose for a picture. Harry pleaded that they were too tired, but the photographer snapped one anyway. In it Harry and Bess, looking uncharacteristically haggard, are standing in the hotel elevator, impatient for the door to close. The photograph, accompanied by a brief story, appeared in the paper the next day. But somehow—perhaps because it was a holiday weekend—the wire services missed it, which is why, outside Washington, Pennsylvania, nobody knew where Harry and Bess were that night.

To get from the Pennsylvania Turnpike to Washington, Harry and Bess took Route 31. Today you take Interstate 70, but you still pass through many of the same towns, including some with the best names in all of the Keystone State: Hunker, Lover, Glyde, and Eighty Four (the last supposedly named to commemorate Grover Cleveland's election in 1884).

The George Washington Hotel is now an apartment building. Remarkably, however, the lobby is still largely intact, complete with a lovely, massive, spindly chandelier. The ballrooms are also intact and can still be rented for wedding receptions and other functions.

12

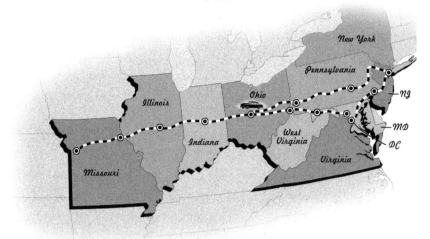

Columbus, Ohio,
July 6–7, 1953

*A*fter their long drive the day before, Harry and Bess took it easy on
Monday, July 6, driving only a little over 150 miles along Highway 40
from Little Washington to Columbus, Ohio. Around noon they checked
into the Deshler, a thousand-room hotel on the northwest corner of Broad
and High streets in downtown Columbus, catty-corner from the Ohio
statehouse. When it opened on August 23, 1916, the Deshler was hailed
as "the most beautifully furnished hotel" in the country. The table service
was gold. The massive Oriental rug in the lobby cost fifteen thousand dollars. (To spare it the ravages of rowdy football fans, the rug was rolled up
on Friday nights before Ohio State home games.)

By 1953, however, the Deshler had grown a bit threadbare, and, just a
week before Harry and Bess checked in, Conrad Hilton bought the hotel,

promising to return it to its rightful place as "one of the finest hotels in the United States." Nobody doubted Hilton would do it. He'd been in the hotel business since he was a boy, helping his father run a boardinghouse in San Antonio, a tiny mining town in the New Mexico Territory. Returning from service in World War I, Hilton bought his first hotel in Cisco, Texas. His sixteenth was the Deshler.

Hilton seemed to have the Midas touch, turning every property he owned into a moneymaker. His secret was simple. He called it "digging for gold." He would squeeze revenue out of every square foot of his hotels. At the Palmer House in Chicago, he converted a newsstand (monthly rent $250) into a bar (yearly revenue $490,000). At the Plaza in New York, he rented out a small showcase in the lobby for eighteen thousand dollars.

He would sink more than two million dollars into it, but, alas, even Conrad Hilton couldn't save the Deshler. It was too late. In 1948, something called a "shopping center" had opened in the Columbus suburb of Whitehall. Another one was on the drawing board for Berwick, with enough parking for two hundred cars. Why bother driving downtown, where parking was a hassle anyway? Businesses began to flee for the suburbs. Suddenly, a thousand-room hotel in downtown Columbus was anachronistic, obsolete.

In 1964 Hilton sold the hotel to Charles "Curly" Cole, a flamboyant businessman who sank his own millions into the Deshler, turning it into a 275-room luxury hotel, where scantily clad women swung from a trapeze in the lobby. Cole's room, 1212, was decorated in a rain forest theme, complete with artificial thunder and lightning. In 1966 Cole threw in the towel and sold the Deshler to Fred Beasley, an auto dealer and horseman who knew nothing about running a hotel but shared Cole's enthusiasm for the outlandish. Beasley, legend has it, once rode one of his show horses through the lobby and into an elevator, demanding to be taken to his room. By the summer of 1968 the Deshler was hopelessly in arrears. Beasley was delinquent in real estate taxes by nearly sixty-five thousand dollars. His overdue sewer and water bill amounted to $13,421.39. At one minute after midnight on July 31, the Deshler closed its doors. The wrecking ball came a little more than a year later. Other historic buildings in downtown Columbus, most notably Union Station and the Neil House, another hotel, would meet the same fate in the following years.

For fifteen years, the site of the Deshler was a parking lot, a macadam metaphor for the fall of downtown Columbus, right next to the statehouse. In 1985 a new office building called One Columbus Center was erected on the site, part of a revitalization effort that has met with mixed success. On the ground floor of One Columbus Center there is, of course, a Starbucks. I stopped in and had a cup of coffee and a piece of lemon cake. It was as close as I would ever get to spending a night in the Deshler.

When they checked into the Deshler, Harry and Bess were greeted in the lobby by dozens of squealing teenage girls. They weren't ex-presidential groupies. The hotel, it turned out, was hosting the annual convention of the Future Homemakers of America. The FHA was founded in 1945 by Edna Amidon, a home economics teacher whose mission in life was to teach girls how to cook and sew and clean. Edna wasn't being sexist. She was being prudent. Surveys at the time indicated that most American men wanted wives who would be "good housekeepers." (Women, for their part, wanted husbands who were "industrious.") So, for young women, learning how to keep house was essential to finding a mate—and, given their limited employment opportunities outside the home, essential to their economic security as well.

More than two thousand girls from forty-five states attended the convention in Columbus. Speaking at the opening session on Friday, July 3, Edna warned the girls that "more families are on the move due to changes in industry, armed forces' requirements and other causes," and that they needed to learn how to "make a good home anywhere" and "put down roots quickly in any community."

The unexpected appearance of the former president and first lady at their convention three days later practically sent the girls into delirium.

They nearly tore the hotel drug store apart in their rush to purchase film for their Brownie cameras. "Man, the place was really jumpin'," was how one of the girls described the Trumans' arrival to a reporter. Said another of Bess, "She was wearing a black dress and didn't look as old as we thought she would."

"We're just on our way home," Harry said as he and Bess checked in, "and frankly we're pretty tired. We're just going to sit down and rest." They went up to room 1663 and asked for room service menus, which the hotel's concierge, Fred Riedal, delivered to them.

"Hiya, captain," said Truman when Riedal came to the door.

"Hello, Mr. President," replied Riedal with great formality.

The Trumans ordered yet more fruit—this time with cottage cheese. Harry had iced tea. Bess had iced Sanka. When Harry tried to pay for the meal, Riedal refused. "No, sir," he said, "it's on the house." Harry didn't press the issue.

A reporter and a photographer came to the room, but Harry still wasn't feeling very talkative. "I think I've said about everything anyway, haven't I?" The photographer asked Harry to autograph a dollar bill, something he had done many times as president, but the now-ex-president demurred. "No," he said, "there's a five-thousand-dollar fine for doing that. When I was president, it was all right. I could even ask someone else to do it. But not any more." (Harry was mistaken. While it was—and still is—illegal to deface currency "with intent to render [it] unfit to be reissued," merely autographing a dollar bill hardly rises to the level of a felony. Harry was probably misinformed by his old army buddy, John Snyder—who also happened to be his secretary of the treasury, and whose signature appeared, quite legally, on every banknote issued from 1946 to 1953.)

After lunch, Harry took a nap while America's future homemakers stalked the corridors of the Deshler in search of him. The hotel stationed two security guards outside his room to keep the girls at bay.

Bess, meanwhile, went down to the beauty salon in the lobby to get her hair done. While the salon manager, Mary Love, washed Bess's hair and put it into pin curls, the two women, perhaps mindful of the future homemak-ers in their midst, discussed the merits of careers for young women. Bess doubted whether it was worth the trouble for women to pursue careers outside the home. "You have to work so hard to get to the top," she said.

Soon Bess had her hair up and was sitting under a big, dome-shaped dryer, reading *The House of Moreys*, a new book by the British novelist Phyllis Bentley. Here, alone, under the dryer, reading, Bess looked per-fectly content. A half hour later she emerged, looking, the *Columbus Dispatch* said, "rested and stylish." "Small curls covered her head," the paper reported. "A fluffy bang topped her forehead." Mary Love described the cut as a poodle, made popular by Mary Martin in the musical *South Pacific*. Bess, however, noted that she had been wearing her hair like that since long before Mary Martin appeared on Broadway. She said she kept it looking nice by washing it once a week—unlike Martin, who had to wash hers every night.

The Trumans had dinner in their room that night and went to bed early. They checked out of the Deshler around nine the next morning, amid more pandemonium in the lobby. Harry said he'd had a "wonderful" time in Columbus—though he'd never even left the hotel. "Everyone here has treated us marvelously." Then he turned to Bess and said, "Missy, let's go."

They climbed into the New Yorker, which was parked under a canopy in front of the hotel. Harry turned the ignition and put it in gear. The car bucked twice, "like a Missouri mule," according to one report. Then it stalled. A roar went up from the crowd that had gathered to send them off. A little embarrassed, Harry restarted the car and pulled away. He honked the horn twice as a final good-bye and headed west on Broad Street, leav-ing in his wake hundreds of future homemakers squealing in delight.

Membership in the Future Homemakers of America peaked at more than five hundred thousand in 1965, when the group merged with the New Homemakers of America, whose members attended black schools in the South. As the times changed, so did the FHA. In 1973 it began to admit boys, and its mission gradually expanded to encompass "personal growth and leadership development." In *Teen Times*, the organization's quarterly magazine, articles like "Glamour for Gray Days" and "Milestones to Marriage" gave way to pieces about teen pregnancy and alcoholism.

In 1999, after much debate, the organization changed its name to Family, Career and Community Leaders of America—the FCCLA. The change was prompted by concerns that the old name "conjured up images of stay-at-home housewives who cook pot roast and darn socks." Today the FCCLA focuses on "character development, creative and critical thinking, interpersonal communications, practical knowledge, and career preparation." In 2007 the group had nearly 230,000 members, 23 percent of whom are male.

Just as the FHA has changed, so, too, have Americans' attitudes toward prospective spouses. Recent surveys have found that both men and women now look for partners who are "intelligent" and "attractive."

About seventy miles west of Columbus, near Dayton, the Trumans passed Wright-Patterson Air Force Base. They didn't stop at the time, but, were they to make the trip today, they most certainly would, for the base now houses Harry's presidential airplanes.

Franklin Roosevelt was the first president to fly in office when he took a Boeing 314 Clipper Ship to the Casablanca Conference in 1943. Named the *Dixie Clipper*, the plane was operated by Pan American Airways. After Casablanca, military leaders thought better of having their commander in chief fly commercial again, so the Army Air Forces specially modified a C-54 transport plane for Roosevelt and delivered it to him in 1944. Nicknamed the *Sacred Cow* by either the White House press corps or AAF personnel, the plane featured a small elevator behind the passenger cabin to make it easier for the president to get on and off the plane in his wheelchair.

Roosevelt used the plane just once, to attend the Yalta Conference in February 1945. When Truman became president, he inherited the *Sacred*

Cow and, on June 19, 1945, a little more than two months after taking office, he flew to Olympia, Washington, on the plane. It was the first domestic flight in the history of the presidency.

Whenever he flew, Harry liked to hang out in the cockpit and chat with the crew. He also liked to have a little fun. The plane's pilot, Lt. Col. Henry Myers, said the president asked to be notified whenever the *Sacred Cow* flew over Ohio, the home state of Truman's nemesis in the Senate, Robert Taft. In *The Flying White House*, J. F. terHorst and Ralph Albertazzie explained why:

> Duly alerted by Myers that the *Sacred Cow* was flying over Ohio, Truman would walk aft to his lavatory. Moments later, after the president had returned to his seat, Myers would get a presidential command over the intercom to activate the waste disposal system. . . . The discharged liquids, of course, evaporated quickly in the cold, dry air outside. But it was Truman's way of having a private joke at Taft's expense.

By late 1946, the *Sacred Cow* was already showing its age, so the air force decided to replace it with a Douglas DC-6, the most advanced long-range airliner then in production. The new plane was even more luxurious than the *Sacred Cow*. Mounted on the wall of the stateroom were instruments—a compass, an altimeter, and a speedometer—that the president could monitor in flight. Powered by four 2,400-horsepower prop engines, it had a cruising speed of 320 miles per hour and a range of 4,400 miles. (The *Sacred Cow*, by comparison, had a cruising speed of 245 miles per hour and a range of 3,900 miles.) The new plane was also equipped with the most modern communications equipment, including a teletype system that could send and receive coded messages. It seemed to have everything—except a name.

The White House and the air force had always hated the name *Sacred Cow*, which they regarded as undignified. Truman's press secretary, Charles

Ross, never failed to point out that "*Sacred Cow* was a nickname for which the White House had no responsibility." According to Ross, Truman simply called the plane "the C-54." The air force wanted to call the new presidential plane the *Flying White House*, or simply refer to it by its air force number (46-505). But Henry Myers, the pilot, suggested the *Independence*, a name that evoked the nation's history and ideals. Of course, it also happened to be the name of the president's hometown. The air force didn't care for the name, but Harry liked it, and that was all that really mattered.

The most striking thing about the *Independence* was its two-tone blue paint scheme. While the *Sacred Cow* looked like every other C-54 (on the outside anyway), its replacement was painted to look like an eagle. The nose was the beak, and the cockpit windows were the eyes. Stylized feathers swept down the fuselage. Douglas Aircraft had come up with the design for American Airlines, whose logo was an eagle. American rejected it, but air force officials who happened to see the design thought it would be perfect for the new presidential plane. The *Independence* looked unlike any other plane in the world. It was flashy, and Harry loved it.

The *Independence* was officially commissioned on the Fourth of July in 1947. Two months later, Harry, Bess, and Margaret flew it to a conference in Rio de Janeiro. On the way home, Harry played a practical joke on Bess, whose fear of flying was well known. The plane had reversible propellers, a new technology that made it possible to land on short runways. Before landing in Belem, Brazil, pilot Henry Myers told Harry that he would have to use the reversible props, and that they would make a lot of noise. "I reminded him especially to warn Mrs. Truman in advance," Myers remembered. "I knew it would worry her otherwise."

But Harry said nothing to Bess.

The plane landed. Bess heard the strange noise.

"Oh, my, what's happening?" she said.

Harry looked out the window and shouted, "The plane's falling apart!"

The *Independence* was Harry's second presidential airplane. Its unusual paint scheme was originally designed for American Airlines. Today the plane is on display at Wright-Patterson Air Force Base near Dayton, Ohio.

But Bess could always tell when Harry was pulling her leg.

"If that's all that happens when this thing falls apart," she said nonchalantly, "then it's not as bad as I expected."

The *Independence* made its most famous presidential flight in October 1950, when it flew Truman to Wake Island for his historic meeting with Douglas MacArthur. In all, Truman flew more than 135,000 miles on sixty-one trips during his presidency.

When Eisenhower took office in 1953, he didn't want Harry's hand-me-down airplane. He ordered a new one, a Lockheed Constellation, which he dubbed *Columbine II*. (The plane he had used as Supreme Commander of Allied Forces in Europe had been named *Columbine*, after the official flower of Mamie Eisenhower's home state of Colorado.) Later that year, Eisenhower's plane, which went by the call sign "Air Force 8610," found itself in the same airspace as Eastern Airlines flight number 8610. The resulting confusion prompted the air force to designate any plane carrying the president "Air Force One." The named presidential airplane went the way of the named highway.

After they were retired from presidential service, both the *Sacred Cow* and the *Independence* continued to be used by high-ranking military and government officials. The *Independence*, in fact, made a brief cameo as Air Force One. On April 27, 1961, with his regular plane undergoing maintenance, President Kennedy flew the *Independence* from Washington to New York. On board, Kennedy marveled at the quaint instruments on the wall of the stateroom.

The *Sacred Cow* was permanently retired in 1961, the *Independence* four years later. Both planes are now on display at the National Museum of the United States Air Force at Wright-Patterson, along with several other presidential airplanes, including the Boeing 707 that flew Kennedy to Dallas on November 22, 1963 (and returned his body to Washington that same day).

The presidential airplanes are stored in a hangar separate from the main museum, so visitors have to take a shuttle bus to see them. My lovely wife and I happened to be visiting in early February, which, based on our experience, is not the peak tourist season in southwestern Ohio. Apart from the driver and a chaperone (it being a military base, after all), we were the only two people on the bus, which was fine with us, because we had the run of the place.

The *Sacred Cow* and the *Independence* have been restored to their original appearance inside and out, and you can actually walk through them, though everything inside is walled off with Plexiglas, leaving a narrow passageway that claustrophobics are wise to avoid. (We were told that larger visitors have been known to get stuck.) Seated in the stateroom of the *Sacred Cow* is a mannequin of FDR in a tuxedo, looking a bit like he's waiting for somebody to bring him a drink. A replica of his wheelchair is parked near the elevator specially installed for him.

Inside the *Independence* there's a mannequin of Harry sitting at a small table in the main compartment, but it's not a very good likeness. He's too skinny and his clothes don't seem to fit. The jacket is too small. If the real Harry saw it, he'd be mortified. But his eyes would brighten at the sight of the newspaper lying on the table in front of the mannequin. It's a copy of *Stars and Stripes* with the banner headline "MacArthur Relieved of Command." Farther down the narrow Plexiglas corridor is a small room marked "Presidential Dressing Area/Lavatory." It must have disappointed Harry that the *Independence*, unlike the *Sacred Cow*, could not discharge its waste in flight.

There's another sight at Wright-Patterson that is connected to Truman, though it is very much off-limits to the public. The remains of crashed UFOs and their occupants are stored inside the secret "Blue Room" in Hangar 18. Or so the story goes. It makes sense, in a way, since Wright-Patterson is where Project Blue Book was based. (Though, it must be noted, Blue Book concluded that there was "no evidence indicating that sightings categorized as 'unidentified' were extraterrestrial vehicles.") Supposedly the debris from Roswell was taken to the Blue Room where, according to some of the wilder accounts, it was personally inspected by Truman. That's highly doubtful. Even the president would have had difficulty gaining entrance to the Blue Room. "I once asked General Curtis LeMay if I could get into that room," Arizona Senator Barry Goldwater told the *New Yorker* in 1988, "and he just gave me holy hell. He said, 'Not only can't you get into it but don't you ever mention it to me again.'"

On the shuttle bus to the presidential planes hangar, I asked our chaperone, half-jokingly, if it would be possible to see Hangar 18, too. All he would say is, "They don't want us to talk about that."

13

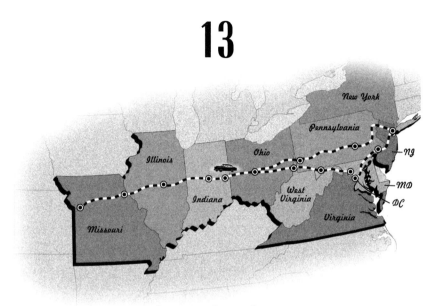

Richmond, Indiana,
July 7, 1953

O n the morning of Tuesday, July 7, Ora Wilson, the sheriff of Wayne County, Indiana, got a call from a friend at the Ohio State Highway Patrol. His friend advised Wilson that Harry and Bess Truman were headed his way, and helpfully supplied a description of their vehicle and an ETA. Like Glenn Kerwin, the police chief in Decatur, Illinois, Ora Wilson was anxious to "look after" the Trumans while they were in his jurisdiction. He also wanted to get his picture in the paper. So he recruited one of his deputies—his son Lowell—to help spring a trap for the Trumans. Father and son sat in a cruiser parked on the east side of Richmond, the county seat, and waited to intercept the couple as soon as they came into town. In the backseat was a photographer for the *Richmond Palladium-Item*.

Richmond, Indiana, population forty thousand, sits on the banks of the Whitewater River, just across the Ohio border. Founded by Quakers in

1806, it was a center of the abolitionist movement. The Wright Brothers grew up here, and Wilbur attended Richmond High School before the family moved to Dayton. It's also where the Reverend Jim Jones, founder of the Peoples Temple, went to high school. But Richmond's two enduring claims to fame are curiously paradoxical: in the 1920s, the city played a key role in the rise of both the Ku Klux Klan and African American music.

During the Roaring Twenties, the Klan enjoyed a resurgence known as the second wave, exploiting white anxiety over the influx of immigrants from Central and Eastern Europe, as well as the mass migration of African Americans from the South to the North. In 1924 there were four million active Klan members, including some five hundred thousand in Indiana— the largest single state contingent. In Richmond roughly half the city's adult white males belonged to the Klan, including the mayor, the county sheriff, and the county prosecutor. On the evening of Friday, October 5, 1923, the Klan staged a spectacular parade through Richmond. It featured more than six thousand hooded and robed Klansmen, as well as marching bands, floats, and, of course, many "fiery crosses." In "magnitude and impressiveness," the *Richmond Palladium-Item* reported the next day, the parade "has had few equals in this city."

The Klan's Svengali in Indiana was David C. Stephenson, a former printer's apprentice and Socialist Party activist who was said to pocket two dollars of each Klansman's ten-dollar membership fee ("klecktoken," in Klan vernacular). It was Stephenson who undoubtedly organized the Richmond parade. By 1924 his power and influence in Indiana were unmatched. That fall he threw his support (and the Klan's money) behind the Republican gubernatorial candidate, a fellow Klansman named Edward Jackson.

Jackson won the election in a landslide. At Jackson's inaugural ball, Stephenson met Madge Oberholtzer, a twenty-eight-year-old former schoolteacher who ran a state anti-illiteracy program. A little more than two months later, on March 25, 1925, Stephenson invited Oberholtzer to his house on the pretext of discussing state business. He drugged her, forced her into a car, and drove her to Union Station in Indianapolis, where they boarded a train bound for Chicago. In a Pullman compartment, Stephenson attacked Oberholtzer, raping her repeatedly and biting her breasts and genitals so viciously that her flesh was torn. They got off the train in Hammond, Indiana, where Oberholtzer tried to poison herself with mercuric chloride. Stephenson took her back to her parents' home in Indianapolis, dropping her off with the warning, "I am the law and the power." Oberholtzer died a month later, either from the poison or from an infection resulting from her wounds. In any event, Stephenson, in a spectacular and lurid trial, was convicted of murder and sentenced to life in prison. He fully expected his fellow Klansman, Governor Jackson, to pardon him. When he didn't, Stephenson, enraged, exposed the Klan's machinations in Indiana politics to the *Indianapolis Times*, helping the paper win a Pulitzer and bringing the Klan's second wave to an inglorious end.

Until Stephenson's downfall, the Klan's political influence was extraordinary, not only in Indiana but throughout the Midwest and, of course, the South. Back in 1922, when he was running for Jackson County judge, Harry Truman himself had paid the ten-dollar initiation fee to join the Klan, membership seeming to be a prerequisite for political success at the time. Informed he could not hire Catholics if elected, Truman, who had commanded many Catholics in World War I, withdrew his application and got his ten dollars back. Later, he claimed he and his old army chaplain, a Dominican priest named Curtis Tiernan, had busted into "many a meeting of the KKK" in Missouri and confronted the speakers. "We were ejected from some of the meetings, but we broke many up."

At the same time Klansmen were parading through Richmond in the 1920s, down in a hollow west of town, in a shack by the Whitewater River, African American jazz and blues musicians were making some of the most epochal recordings in the history of American music.

Back in 1872, an Alsatian piano maker named George M. Trayser, with the help of two local businessmen, Richard Jackson and James Starr, opened a factory in Richmond. The Starr Piano Company, as it came to be known, quickly became one of the country's leading piano manufacturers, at a time when the piano was a status symbol akin to the iPhone today. In 1893, the company was acquired by Henry Gennett, a Nashville business-man who moved to Richmond to oversee his new business.

By 1915 Starr was selling fifteen thousand pianos a year. The business seemed impregnable.

Then the phonograph came along.

Thomas Edison had invented the cylinder phonograph in 1877, but it wasn't until a German immigrant named Emile Berliner invented a machine he called the gramophone that the recording industry began to develop. Berliner's invention played music recorded on flat discs instead of cylinders. The discs were easier to duplicate and store, and, since both sides could be used, they held more recording space than cylinders. Berliner's invention touched off a war between the two formats not unlike the Beta/VHS and Blu-ray/HD DVD wars of more recent generations. When the dust finally settled in the late 1910s, Berliner's format had prevailed.

Back in Richmond, Henry Gennett, the owner of the Starr Piano Company, followed the phonograph wars with intense interest. He knew the phonograph would replace the piano in respectable parlors, and he wanted a piece of the action. By 1916 the company was already man-ufacturing its own brand of phonograph players. It also established a record division to produce seventy-eight-rpm discs for its (and, of course, other companies') phonograph players. The recording label was named Gennett.

Gennett records were recorded in a small wooden studio that sat next to the railroad tracks that ran through the Starr complex in Richmond. Huge draperies were hung on the walls to afford at least some soundproof-ing, though many recording sessions were still interrupted when trains passed. Some audiophiles swear they can hear the sound of passing trains in the background of old Gennett recordings.

Since the bigger record labels like Victor and Columbia signed the most famous names in the music business to exclusive contracts, Gennett recorded lesser-known artists who happened to be passing through town, usually on their way to or from gigs in Indianapolis or Chicago. Fortunately for Gennett, as well as posterity, some of the musicians who passed through Richmond in those days went on to become legends in jazz and blues: Louis Armstrong, Duke Ellington, Fletcher Henderson, Blind Lemon Jefferson, Jelly Roll Morton. Their recordings for Gennett have become landmarks in American music.

The performers were not lavishly compensated. Many received a flat fee of fifteen to fifty dollars per recording session. The Gennett label, however, flourished. The records, recognizable by a parrot logo on the cover, sold for about a dollar each in hundreds of stores nationwide. Advertised under the dubious slogan "The Difference Is in the Tone," Gennett sold three million records in 1920.

The emergence of radio, and later, the Great Depression, hit the Starr Piano Company hard, and Starr sold its recording division to Decca Records in 1935. The company was finally sold at auction in 1952, and the Richmond factory was closed.

Around noon, Ora and Lowell Wilson spotted the Trumans' Chrysler heading into Richmond on East Main Street. They pulled it over.

"Sheriff," asked Harry with some exasperation, "what did I do wrong?"

"We just wanted to welcome you to Richmond," said the elder Wilson, who added that it would be awfully nice if Harry and Bess would pose for a picture with him in front of the Madonna of the Trail statue. Harry had come to Richmond to help choose the site for the statue back in 1928, when he was president of the National Old Trails Road Association. He had been scheduled to return to Richmond later that year for the dedication of the statue, but, just a few days before the October 28 ceremony, he sent his regrets, saying he was "very busily engaged in politics" at the moment. Seventeen years later, on April 2, 1945, it was announced that Truman, now vice president of the United States, had accepted an invitation to speak at a soil conservation conference being held by the local Kiwanis club in Richmond on May 9. Again Truman would have to send his regrets. Roosevelt died on April 12. Instead of speaking about soil conservation in Richmond, Indiana, on May 9, 1945, Truman, now president, was in the Oval Office signing a bill extending the draft. He had announced the surrender of Germany just the day before.

So, by stopping in Richmond (albeit involuntarily), Harry was making good on unfulfilled obligations. The Wilsons escorted the Trumans to Glen Miller Park, where the *Palladium-Item* photographer snapped a picture of Ora, Harry, and Bess posing in front of the larger-than-life Madonna. (The park was named after a local businessman, not the big band leader.) Afterward, the Wilsons escorted the Trumans to the Leland Hotel in downtown Richmond, where Harry and Bess had lunch. At their table, they posed for another picture for the *Palladium-Item* photographer. After the customary plea for "one more shot," Harry turned to Bess and said, "This may break the camera," bringing a wide smile to Bess's face. Harry was in a jovial mood. He told the photographer that Manley Stampler, the state trooper who had pulled him over on the Pennsylvania Turnpike, "got the wrong man."

After lunch, the hotel provided the Trumans a room so they could rest a bit before resuming their journey.

On the whole, Richmond treated Harry much better than it treated another former president who came to town. In June 1842, a little more than a year after leaving the White House, Martin Van Buren passed through Richmond on his way to Indianapolis. He was on a tour to gauge support for another presidential bid. He didn't find much in Richmond, mainly because he had vetoed several bills to fund improvements to the National Road, which had been extended through Indiana in 1834. By the time Van Buren became president, the road had deteriorated so badly that Hoosiers called it a "buttermilk lane." But Van Buren, like Monroe before him, did not believe it was the federal government's responsibility to repair the road. David P. Holloway, the editor of the *Richmond Palladium*, did not encourage the town to roll out the red carpet for Van Buren. In an editorial ahead of the former president's visit, Holloway wrote, "To welcome such a man whose official conduct has spread misery and desolation throughout the land and is seeking power again to enthrall the people is repugnant." On June 9, Van Buren gave a speech in Richmond that Holloway dismissed as "cold and indifferent." That night, a "mysterious chap" partially sawed through one of the crossbars underneath the former president's carriage. The next morning, Van Buren was about two miles west of town when the crossbar snapped. The former president was forced to walk through deep mud for help. "Perhaps it might cure him of his oppositions for the old National Road's completion," sniffed Holloway. (Something similar is said to have happened to Old Kinderhook a little farther west in Plainfield, Indiana, as well.)

David C. Stephenson, who was so instrumental in the rise (and fall) of the Ku Klux Klan in Indiana in the 1920s, was released from prison in 1950, after serving twenty-five years for the murder of Madge Oberholtzer. He was arrested on a parole violation shortly thereafter and returned to prison. He was paroled again in 1956. In 1961 he was charged with attempting to molest a sixteen-year-old girl—in Independence, Missouri, of all places. He was fined three hundred dollars and ordered to leave the state. He died five years later in Jonesboro, Tennessee.

The Ku Klux Klan has never come close to approaching the heights of its popularity in the 1920s. In 2007, however, the Anti-Defamation League reported that the Klan "has experienced a surprising and troubling resurgence due to the successful exploitation of hot-button issues, including immigration, gay marriage, and urban crime." Indiana, the report notes, was one of the states "notable for active or growing Klan chapters."

The remnants of the Starr Piano Factory in Richmond, Indiana. The Gennett Records logo is still visible on the building.

Photo by author

After it was abandoned in 1952, the sprawling Starr Piano Factory along the Whitewater River quickly fell into disrepair. Most of the structures were torn down in the 1960s and '70s. All that remains is the factory's sixty-foot-tall smokestack and the shell of a building once used for making player pianos. The Gennett Records parrot logo is still clearly visible on the building.

The Leland Hotel, where the Trumans stopped for lunch, still stands, though it has been converted into a retirement home. The seven-story brick building on the corner of Ninth and South A is now known as the Leland Residence—"The Elegant Retirement Community." Its residents belong to that rapidly vanishing segment of the American population with firsthand memories of the Truman presidency.

Residents of the Leland are served meals in what used to be the hotel's restaurant. I called the home to see if it would be possible for me to have lunch there, as Harry and Bess had. "Of course you can," said the cheerful manager, Judy Sherrow. All she asked in return was that I give a brief presentation on the Trumans' trip to the home's residents. In other words, I was to be an "activity." It struck me as a perfectly reasonable exchange, and I agreed at once.

Lunch was served at eleven-thirty in the morning. (It seems the elderly, in Richmond, Indiana, at least, like to take their meals early. At the Leland, dinner is served at four-thirty.) I sat at a small table with Judy and one of the home's residents, a woman recovering from a recent fall and having difficulty mastering the walker she was now forced to use.

"I'm not used to needing help!" she said.

"It's just part of the process of getting old," said Judy reassuringly. She spoke in a soothing tone perfectly suited to her position.

"Well, I don't like it," the woman said.

Then, out of the blue, the woman insisted Judy guess her age. Judy was hesitant, but the woman prodded her.

"Seventy-seven," Judy proffered.

"No," said the woman, now suddenly quite pleased. "*Eighty*-seven!"

Over grilled ham and cheese sandwiches and chicken soup, Judy told me about the Leland. Built on the site of an old casket factory in 1928, it was widely regarded as the finest hotel in all of Indiana when it opened. But it couldn't compete with the motels that sprouted on the outskirts of town in the 1960s and '70s. It closed in 1984, reopened in 1986, closed again in 1990, reopened again in 1993, and finally closed for good in 2000. It was reborn as a retirement home in 2001, which is when Judy was hired. I asked her what she'd done before that. She smiled. "I ran a nursery school for twenty-eight years," she said. "The jobs really aren't that different. You just need to meet their needs and try to make them happy."

After lunch I gave my presentation in the Leland's "living room," which used to be the hotel's lobby. It was attended by seven women—all quite elderly, naturally. They were scattered about on sofas and easy chairs. Two of them dozed intermittently throughout the talk. But I thought I did a pretty good job, and when I concluded, I was rewarded with a round of applause, which, besides making me feel good, had the added benefit of awakening the two drowsy attendees.

Around two o'clock the Trumans left Richmond. That night, they would do what countless other road trippers have done: they would crash with friends.

14

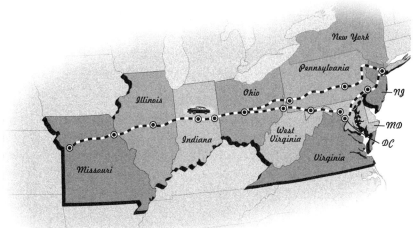

Indianapolis, Indiana, July 7–8, 1953

*A*round four o'clock in the afternoon of Tuesday, July 7, Harry and Bess pulled into the driveway behind the McKinney home on North Meridian Street in Indianapolis. At six—after Harry's nap, of course—the McKinneys hosted a reception for the former president and first lady in their backyard. The weather was lovely. The heat that had seemed to follow the Trumans ever since they left Independence had finally abated. The temperature was in the seventies.

About a hundred people attended the party, which the *Indianapolis Times* called "one of the season's most exclusive and loveliest." It was a swanky affair. Harry wore a white Palm Beach suit, a gray and white silk tie, and spotless white shoes. Bess wore a pale gray dress. "Everybody at the party looks so good," cracked one attendee, "we look like a bunch of

Republicans." But it wasn't strictly a political event. Several prominent Indianapolis Republicans were on hand, including the city's thirty-seven-year-old mayor, Alex Clark.

Nineteen-year-old Claire McKinney, the McKinneys' eldest daughter, was at the party that evening, dressed in a "gay summer frock," according to the next day's *Indianapolis Times*. She remembered one of the guests turning to Mayor Clark in the receiving line and asking, a bit accusatorily, "What are you doing here?" Truman overheard the remark and grabbed the mayor's hand, saying, "It'd be a hell of a country, wouldn't it, Mayor, if there wasn't a two-party system?" "Then he talked to him for a long time," Claire said. "Harry Truman didn't choose his friends by their party affiliation."

Harry ordered a Wild Turkey (allegedly watered down) from the makeshift bar that was set up in the driveway. Bess had a ginger ale. The guests broke into two groups, the men surrounding Harry, the women encircling Bess. The mood was convivial. When someone told Harry he'd done a good job raising Margaret, Harry held his hand up. When it comes to raising daughters, he said, "The important thing is the mother. . . . It doesn't matter about the father." A local Democratic Party official named Harry Gasper introduced himself to Truman, noting that they shared the same first name. "Only," Gasper said, "my mother wanted me to be president and I never got farther than a ward chairman."

"I'll tell you something," the other Harry replied. "My mother didn't care what I became."

At Bess's circle, one of the guests asked her for the secret to a happy marriage. "Well," she answered, "I just let him alone." She said she and Harry were enjoying their cross-country trip immensely, but they were looking forward to going home. "There are just two of us and we sort of rattle around the old house." When she noticed the ice in her ginger ale had melted, Bess announced, "We need more ice," and led the pack of women to the bar. When one couple came to say good-bye to her, the wife said, "When we come through Missouri we're going to drive by your house."

"Don't drive by," said Bess. "Come in."

After the hour-long reception, the Trumans, the McKinneys, and two other couples went inside for dinner. Claire McKinney, meanwhile, went out dancing with friends. Later that night, she bumped into Alex Clark, the Indianapolis mayor, at a nightclub. "You need to meet my little brother," the mayor told her. His name was Jim. He had just returned from Korea. Claire said it would be fine if Jim gave her a call sometime.

When Claire returned home around midnight, the former president of the United States was playing the piano, quite loudly, in her living room, much to the amusement of the rest of the dinner party. "They were all singing and laughing and having the best time," says Claire. "It was—there couldn't be anything more normal." Claire went upstairs and tried to get some sleep while Harry Truman banged away on the piano downstairs.

The Trumans slept in Frank and Margaret McKinneys' bedroom that night. Frank slept on a couch in his study. Margaret slept in Claire's room. The McKinneys' bedroom was en suite, so the rest of the household was spared the sight of a slightly tipsy Harry Truman padding around the second floor in his pajamas in the middle of the night, searching for the bathroom.

At 7:20 the next morning, Harry emerged from the McKinney home for his morning constitutional. Accompanied by Frank McKinney and the *Indianapolis News*'s political reporter, Ed Ziegner, Harry covered about twelve blocks in the neighborhood around the McKinney home. He slowed his usual 120-step-a-minute pace, he said, "to be considerate of the others." Along the way Truman and his companions discussed the Civil War, World War I, the trials and tribulations of other ex-presidents, and his former associates in Washington. Returning to the McKinney home after thirty minutes, Harry turned to his host and said, "Frank, this will cost you a big breakfast." But McKinney was in no shape to cook. He was winded. "It was the first walk I've taken in I don't know how long," he said. "I didn't even know what streets had sidewalks."

After breakfast Truman held a press conference in the McKinneys' living room. He said the Democrats lost in 1952 because the "people were prosperous, fat, and easygoing." "They thought maybe they would like a change," he said. "They let glamour and demagoguery get the best of them."

Asked if he was "optimistic about the future of this country," he said, "I'm always optimistic about this great country of ours. I've always said I wish I could see the next 50 years—it will be the greatest period in the history of the world." Asked if he didn't "expect to see most of it," Truman laughed. "Well, I'm in pretty good health now. But according to the Bible after next year I'll be living on borrowed time."

At one point the press conference was interrupted when the McKinneys' two-and-a-half-year-old daughter, Kathy, came bounding into the living room. Her mother set her on the couch next to Truman, but Kathy would have none of it. She jumped off the couch and began screaming "Mommy!"

"Smart young lady," observed Truman.

But her mother put her back on the couch, and this time Kathy took to the grinning stranger in the crisp white suit. The press conference continued with Harry bouncing Kathy on his knee.

He reiterated that he would not accept any position on the board of directors of any organization, out of respect for the presidency. He said he would spend the rest of the year working on his memoirs, or his "statement of fact," as he referred to it.

He said he'd had "a very pleasant visit" in Indianapolis but was eager to return to Independence, "the finest place in the world to live." ("You people ought to think that about Indiana," he added, good politician that he was.) He declined to say which route he planned to take home. He only said he hoped to make it back before the end of the day. But Independence was nearly five hundred miles away. He needed to leave soon. He excused himself and went upstairs to finish packing.

At eleven o'clock, the big black Chrysler swung out of the McKinneys' driveway and onto 49th Street. The Trumans waved good-bye and headed home.

A few weeks later, Claire McKinney got a call from Jim Clark, the mayor's brother. They went out on a date and, according to Claire, they didn't have a very good time. "But," Claire said, "after I graduated from college a couple years later we were thrown together again by his brother and actually had a very good time. But it never would have happened if it hadn't been for that reception for Harry Truman!" Claire and Jim were married in 1957. Harry and Bess sent them a silver tray as a wedding present. They still have it.

There was just one tiny problem with Claire's new husband: he was a Republican. And when he ran for a seat in the state legislature in the early 1960s, Claire joined him. "I jumped ship," Claire told me. "I had to." She was nervous about telling her father, so she made an appointment to see him in his downtown office. "I thought I'd better be proper about this," Claire said. "I said, 'I just wanted to let you know that I'm changing my registration.' He said, 'You damn well better!' He and my husband were very good friends and he was very proud to vote for him." In 1962, Jim Clark was elected to the Indiana House of Representatives.

Claire and Jim have four children. The eldest, J. Murray Clark, is the chairman of the Indiana Republican Party.

The McKinneys sold their home on North Meridian Street in 1954, but the current owner was kind enough to allow Claire and me to take a look around. Claire still lives in Indianapolis and passes the house often, but she hadn't been inside it in more than fifty years. As she surveyed the first floor, she made the observation that everybody seems to make upon returning to a childhood home after a long absence. "It feels small," she said softly. "Isn't that funny?"

I felt it would have been a tad presumptuous of me to ask the owner of the house if Claire and I could stay for dinner, but Claire suggested an appealing alternative. She invited me to join her and Jim for dinner at their house. She would invite Murray and his wife, Janet, too. And there was a guest room in the basement, so I could even spend the night. It was a generous offer and one that I did not hesitate to accept.

I arrived at Claire and Jim's house at five-thirty. Claire and I chatted about the weather—a series of violent storms had recently passed through Indianapolis—while Jim prepared a round of cocktails (vodka and Fresca).

A few minutes later Murray and Janet arrived. Murray looked like a politician—and I mean that in a good way. His appropriately gray hair was perfectly coiffed, his tan suit still crisp even at the end of a long day at the office. His attractive blond wife, Janet, was a pediatric dentist. We all took seats in the living room. Murray seemed a little wary of me at first. Who, after all, was this stranger who kept pestering his mother? But, abetted by a Coors Light or two, he lightened up. He talked about the Eric Clapton concert he and Janet had gone to the previous Friday. "He's my all-time favorite," Murray said. "He played 'Layla'—the greatest rock 'n' roll song ever written." The only bummer was that the concert ended early because of the storms.

Murray is a partner in an Indianapolis law firm, where he specializes in real estate law. He served eleven years in the Indiana Senate and ran for lieutenant governor in 2000 (he lost). In 2004 he was the chairman of Mitch Daniels's gubernatorial campaign (Daniels won). Since then he's been chairman of the state Republican Party.

I asked Murray how it came to be that he, the grandson of the chairman of the Democratic National Committee, came to be the head of the GOP in Indiana. He told me he'd been interested in politics since he was a child. It was practically the family business, after all. At nine years old he worked on his Uncle Alex's second mayoral campaign, and at sixteen he worked on Richard Lugar's first senatorial campaign (losing efforts, both). He was close to his grandfather, he said, but he never even considered being a Democrat. "I strongly believe, however, he would truly be proud that I am state chair," Murray said. "Even if it is the GOP."

Murray had recently chaired the state convention (it was held the same weekend as the Clapton concert). At the convention, delegates to the 2008 Republican National Convention in St. Paul were chosen. Murray had had to cope with an insurgent faction of Republicans loyal to the irrepressible presidential candidate Ron Paul. The "Paulites" had tried to elect "stealth delegates" who would vote for Paul instead of John McCain at the national convention. "They're true believers," Murray sighed. He sounded more than a little exasperated with that faction of the party. It reminded me of how his grandfather had had to keep the fractured Democrats together at the 1952 national convention. It seems that being a party leader, Republican or Democratic, is less about politics than peacekeeping—or herding cats.

It was time for dinner. Claire asked if we would like red wine or white. The consensus was that both bottles should be opened. We enjoyed a lovely meal of chicken cordon bleu and roasted vegetables, with Apple Brown Betty and vanilla gelato for dessert. Throughout dinner I told Truman stories at an ever-increasing volume while my companions pretended not to be bored. We also talked about how politics has changed since 1953, how it seems to have become more personal and less personable.

"Politics was different then," Claire said. "It wasn't as mean. Politics today is mean. People respected each other. I remember one night my father came home for dinner and he said, 'A terrible thing happened in our town today. A man who was running for president of the United States came to our town to talk today—and people threw eggs at him.' It was Wendell Willkie, the Republican candidate. My father said, 'Respect is owed to anybody who is running for this office.' It was respect. It wasn't personal."

It was a wonderful evening. I had been treated like a king—or, better yet, an ex-president. I slept like a baby in Claire's guest room that night, which is probably how Harry slept the night he stayed with Claire's parents all those years before.

Harry Truman and Frank McKinney remained close friends for the rest of their lives. And, like Harry, Frank remained active in Democratic Party politics. Over the years he was offered a number of prominent political positions, including a seat on the Securities and Exchange Commission, but he declined them all to stay in Indianapolis. In 1968, at Truman's urging, President Johnson appointed McKinney ambassador to Spain. It was a challenging assignment. At the time the United States was negotiating with the Franco regime to keep its military bases in Spain. The Senate confirmed McKinney's appointment, but he was too ill to take the post. He died of cancer in 1974. He was sixty-nine.

15

St. Louis, Missouri,
July 8, 1953

*I*nstead of backtracking along Highway 36 through Decatur and Hannibal, the Trumans took Highway 40 home from Indianapolis. That took them on a more southerly route through Illinois and into St. Louis. Maybe they chose the different route to throw the press off their trail. If so, it worked. Harry and Bess went "missing" again that afternoon. After they left the McKinneys, there were no more reported sightings of the couple until they stopped for dinner in St. Louis at four o'clock, about five hours later.

It was on an earlier trip to St. Louis that the single most enduring image of Harry Truman was captured. On the afternoon of Thursday, November 4, 1948, less than forty-eight hours after his stunning upset in the presidential election, Truman was headed back to Washington on the *Ferdinand*

Magellan when the train stopped briefly at Union Station in St. Louis. A crowd of several thousand turned out to greet the triumphant candidate. Among those who met Truman at the station that afternoon was his friend Charles Arthur Anderson, a World War I veteran and former Democratic congressman from Missouri. Somehow Anderson had obtained a copy of the early edition of the previous day's *Chicago Tribune*. After Truman gave a short speech from the rear platform of the train, Anderson handed him the paper. Beaming, the newly elected president turned toward the crowd and held the paper aloft with both hands for all to see its famously erroneous headline: "DEWEY DEFEATS TRUMAN." A roar went up. "That's one for the books," said Truman laughing. At least three photographers standing shoulder to shoulder directly beneath the president captured the moment: Frank Cancellare of United Press, Pierce Hangge of the *St. Louis Globe-Democrat*, and Byron Rollins of the Associated Press. Their photographs, so identical as to be nearly indistinguishable, would become iconic, a timeless commentary on the fallibility of polls, the virtues of perseverance, and the trustworthiness of the press.

Now, less than five years later, Harry had returned to St. Louis under considerably more modest circumstances. For dinner, he and Bess went to Schneithorst's, a popular German restaurant at Lambert Field—the St. Louis airport. Yes, once upon a time airports were renowned for their fine dining. Air travel, after all, was glamorous and sophisticated. At the dawn of the jet age, people dressed up to fly, and the airport was a place for the beautiful and the rich, not metal detectors. (The FAA didn't even require airlines to search passengers and baggage until 1973, after the D. B. Cooper hijacking.) Airports were tourist attractions, too. Thousands came to Lambert Field every month simply to stare in slack-jawed amazement at such modern marvels as the enormous four-engine Douglas DC-6s and Lockheed Constellations.

Schneithorst's occupied a prized corner of Lambert Field's terminal, a rectangular two-story brick building that resembled a high school. The restaurant looked out on the runway, so diners could enjoy the spectacle of takeoffs and landings with their Wiener schnitzel à la Holstein and potato pancakes. It was owned by Arthur Schneithorst, who'd held the airport concession since 1940. (As part of the deal, Schneithorst also provided in-flight meals for the airlines based in St. Louis.) He'd seen the restaurant through some lean years during the war, but now business was booming, and Schneithorst's had become a St. Louis favorite.

How Harry Truman ended up at Schneithorst's is anybody's guess. Maybe it was recommended to him when he stopped for gas. Harry tended to regard the recommendations of service station attendants most highly. In any event, as had happened so often on their trip, Harry and Bess weren't even recognized when they entered the restaurant. But a buzz soon filled the room, and all eyes turned from the runway to the middle-aged couple seated at a table in waitress Virginia Sullins's section. They ordered veal cutlets.

One bold customer walked up to them to confirm their identities. Harry "admitted the charge," as he liked to say, and thereafter their meal was constantly interrupted. This had become their usual dining experience. But if they were perturbed, they never showed it. They "laughed and joked with other less famed customers," the *St. Louis Post-Dispatch* reported. They even stayed for dessert, though Mrs. Sullins was by that point so flustered that she had difficulty remembering their order: chocolate ice cream for Harry, more fruit (cantaloupe) for Bess.

The brick terminal at Lambert Field was replaced in 1956 with a striking new building designed by the St. Louis architectural firm of Hellmuth, Yamasaki, and Leinweber. (George Hellmuth would later form HOK, the firm that designed the Abraham Lincoln Museum as well as many ballparks. Minoru Yamasaki went on to design the World Trade Center.) With its vaulted ceilings and glass walls, the terminal suggests a sense of flight. It was one of the firm's first big projects, and it was an unqualified success. The Lambert Field terminal has been cited as an architectural masterpiece. (Another of the firm's early projects in St. Louis, the Pruitt-

Igoe public housing project, was less well received. It was demolished in 1973.)

Arthur Schneithorst was not awarded the restaurant concession in the new terminal. Undeterred, he built a new, half-million-dollar German restaurant at the intersection of Clayton Road and Lindbergh Boulevard in western St. Louis County. He called it the Hofamberg Inn. St. Louis had never seen anything like it. The sprawling building looked like something straight out of Bavaria, with a clock tower, turrets, and a red-tiled roof. It had three separate dining rooms and two bars, one of which was paneled in walnut and pigskin, with brass figures in bas-relief on the walls. And that was just the first floor. Upstairs were nine banquet rooms. The Hofamberg Inn became a St. Louis institution, but when Arthur's grandson Jim Schneithorst Jr. took over the business in 2002, the first thing he did was tear the place down. He really didn't have much choice. The building had become too expensive to maintain, and the demand for schnitzel just wasn't what it used to be. A "mixed-use development" was built in its place. It includes a very nice restaurant, but, as St. Louisans will tell you, it's just not the same.

The restaurant concession at Lambert Field is now held by HSMHost, a Maryland-based company that operates restaurants in airports and highway rest stops—sorry, "travel venues"—all over the world. Based on my extensive research, which consisted of asking somebody in the airport's management office, a restaurant called the Rib Café is roughly where Schneithorst's used to be. The day I visited happened to be Valentine's Day, and, by a happy coincidence, Allyson was traveling with me. We planned to return to the airport that night and enjoy a romantic dinner at the Rib Café. Reservations, we assumed, would not be necessary.

If you've ever wondered what kind of restaurant would be closed on Valentine's night, it would be the kind in the St. Louis airport. As Allyson and I discovered when we showed up for dinner at eight, the Rib Café closes at 6:30 P.M. every day. Even Valentine's Day. How this fits into HSMHost's master plan, I don't know.

Disappointed, we took the shuttle back to our hotel, where we had a completely forgettable dining experience.

The next day we returned to the Rib Café—for lunch. And, as airport restaurants go, it wasn't half bad. It overlooks the runway, just like Schneithorst's did, so we could watch planes take off and land while we dined. We ordered ribs, naturally, and they were pretty good. We also enjoyed a tangy coleslaw. The service was efficient. All in all, it was a lovely meal—except for the dead bird on the ledge just outside our window. It lay on its back, in the mid- to late stages of decomposition.

After dinner at Schneithorst's, Harry and Bess signed a few autographs, then walked out to their car. Harry asked the parking lot attendant for directions back to Highway 40. (Highway 40 and Interstate 64 are now the same road in St. Louis, but the city's residents—much to their credit—still refer to it as "40," not "64.")

Harry and Bess took 40 all the way back to Independence.

They drove straight into the setting sun.

Epilogue

The Trumans reached 219 Delaware Street at 9:00 P.M. on Wednesday, July 8. They'd been gone nineteen days. They'd driven some twenty-five hundred miles. Bess's brothers George and Frank, who lived around the corner, helped them unpack. "It was a wonderful trip," Bess told the *Independence Examiner*. Harry skipped his walk the next morning and slept in. He didn't leave for work until around ten. On the way in, he dropped off his suits at the cleaners. In one of his jacket pockets he discovered the key to his room at the Waldorf. He mailed it back.

Harry and Bess would never take another long car trip. Harry was forced to admit that it was virtually impossible for them to travel incognito anymore. He lamented the loss of anonymity in a letter to his old friend Vic Householder, who had invited Harry to visit him in Arizona. "I'd give most anything to pay a visit to Arizona," Harry wrote. "But Vic I'm a nuisance to my friends. I can't seem to get from under that awful glare that shines on the White House. . . . So, Vic, we've decided that until the glamour wears off we'll only do the official things we have to."

But as Harry discovered, the glamour of the presidency never wears off. He and Bess did continue to travel, but the trips were choreographed. In 1956 they went to Europe, accompanied by Stanley Woodward, Harry's former chief of protocol, and Woodward's wife, Sara. Harry had been to Europe twice before, as an officer in World War I and to confer with Churchill and Stalin at Potsdam, but it was Bess's first trip overseas. They toured Paris, Rome, and London, meeting with dignitaries including Churchill and Pope Pius XII. On June 20, 1956—exactly three years after he and Bess had driven from Decatur to Wheeling, stopping at the McKinneys' house for lunch—"Harricum" Truman was awarded an honorary degree at Oxford. "Never, never in my life," he said, "did I ever think I'd be a Yank at Oxford." "Give 'em hell, Harricum!" the students shouted.

Harry, of course, never ran for office again, but he remained active and vocal—some would say too vocal—in the Democratic Party for the rest of his life. He never really stopped being a politician (an honorable profession in his estimation), but he grew less politic. He caused a minor flap in the 1960 presidential campaign when he said anybody who voted for his bitter enemy Richard Nixon "ought to go to hell." John Kennedy was asked about the comment in one of his famous televised debates with Nixon. "Well," he said, "I must say that Mr. Truman has his methods of expressing things. . . . I really don't think there's anything I can say to President Truman that's going to cause him at the age of seventy-six to change his particular speaking manner. Maybe Mrs. Truman can, but I don't think I can." (Nixon, whom the Watergate tapes would reveal to be spectacularly profane, responded with his usual sanctimony: "I can only say that I am very proud that President Eisenhower restored dignity and decency and, frankly, good language to the conduct of the presidency of the United States.")

The first volume of Truman's memoirs, *Year of Decisions*, was published in 1955. The second, *Years of Trial and Hope*, came out the following year. Sales were strong, but the reviews were tepid. His army of ghostwriters—more than a dozen, by some estimates—had watered down the prose, rendering it a bland imitation of the pugnacious and opinionated president that America had come to know. Harry knew it, too. Across one page of an early draft he scribbled, "Good God, what crap!" (A third book, *Mr. Citizen*, which chronicled his life after the White House, better represented the man.)

In 1955 Harry traded in his 1953 Chrysler New Yorker—for the 1955 model. (If you happen to see the '53, please let me know.) It was in the new Chrysler that Harry chauffeured Margaret to Trinity Episcopal Church in Independence on April 21, 1956, for her marriage to Clifton Daniel. It was the same church in which Harry and Bess had been married thirty-seven years earlier. Margaret had met Clifton in New York. He was an editor at the *Times*. "Margie has put one over on me and got herself engaged to a news man!" Harry wrote his old friend Dean Acheson. But, he hastened to add, "He strikes me as a very nice fellow and if Margaret wants him I'll be satisfied." Margaret and Clifton would bless Harry and Bess with four grandsons, on whom they doted relentlessly.

The Harry S. Truman Library was dedicated on July 6, 1957. It wasn't built on the Truman family farm as Harry had hoped. His brother and sister had vetoed that idea. The land was too valuable. "Ain't no use wastin' good farmland on any old dang library," said his brother Vivian. So instead the library was built on thirteen acres donated by the city of Independence, just a mile down the road from the Truman home on Delaware Street.

Sitting next to Truman on the dais at the library's dedication was Herbert Hoover. The only two living ex-presidents had reconciled in 1955, when Harry invited Hoover to attend a fundraising dinner for the library in San Francisco. Hoover, who was raising funds for his own library in West Branch, Iowa, accepted the invitation. "I have a fellow feeling," he wrote Truman, "for I have one of those burdens of my own." Thereafter, Truman and Hoover corresponded regularly, and their mutual admiration, grudging at first, blossomed into genuine friendship. When Harry invited him to attend the library's dedication, Hoover replied, "One of the important jobs of our very exclusive Trade Union is preserving libraries." Harry returned the favor when he attended the dedication of Hoover's library in 1962. "I feel sure that I am one of his closest friends and that's the reason I am here," Harry told the crowd.

Later that year, Hoover wrote Harry to thank him for sending him a copy of *Truman Speaks*, a compilation of lectures Harry had delivered at Columbia University. "This is an occasion when I should like to add something more," Hoover wrote after the obligatory thank you, "because yours has been a friendship which has reached deeper into my life than you know. . . . When you came to the White House within a month you opened the door to me to the only profession I knew, public service, and you undid some disgraceful action that had been taken in the prior years. For all of this and your friendship, I am deeply grateful." Coming from one as reserved as Hoover, it was an extraordinary letter, and it moved Truman deeply. He had it framed, and he displayed it in his office at the library.

Like a marble statue suddenly come to life, Truman delighted in surprising visitors to the library, especially schoolchildren, with whom he would hold impromptu question-and-answer sessions—with Harry asking as many questions of the children as they asked of him. He always pointed out that one of them could be president one day—after all, he had never expected to be president himself. Sometimes he would play the piano for them, too.

Truman kept an office at the library, which finally freed him of the financial burden of renting one in downtown Kansas City. However, other expenses, including postage, were still his responsibility, and his finances continued to trouble him. In January 1958, Truman and his brother and sister sold off the family farm in Grandview. It broke Harry's heart, but he had no choice. If the farm hadn't been sold, he wrote, "I would practically be on relief." The land was purchased by a developer who turned it into a shopping center called Truman Corners. Only the family's farmhouse was preserved. Today it sits within spitting distance of a McDonald's, a Sam's Club, an Applebee's, and an IHOP.

Harry and Bess on the porch of their house in Independence on Valentine's Day 1960. When a friend once offered to arrange a private screening of the movie *Gentlemen Prefer Blondes*, Harry declined. "Real gentlemen," he said, "prefer gray hair."

Photo courtesy of the Harry S. Truman Library

Ever more openly, Harry continued to lobby his friends in Congress for financial assistance. To his close friend House Speaker Sam Rayburn he bluntly confessed to needing assistance "to keep ahead of the hounds." In the summer of 1958, Rayburn, working with Senate Majority Leader Lyndon Johnson, finally got a presidential pension bill through Congress. House Majority Leader John McCormack said an outgoing president should not be expected to "engage in any business or occupation which would demean the office he once held." Dwight Eisenhower, perhaps mindful of his own impending retirement, signed the Former Presidents Act into law on August 25. "The world's richest nation has finally made sure that never again will an ex-president have to live off the charity of relatives," began the UPI report on the new law, which entitled ex-presidents to "a monetary allowance" of twenty-five thousand dollars, as well as fifty thousand dollars for office expenses and unlimited franking privileges. (Since it is not a contributory pension, the "allowance" is taxed as if it were a salary.)

At long last, Harry Truman was financially secure.

Herbert Hoover, of course, didn't need the money. He hadn't even taken a salary as president. But he accepted the pension anyway, to spare his friend Harry any embarrassment.

On November 22, 1963, Truman was having lunch at the Muehlebach Hotel in Kansas City when he was told that President Kennedy had been shot. In the car on his way home he heard on the radio that Kennedy had died.

Harry flew to Washington to attend Kennedy's funeral. Eisenhower was there too, and the two old adversaries ended up sharing the same limousine to the graveside service at Arlington National Cemetery. Margaret Truman Daniel and Mamie Eisenhower rode with them. (Bess wasn't feeling well, so she stayed home.) They discussed whether Kennedy's assassination was the work of a conspiracy or a lone gunman. They agreed it was most likely the latter.

After the service, Margaret invited the Eisenhowers to join her and her father for lunch at the Blair House, where they were staying. Ike and Mamie accepted the invitation. Sandwiches were served, along with coffee and, perhaps, something stronger. For an hour, Harry and Ike chatted amiably, reminiscing about old battles, political and otherwise.

"I thought it would never end," recalled Admiral Robert Dennison, a White House aide who was also there, "but it was really heartwarming . . . you'd think there had never been any differences between them. . . . It was really wonderful."

When it was time for the Eisenhowers to go, Harry and Margaret walked them to their car. The two former presidents chatted some more. Then they shook hands, "a long, lingering, silent handshake," according to one account. Margaret kissed Ike on the cheek. Mamie kissed Harry.

Harry and Ike had made peace, though they would never see each other again.

In 1965, in the wake of the assassination, Congress passed a law authorizing the Secret Service to protect former presidents and their wives. This did not please the Trumans. When an agent showed up at their house and told Harry that he no longer had a need for Mike Westwood, the Independence cop who'd been his part-time bodyguard for twelve years, Harry told the agent, "Well, I no longer have a need for you, so get out of here." Bess was equally opposed to the return of the Secret Service. "Mother reacted as if they had just told her she was going to have to spend four more years in the White House," Margaret wrote. "She refused to allow the Secret Service men on the property." Harry read the new law carefully and discovered a provision allowing him and Bess to refuse the protection. On September 21, he wrote the Secret Service requesting that their detail be "discontinued." (Ironically, less than three weeks earlier, he had received a letter threatening to have him "rubbed out" to avenge Hiroshima and Nagasaki.)

Then one night, the phone in the hall rang. Bess answered.

"Bess," purred a familiar voice, "this is Lyndon." Perhaps the president mentioned Harry and Bess's road trip in 1953, and how worried the Secret Service had been even back then. Perhaps he told her how helpful it would be to have the agents around now, how they could run errands or help around the house. And, of course, there was the matter of safety. Whatever he said, Johnson must have been at his persuasive best, for he convinced the stubborn couple to allow the Secret Service back into their lives.

But, at Harry's insistence, Mike Westwood stayed.

Harry and Bess often returned to New York to visit Margaret, Clifton, and the grandchildren. They usually traveled by plane. Harry still took a walk most mornings, accompanied by a pack of reporters, including, now, television crews. But, as the years passed, his pace slowed, the walks grew shorter, and his famously acidulous observations occasionally gave way to simpleminded crotchetiness. Civil rights demonstrators were "busybodies," antiwar protestors were "silly."

He became something of a grumpy old man, yet the nation's fondness for him only grew, perhaps because he represented a bygone era whose passing, given the tumultuous times, was bemoaned. He was humble, too, in a way his successors were not. Harry had become an elder statesman, though he hated the term. To him, a statesman was just a politician who was dead.

In 1969 Harry ranked seventh in the Gallup Poll's annual list of America's "Most Admired Men." (For what it's worth, Nixon ranked first.) More recently, a 2004 poll by Greenberg Quinlan Rosner found that 58 percent of Americans viewed Truman favorably.

Historians began to reassess Harry too. In 1962, Arthur Schlesinger polled seventy-five historians to rank the presidents. The top five were Lincoln, Washington, FDR, Wilson, and Jefferson. According to the historians, they were the "great" presidents. Harry—whom Walter Trohan had called "one of the most mediocre men ever to inherit power"—ranked ninth. He was one of the "near great" presidents. The results were published in the *New York Times Sunday Magazine* that July. On file at the Truman Library is a copy of the article with notations made in Harry's characteristic slashing script. Harry's top five were Washington, Lincoln, Jefferson, Wilson, and Jackson. Above the picture of John Adams, whom the historians ranked tenth, he scribbled, "Should be about 18." Above the picture of himself he wrote, "Not to be considered." It was Harry's belief that a president should be dead "about thirty years" before his administration could be fairly assessed.

It is delightful to imagine the aging ex-president, pencil in hand, sitting on his porch on a sultry summer Sunday morning in Missouri, correcting the rankings.

On October 13, 1964, Harry slipped and fell in his second-floor bathroom. His head smashed against the sink, shattering his glasses and cutting his forehead. He fell against the bathtub, fracturing two ribs. The next day he received a telegram from Herbert Hoover:

Bathtubs are a menace to ex-presidents for as you may recall a bathtub rose up and fractured my vertebrae when I was in

Venezuela on your world famine mission in 1946. My warmest sympathy and best wishes for your speedy recovery.

Those were the last words Herbert Hoover is known to have written. Three days later he collapsed. Massive internal bleeding was the cause. He never regained consciousness and died on October 20. He was ninety. At 31 years and 231 days, Hoover's is the longest ex-presidency in history. Truman, of course, was unable to attend the funeral. He sent a telegram to Hoover's two sons. "He was my good friend and I was his," he wrote.

Harry was back home in a few days, but he never fully recovered from the fall. His morning walks grew less frequent, and he went into his office at the library less often. He grew thin and frail, his face gaunt behind massive horn-rimmed glasses. The man who had found it impossible to travel incognito in 1953 was now unrecognizable, even to many of his neighbors in Independence.

In 1968 Richard Nixon, one of the two men in politics he truly hated, was elected president. It was a bitter pill for Harry to swallow. He had wanted Lyndon Johnson to run for reelection, to take his case directly to the people, just as Harry had twenty years before. Instead, Harry felt, LBJ had let the "silly" war protesters drive him from office.

But when the new president, quite unexpectedly, asked if he could visit the Trumans, Harry could hardly refuse. As Margaret put it, "That special bond which links the residents of the White House prevailed over old animosities." On March 22, 1969, the Nixons came to Independence. They spent about twenty minutes at the house on Delaware Street. The two men chatted while Bess showed Pat Nixon around the house. Then they went to the library, where Nixon presented Harry with a Steinway piano that had been in the White House when the Trumans lived there. Nixon sat down and played "The Missouri Waltz." Truman disliked the song, of course, but that didn't matter. His hearing wasn't what it used to be. When Nixon finished, Harry turned to Bess and asked her what song he'd played.

A week later, Dwight Eisenhower died. Truman could not attend the funeral, but his public statement was characteristically both candid and generous. "General Eisenhower and I became political opponents but before that we were comrades in arms, and I will not forget his service to his country and to Western civilization."

On June 28, 1969, Harry and Bess celebrated their golden wedding anniversary, quietly as usual. By the end of that year, Harry had stopped going to his library altogether. The morning walks stopped too, as he retreated into 219 Delaware Street.

On the afternoon of December 5, 1972, Harry left the house for the last time. He was taken by ambulance to Research Hospital in Kansas City to be treated for lung congestion. His condition deteriorated.

On the day after Christmas, Harry S. Truman died. He was eighty-eight.

Lyndon Johnson, now the only living ex-president, attended the funeral. He did not look well, and, less than a month later, on January 22, 1973, he died of a heart attack. He was sixty-four. For the first time since the death of Calvin Coolidge forty years earlier, America had no living ex-president. Nixon would rectify that by resigning on August 9, 1974.

Now alone in the big house on Delaware Street, Bess continued to follow politics and baseball closely. She was honorary chairman of Missouri Senator Thomas Eagleton's 1974 reelection campaign. "She knew every player in the Kansas City Royals starting lineup and had very strong opinions of the plusses and minuses of each one," marveled Eagleton. Arthritis confined her to a wheelchair, but she was active until a fall and a stroke in the early 1980s.

The longest-lived first lady in American history, Bess Truman died on October 18, 1982. She was ninety-seven.

Harry and Bess are buried next to each other in the courtyard of the Truman Library.

Harry is on the driver's side.

Postscript

On April 4, 2008, in the midst of her bruising campaign for the Democratic presidential nomination, New York Senator Hillary Clinton released her and her husband's tax returns for the previous eight years. The returns showed that the former president and first lady had earned a combined $109 million.

Harry Truman must have been spinning in his grave.

The Clintons' income included thirty million from their bestselling books, and as much as fifteen million from an investment partnership with one of their top campaign fundraisers. Bill Clinton earned more than ten million in speaking fees alone. The former president was paid $650,000 by the investment firm Goldman Sachs for giving just four speeches.

"We've come a long way from Harry Truman," former Clinton aide Leon Panetta wryly observed. Indeed, being an ex-president has changed a lot since the Secret Service dropped off the Trumans at Union Station in Washington on January 20, 1953. As the *Washington Post* noted, the

Clintons had transformed themselves into a phenomenally successful global brand. Today's ex-president is a small corporation unto himself, with annual revenues of seven (or more) figures and a sizeable workforce.

Ironically, the last president to follow Harry Truman's example of refusing to "commercialize" the presidency in retirement was Richard Nixon. Like Harry, Nixon refused to sit on corporate boards or accept exorbitant speaking fees. His income came primarily from book sales. In 1985, he even gave up his Secret Service detail and hired his own bodyguards. In 1980, the Nixons moved from California into a Manhattan townhouse. The still-brooding former president often took brisk early-morning walks, but there were few shouts of "Hiya, Dick!" Instead his presence was often met with speechless incredulity, as if, one writer said, he had risen from the dead.

It was Nixon's successor who turned the ex-presidency into a gold mine. Gerald Ford cashed in on his status as a "former" in a way none of his predecessors ever had. Besides the obligatory book deal, he accepted seats on the boards of more than a dozen corporations, including American Express and 20th Century Fox, receiving lucrative compensation for little work. He also commanded speaking fees of fifteen thousand dollars or more and worked the "mashed potato circuit" relentlessly, becoming the first ex-president since Theodore Roosevelt to earn substantial income in that manner. He even lent his name to a series of presidential commemorative coins. By the early 1980s, Ford was raking in more than a million dollars a year. Nixon accused Ford of "selling the office," but Ford was unapologetic. "I'm a private citizen now; it's nobody's business," he said. "In effect," wrote historian and journalist Mark K. Updegrove, "he became the first to make a job—a very lucrative one—out of being a former president."

Meanwhile, the "exclusive trade union" continued to grow. When George W. Bush took office in 2001, America had five formers (Ford, Carter, Reagan, Bush, and Clinton), tying the record set when Clinton took office in 1993 (Nixon, Ford, Carter, Reagan, Bush) and when Lincoln took office in 1861 (Van Buren, Tyler, Pierce, Fillmore, Buchanan). As with

Harry and Herbert, unlikely bonds were formed. Carter and Ford became such close friends that Carter once said they were "almost like brothers" and challenged historians "to find any former presidents who . . . have formed a closer and more intimate relationship" than he and Ford. The elder Bush and Clinton also formed an unlikely alliance, working together on humanitarian relief efforts around the world. Occasionally, all the formers have joined forces. At the dedication of the Reagan Library in 1991, the sitting president, George H. W. Bush, was photographed standing in front of the library with his four immediate predecessors. It was a historic moment, the first gathering of five presidents. The Associated Press later revealed that Bush and the four formers had cut a deal: A limited number of copies of the photo had been made, no more than fifteen hundred. Each of the five was to sign each of the copies. All agreed to sign no other copies, driving up the price of the photos they'd already signed. One autograph collector estimated the deal would net each man as much as $1.5 million. The presidents insisted the pact was only intended to raise money for their libraries.

In 1961 Harry was asked to sign a photograph of him standing on the dais with Hoover, Eisenhower, and Nixon at Eisenhower's first inaugural. The other three men had already signed it, but Harry refused. "I wouldn't sign a picture with that son-of-a-bitch Nixon in it," he said by way of explanation. "He called me a traitor." Then he cocked his fist as if to throw a punch. "This is what I'd like to do to him."

All the while, the presidential pension package has continued to grow. Today an ex-president receives an annual pension equivalent to the salary of a cabinet officer—around $190,000. He also gets money to pay for office expenses, staff salaries, travel, and postage. It can amount to more than a million dollars a year. In 2008 the rent on Bill Clinton's office in Harlem alone was more than $500,000. (Carter's in Atlanta was $102,000. The elder Bush's in Houston was $175,000.)

The total amount of money the federal government spends on its ex-presidents has risen from $160,000 in 1959 to an estimated $2.5 million in 2008. And that's not counting Secret Service protection, which, in 2000, when four formers were living, cost nearly twenty-six million dollars altogether.

Harry thought presidents deserved pensions, but probably not that much. Given the earning power of the modern ex-president, it's doubtful such lucrative pensions are even necessary anymore. Yet, just as it was loath to grant the pensions in the first place, Congress is now loath to take them away. In 1994 President Clinton signed a bill that would have ended an ex-president's office allowance in 2003 or five years after leaving office, whichever was later. But the legislation was quietly repealed three years later, reportedly at the urging of the ex-presidents. The only perk the exes have ever lost is one they didn't want. For several years in the 1980s, the government rented a townhouse in Washington exclusively for their use when they visited the capital. In 1988 the funding was cut because the property was almost never used.

When he was in office, America's newest ex-president was often fond of comparing himself to Harry Truman. In some ways the comparison is apt. Both George W. Bush and Harry Truman were mocked by critics as inarticulate and bumbling. Both presided over unpopular wars. (Of course, Truman was repelling an invasion, while Bush launched one.) As a result of those wars (and other factors), Bush and Truman both saw their approval ratings plummet. (In 2008, Bush's sank to 22 percent, matching Harry's low in 1952.)

In a commencement address at West Point in 2006, Bush invoked Harry's name seventeen times. He claimed his administration was "building on the legacy of Harry Truman." And he equated the cold war with what he called "today's war." "Like the cold war," Bush said, "we are fighting the followers of a murderous ideology that despises freedom, crushes all dissent, has territorial ambitions, and pursues totalitarian aims."

The younger Bush believes history will vindicate him just as it has, in the eyes of many historians, vindicated Harry.

Some historians are skeptical. "The only connection between Harry Truman and George Bush is that they left office with low opinion numbers," Douglas Brinkley of Rice University told the *Washington Post.* "That's a very thin reed."

However, as ex-presidents, Bush and Truman will definitely have at least one thing in common. Under legislation passed in 1995, all ex-presidents after Bill Clinton will receive Secret Service protection for only ten years after leaving office. (They can keep the rest of their generous pension packages.)

So, on January 20, 2019, George W. Bush will become the first ex-president since Harry Truman with no legal right to taxpayer-funded protection.

But I doubt we'll see him and Laura driving back to Washington by themselves anytime soon.

Acknowledgments

On my travels I was blessed with an abundance of hospitality, helpfulness, and humor. Thank you Daniel Barber, Nancy and Norman Barter, James Blauvelt, Steve Chou, Jim Clark, Murray Clark, Jill Cordes and Phil Johnston, Clifton Truman Daniel, Jim Grass, Mary Griffin, Bill Herman, the Hohman family, Elise and Robert Kauzlaric, Carroll Kehne Jr., Rodney Manfredi, DiAnne McDaniel, Frank McKinney III, Martin Rothstein, Jim Schneithorst Sr., Judy Sherrow, Max Skidmore, Lynn Smith, Christopher Squire, Scott Strong, Harvey Sunday, Mitch Teich, Doug Tucker, Richard Weingroff, Randi Wight, Lowell Wilson, Herbert Zearing, and Floyd Zerfowski.

The following institutions provided invaluable support: Allegany County Library, Cumberland, Maryland; Citizens Library, Washington, Pennsylvania; Columbus Metropolitan Library, Columbus, Ohio; Decatur Adult Transition Center, Decatur, Illinois; Decatur Public Library, Decatur, Illinois; District of Columbia Public Library, Washington, D.C.; Federal Highway Administration, Washington, D.C.; Frederick County Public Library, Frederick, Maryland; Hannibal Free Public Library, Hannibal,

Missouri; Harry S. Truman Library and Museum, Independence, Missouri; Harry S Truman National Historic Site, Independence, Missouri; Herbert Hoover Presidential Library and Museum, West Branch, Iowa; Historical Society of Dauphin County, Pennsylvania; Historical Society of Frederick County, Maryland; Indiana Historical Society, Indianapolis, Indiana; Indianapolis–Marion County Public Library, Indianapolis, Indiana; Kansas City Public Library, Kansas City, Missouri; Leland Residence, Richmond, Indiana; Library of Congress, Washington, D.C.; Mid-Continent Public Library, Independence, Missouri; Morrisson-Reeves Library, Richmond, Indiana; Office of the Senate Curator, Washington, D.C.; Ohio County Public Library, Wheeling, West Virginia; Pennsylvania State Police Historical, Educational & Memorial Center, Hershey, Pennsylvania; St. Louis Mercantile Library, St. Louis, Missouri; State Library of Pennsylvania, Harrisburg, Pennsylvania; Van Pelt Library, University of Pennsylvania, Philadelphia, Pennsylvania; Waldorf-Astoria Hotel, New York, New York; Washington County Historical Society, Washington, Pennsylvania; and Wayne County Historical Museum, Richmond, Indiana.

Special thanks to Liz Safly and her colleagues at the Truman Library, who made my time there so productive and pleasurable, as well as to my friends in Bamako, who suffered my Truman tales with good humor for two years.

For going above and beyond the call of duty, I am especially indebted to Claire McKinney Clark, Alan Hais, George W. Pappas, Manley Stampler, and Toni Walker.

To my parents, Tracy and Jim Algeo, as well as my brothers, sisters, nieces, and nephews: I couldn't have picked a better family. Same goes for my in-laws, Gigi and Frank McCollum.

To my agent, Jane Dystel: you're an all-star in my book. To my editor, Jerome Pohlen, and everyone at Chicago Review Press, thank you for your kind support, superior advice, and constant encouragement.

Allyson, *grazie amore mio*.

Lastly, thank you Harry and Bess Truman. You have been wonderful traveling companions.

Sources

My account of Harry and Bess Truman's 1953 road trip is based on contemporaneous newspaper reports, interviews with surviving witnesses, previously published accounts, and material on file at the Harry S. Truman Library in Independence, Missouri, particularly the post-presidential papers and oral history interviews.

Eyewitness Interviews

Most eyewitnesses were interviewed multiple times. Interviews were conducted in person, over the phone, and by e-mail.

Claire McKinney Clark (saw the Trumans in Indianapolis)
Mary Griffin (Hannibal, Missouri)
Bill Herman (Indianapolis, Indiana)

Carroll Kehne Jr. (Frederick, Maryland)
George Pappas Jr. (Frostburg, Maryland)
Martin "Doc" Rothstein (Frostburg, Maryland)
Manley Stampler (near Bedford, Pennsylvania)
Harvey Sunday (New Kingstown, Pennsylvania)
Toni Walker (Hannibal, Missouri)
Randi Wight (Bethesda, Maryland)
Lowell Wilson (Richmond, Indiana)
Floyd Zerfowski (Decatur, Illinois)

Newspapers

Bedford (Pennsylvania) *Gazette*
Columbus (Ohio) *Citizen-Journal*
Columbus (Ohio) *Dispatch*
Cumberland (Maryland) *Evening Times*
Decatur (Illinois) *Herald*
Decatur (Illinois) *Review*
Frederick (Maryland) *News*
Frederick (Maryland) *Post*
Hannibal (Missouri) *Courier-Post*
Harrisburg (Pennsylvania) *Evening News*
Harrisburg (Pennsylvania) *Patriot*
Independence (Missouri) *Examiner*
Indianapolis News
Indianapolis Star
Indianapolis Times
New York Daily Mirror
New York Herald Tribune
New York Journal-American
New York Post

New York Times
New York World-Telegram and Sun
Ohio State Journal (Columbus, Ohio)
Philadelphia Daily News
Philadelphia Evening Bulletin
Philadelphia Inquirer
Pittsburgh Post-Gazette
Pittsburgh Press
Richmond (Indiana) *Palladium-Item*
Richmond (Indiana) *Palladium-Item and Sun-Telegram*
St. Louis Globe-Democrat
St. Louis Post-Dispatch
Washington Daily News
Washington Evening Star
Washington Post
Washington Times-Herald
Washington (Pennsylvania) *Observer*
Washington (Pennsylvania) *Reporter*
Wheeling (West Virginia) *Intelligencer*
Wheeling (West Virginia) *News-Register*

Oral History Interviews

Almost since its inception, the Truman Library has been recording and transcribing interviews with people associated with Harry and Bess Truman. Now numbering around five hundred, these interviews are a priceless resource for researchers.

Floyd M. Boring
William J. Bray
Matthew Connelly

E. Clifton Daniel
Mildred Lee Dryden
Stanley R. Fike
Edgar G. Hinde
Frank Holeman
Robert B. Landry
Charles S. Murphy
Robert G. Nixon
Mize Peters
Harold M. Slater
Isaac N. P. Stokes
James L. Sundquist
Harry H. Vaughan
Nathan Thomas (Tom) Veatch
Paul Mike Westwood

Bibliography

Alexander-Bloch, Benjamin. "Former Presidents Cost U.S. Taxpayers Big Bucks; Tab from 1977 to 2000 Is Pegged at $370 Million." *Toledo Blade*, January 7, 2007. (Retrieved from www.toledoblade.com/apps/pbcs.dll/article?AID=/20070107/NEWS09/70107004.)

Arnold, John Patton. *Motor Tourist's Guide*. Chicago: Popular Mechanics Press, 1953.

Arter, Bill. "The Death of the Deshler." *Columbus Dispatch Magazine*, October 5, 1969.

Auto editors of Consumer Guide. *History of the American Auto*. Lincolnwood, IL: Publications International, 2004.

"Back Home with the Neighbors: Quiet Life for Harry and Bess." *Newsweek*, February 2, 1953.

Bailey, Diana L. *The Mayflower: Washington's Second Best Address*. Virginia Beach, VA: Donning Company Publishers, 2001.

Baker, Peter. "Disfavor for Bush Hits Rare Heights." *Washington Post*, July 25, 2007. (Retrieved from www.washingtonpost. com/wp-dyn/content/article/2007/07/24/AR2007072402263. html?nav=hcmodule.)

Bernard, Sid. *Your Guide to New York*. New York: Bernard Publications, 1951.

Brewster, Mike. "Kemmons Wilson: America's Innkeeper." *Business Week*, October 11, 2004. (Retrieved from www.businessweek.com/bwdaily/ dnflash/oct2004/nf2004111_3044_db078.htm.)

Brilley, Don. "Truman Had Special Place in City's Heart." *Decatur* (Illinois) *Herald & Review*, October 5, 1975.

Bromley, Michael L. *William Howard Taft and the First Motoring Presidency, 1909–1913*. Jefferson, NC: McFarland & Company, 2003.

Brune, Lester H. *Chronology of the Cold War, 1917–1992*. New York: Routledge, 2006.

Bumiller, Elisabeth. "At West Point, Bush Draws Parallels with Truman." *New York Times*, May 28, 2006. (Retrieved from www.nytimes. com/2006/05/28/washington/28bush.html?_r=1&oref=slogin.)

Carlson, Peter. "50 Years Ago, Unidentified Flying Objects from Way Beyond the Beltway Seized the Capital's Imagination." *Washington Post*, July 21, 2002.

Caro, Robert A. *The Years of Lyndon Johnson: Master of the Senate*. New York: Alfred A. Knopf, 2002.

Caro, Robert A. *The Years of Lyndon Johnson: Means of Ascent*. New York: Alfred A. Knopf, 1990.

Chambers, John Whiteclay II. "Presidents Emeritus." *American Heritage*, June/July 1979. (Retrieved from www.americanheritage. com/articles/magazine/ah/1979/4/1979_4_16.shtml.)

Chou, Steve. *Hannibal: The Otis Howell Collection*. Charleston, SC: Arcadia Publishing, 2004.

Coffey, Frank, and Joseph Layden. *America on Wheels: The First 100 Years: 1896–1996*. Los Angeles: General Publishing Group, 1996.

Cohodas, Nadine. *Strom Thurmond and the Politics of Southern Change.* New York: Simon & Schuster, 1993.

Costa, Dora L. *The Evolution of Retirement: An American Economic History, 1880–1990.* Chicago: University of Chicago Press, 1998.

Culver, John C., and John Hyde. *American Dreamer: The Life and Times of Henry A. Wallace.* New York: Norton, 2000.

Cupper, Dan. *The Pennsylvania Turnpike: A History.* Lebanon, PA: Applied Arts Publishers, 2001.

Dakelman, Mitchell E., and Neal A. Schorr. *The Pennsylvania Turnpike.* Charleston, SC: Arcadia Publishing, 2004.

Daniel, Clifton Truman. *Growing Up with My Grandfather: Memories of Harry S. Truman.* Secaucus, NJ: Carol Publishing Group, 1995.

Davies, Pete. *American Road: The Story of an Epic Transcontinental Journey at the Dawn of the Motor Age.* New York: H. Holt, 2002.

Dicker, John. *The United States of Wal-Mart.* New York: Jeremy P. Tarcher/Penguin, 2005.

Doherty, Thomas. *Cold War, Cool Medium: Television, McCarthyism, and American Culture.* New York: Columbia University Press, 2003.

Duncan, Dayton. *Horatio's Drive: America's First Road Trip.* New York: Alfred A. Knopf, 2003.

Eggen, Dan. "Citing History, Bush Suggests His Policies Will One Day Be Vindicated." *Washington Post,* June 9, 2008.

Ellis, Richard J. *Presidential Travel: The Journey from George Washington to George W. Bush.* Lawrence, KS: University Press of Kansas, 2008.

Ferrell, Robert H., ed. *The Autobiography of Harry S. Truman.* Columbia, MO: University of Missouri Press, 2002.

Ferrell, Robert H., ed. *Dear Bess: The Letters from Harry to Bess Truman, 1910–1959.* New York: Norton, 1983.

Ferrell, Robert H. *Harry S. Truman: A Life.* Columbia, MO: University of Missouri Press, 1994.

Ferrell, Robert H., ed. *Off the Record: The Private Papers of Harry S. Truman.* New York: Penguin, 1980.

Forrest, Earle R. *History of Washington County, Pennsylvania*. Chicago: S. J. Clarke Publishing Company, 1926.

Freeland, Richard M. *The Truman Doctrine and the Origins of McCarthyism: Foreign Policy, Domestic Politics, and Internal Security, 1946–1948*. New York: New York University Press, 1985.

Fried, Albert, ed. *McCarthyism: The Great American Red Scare: A Documentary History*. New York: Oxford University Press, 1997.

Frost, Stanley. "The Klan Shows Its Hand in Indiana." *The Outlook*, June 4, 1924.

Garrison, Chad. "Schneithorst Helps Family Business Evolve." *St. Louis Business Journal*, January 17, 2003. (Retrieved from http://stlouis.bizjournals.com/stlouis/stories/2003/01/20/focus7.html.)

Geselbracht, Raymond H. "Celebrating the Harry S. Truman Library: The First Fifty Years." *The Public Historian*, Vol. XXVIII, No. 3 (Summer 2006).

Goode, James F. *The United States and Iran: In the Shadow of Musaddiq*. New York: St. Martin's Press, 1997.

Goodman, Rachel Ann. "The Very First Motel." *The Savvy Traveler*, Public Radio International, July 28, 2000. (Retrieved from http://savvytraveler.publicradio.org/show/features/2000/20000728/motel.shtml.)

Graebner, William. *A History of Retirement: The Meaning and Function of an American Institution, 1885–1978*. New Haven, CT: Yale University Press, 1980.

"The Great Plains Drain." *The Economist*, January 19, 2008.

Greene, Bob. *Fraternity: A Journey in Search of Five Presidents*. New York: Crown Publishers, 2004.

Guillory, Dan. *Decatur*. Charleston, SC: Arcadia Publishing, 2004.

Hackes, Peter. "They Left the White House Broke." *Parade*, February 22, 1959.

Halberstam, David. *The Fifties*. New York: Fawcett Books, 1993.

Hamburger, Philip. "Good of You to Do This for Us, Mr. Truman." *The New Yorker*, November 19, 1955.

Hamby, Alonzo L. *Man of the People: A Life of Harry S. Truman.* New York: Oxford University Press, 1995.

Hepburn, Andrew. *A Complete Guide to New York City, Including Westchester County and Long Island.* New York: Travel Enterprises, 1952.

Hepburn, Andrew. *The American Travel Series: Washington, D.C., Virginia, Maryland.* New York: Travel Enterprises, 1953.

Hinckley, Jim, and Jon G. Robinson. *The Big Book of Car Culture: The Armchair Guide to Automotive Americana.* St. Paul, MN: Motorbooks, 2005.

Horgan, James J. *City of Flight: The History of Aviation in St. Louis.* Gerald, MO: Patrice Press, 1984.

Ierley, Merritt. *Traveling the National Road: Across the Centuries on America's First Highway.* Woodstock, NY: Overlook Press, 1990.

Jacoby, Jeff. "Harry Truman's Obsolete Integrity." *International Herald Tribune*, March 2, 2007. (Retrieved from www.iht.com/articles/2007/03/02/opinion/edjacoby.php.)

Jakle, John A., Keith A. Sculle, and Jefferson S. Rogers. *The Motel in America.* Baltimore: Johns Hopkins University Press, 1996.

Jenkins, Roy. *Truman.* New York: Harper & Row, 1986.

Johnson, Clarence A. "Truman Works Long Hours in Role of Ordinary Citizen." *Atlanta Journal and Constitution*, May 31, 1953.

Johnson, Niel M. "Truman and the Trails." *Overland Journal*, Vol. VI, No. 2 (1988).

Johnson, Richard A. "The Outsider." *Invention & Technology*, Summer 2007. (Retrieved from www.americanheritage.com/people/articles/web/20070716-robert-mcnamara-ford-motor-company-vietnam-thunderbird-edsel-whiz-kids-henry-ford-II.shtml.)

Jordan, Philip D. *The National Road.* Indianapolis: Bobbs-Merrill Company, 1948.

Joseph, Gar. "Youngblood's Assault on Negro Mountain." *Philadelphia Daily News*, July 13, 2007.

Kennedy, Janice. "Fame and Infamy at Mayflower Hotel." Windsor (Ontario) *Star*, May 3, 2008. (Retrieved from www.canada.com/windsorstar/news/travel/story.html?id=5f99afae-e467-4a15-b942-0546efe00ec1.)

Kennedy, Rick. *Jelly Roll, Bix, and Hoagy: Gennett Studios and the Birth of Recorded Jazz*. Bloomington, IN: Indiana University Press, 1994.

Kershaw, Sarah, and Michael Powell. "Just a Hotel? For Some, It's an Adventure." *New York Times*, March 20, 2008.

Kirkendall, Richard S. *The Harry S. Truman Encyclopedia*. Boston: G. K. Hall, 1989.

Knestrick, Ray E. *Old Buildings on Main Street, Washington, Pa.* Washington, PA: Observer-Reporter, 1975.

Knight, Amy W. *How the Cold War Began: The Igor Gouzenko Affair and the Hunt for Soviet Spies*. New York: Carroll & Graf, 2005.

Leviero, Anthony. "Behind the Door Marked 'Harry S. Truman.'" *New York Times Sunday Magazine*, August 16, 1953.

Lubove, Roy. *The Struggle for Social Security, 1900–1935*. Pittsburgh, PA: University of Pittsburgh Press, 1986.

Lutholtz, M. William. *Grand Dragon: D. C. Stephenson and the Ku Klux Klan in Indiana*. West Lafayette, IN: Purdue University Press, 1991.

Margolies, John. *Home Away from Home: Motels in America*. Boston: Little, Brown, 1995.

McCullough, David. *Truman*. New York: Simon & Schuster, 1992.

McDermott, Kevin. "Decatur, Down and Out." *Illinois Issues*, November 2001. (Retrieved from http://illinoisissues-archive.uis.edu/features/2001nov/decatur.html.)

Meisler, Stanley. *United Nations: The First Fifty Years*. New York: Atlantic Monthly Press, 1995.

Melanson, Philip H. *The Secret Service: The Hidden History of an Enigmatic Agency*. New York: Carroll & Graf, 2002.

"The Missouri Traveler." *Time*, June 29, 1953.

"Mr. Truman." *The New Yorker*, July 11, 1953.

Model, F. Peter. "The United Nations at 50: The Zeckendorf Connection." *Real Estate Weekly*, November 1, 1995. (Retrieved from http://findarticles.com/p/articles/mi_m3601/is_n13_v42/ai_18530577.)

Morris, Jan. *Coast to Coast: A Journey Across 1950s America*. San Francisco: Travelers' Tales, 2002.

Mui, Ylan Q. "A Hotel Boosted by a Bedtime Story." *Washington Post*, April 3, 2008.

Murphy, Ryan G. "The History of Retirement." *Investment Advisor*, April 2006. (Retrieved from www.investmentadvisor.com/article.php?article=6193.)

Neal, Steve. *Harry and Ike: The Partnership That Remade the Postwar World*. New York: Scribner, 2001.

Okrant, Mark J. *Sleeping Alongside the Road: Recollections by Patrons and the Owners of Motels in That Era When Motels Were Americans' First Choice*. Manchester, NH: Oak Manor Publishing, 2006.

Ortega, Bob. *In Sam We Trust: The Untold Story of Sam Walton, and How Wal-Mart Is Devouring America*. New York: Times Business, 1998.

O'Sullivan, Christopher D. *The United Nations: A Concise History*. Malabar, FL: Krieger Publishing Company, 2005.

"Outside Looking In." *Time*, July 6, 1953.

Parker, Vern. "1953 New Yorker Deluxe Almost Got Away." *Washington Times*, October 21, 2005.

Pemberton, William E. *Harry S. Truman: Fair Dealer and Cold Warrior*. Boston: Twayne Publishers, 1989.

Pennsylvania State Police Historical, Educational & Memorial Center. *The Pennsylvania State Police: A History of the First Uniformed Organization of Its Kind in the Nation, 1905–2005*. Hershey, PA: Pennsylvania State Police Historical, Educational & Memorial Center, 2005.

Pett, Saul. "Leaving White House No Jolt to 'Mr. Average Man' Truman." *Sunday Oregonian* (Portland, OR), August 27, 1961.

Phillips, Cabell. *The Truman Presidency: The History of a Triumphant Succession*. New York: Macmillan, 1966.

Poen, Monte M., ed. *Letters Home by Harry Truman*. New York: G. P. Putnam's Sons, 1984.

Raitz, Karl, ed. *A Guide to the National Road*. Baltimore: Johns Hopkins University Press, 1996.

Reams Jr., Bernard D., and Paul E. Wilson, eds. *Segregation and the Fourteenth Amendment in the States: A Survey of State Segregation Laws, 1865–1953*. Buffalo, NY: W. S. Hein, 1975.

Risen, James. "Secrets of History: The C.I.A. in Iran." *New York Times* Web site. www.nytimes.com/library/world/mideast/041600iran-cia-index.html (retrieved July 5, 2008).

Robbins, Charles. *The Last of His Kind: An Informal Portrait of Harry S. Truman*. New York: William Morrow, 1979.

Robbins, Jhan. *Bess & Harry: An American Love Story*. New York: G. P. Putnam's Sons, 1980.

Roberts, Marcia. *Looking Back and Seeing the Future: The United States Secret Service, 1865–1990*. Des Moines, IA: Association of Former Agents of the United States Secret Service, 1991.

Robertson, Tom. *Frostburg, Maryland*. Charleston, SC: Arcadia Publishing, 2002.

Rose, Lisle A. *The Cold War Comes to Main Street: America in 1950*. Lawrence, KS: University Press of Kansas, 1999.

Rugh, Susan Sessions. *Are We There Yet? The Golden Age of American Family Vacations*. Lawrence, KS: University Press of Kansas, 2008.

Sand, G. W. *Truman in Retirement: A Former President Views the Nation & the World*. South Bend, IN: Justice Books, 1993.

Sandler, Neal. "Memories of a Gas Station Owner." *Frederick* (MD) *Post*, June 2, 1975.

Schofield, Matthew. "Some Say Truman the Driver Was a Hit." *Kansas City Star*, September 22, 1985.

Sheeley, Rachel E. "Remembering Truman." *Richmond* (IN) *Palladium-Item*, July 8, 2003.

Sherrod, Robert. "A Day in a Former President's Busy Life." *Saturday Evening Post*, June 13, 1964.

Singer, Mark. "Town on a String." *The New Yorker*, October 30, 2000.

Skidmore, Max J. *After the White House: Former Presidents as Private Citizens*. New York: Palgrave Macmillan, 2004.

Smith, Stephanie. "Former Presidents: Federal Expenditures for Pensions, Office Allowances, and Protection." Congressional Research Service Report for Congress, June 5, 2007.

Sparks, Glen. "Old Bavaria Meets Modern Commerce." *St. Louis Commerce Magazine*, August 2004. (Retrieved from www.stlcommercemagazine.com/archives/august2004/bavaria.html.)

Stewart, George. *U.S. 40: Cross Section of the United States of America*. Boston: Houghton Mifflin, 1953.

Stone, Martin. "Could Truman Pay His Bills?" *New York Times*, August 5, 1989.

Stover, Dawn. "50 Years After Roswell." *Popular Science*, June 1997.

terHorst, J. F., and Ralph Albertazzie. *The Flying White House: The Story of Air Force One*. New York: Coward, McCann & Geoghegan, 1979.

Theoharis, Athan. *Seeds of Repression: Harry S. Truman and the Origins of McCarthyism*. Chicago: Quadrangle Books, 1971.

Thomas, Robert D., ed. *Columbus Unforgettables: A Collection of Columbus Yesterdays and Todays*. Columbus, OH: Robert D. Thomas, 1983.

Tishler, Hace. *Self-Reliance and Social Security, 1870–1917*. Port Washington, NY: Kennikat Press, 1971.

Truett, Randle. *The Washington Pocket Guide*. New York: Hastings House, 1953.

Truman, Harry S. *Memoirs. Vol. I: Year of Decisions*. Garden City, NY: Doubleday, 1955.

Truman, Harry S. *Memoirs. Vol. II: Years of Trial and Hope*. Garden City, NY: Doubleday, 1956.

Truman, Harry S. "Mr. Citizen." *The American Weekly*, September 20
and 27, October 4, 11, and 18, 1953.

Truman, Harry S. *Mr. Citizen*. New York: Geis Associates, 1960.

Truman, Harry S. *Public Papers of the Presidents of the United States. Harry
S. Truman. Containing the Public Messages, Speeches, and Statements
of the President, April 12 to December 31, 1945*. Washington: U.S.
Government Printing Office, 1961.

Truman, Harry S. *Truman Speaks*. New York: Columbia University Press,
1960.

Truman, Margaret. *Bess W. Truman*. New York: Macmillan, 1986.

Truman, Margaret. *Harry S. Truman*. New York: William Morrow, 1972.

Truman, Margaret, ed. *Where the Buck Stops: The Personal and Private
Writings of Harry S. Truman*. New York: Warner Books, 1989.

Tyarks, Fredric. *Harian's American Travel Guide: Where to Find the Best
in the U.S., Canada & Mexico*. Greenlawn, NY: Harian Publications,
1953.

U.S. Department of Transportation. *America's Highways, 1776–1976: A
History of the Federal-Aid Program*. Washington: U.S. Department of
Transportation, Federal Highway Administration, 1976.

U.S. Department of Transportation. *Roads to Serve the Nation: The
Story of Road Development in the United States*. Washington: U.S.
Department of Transportation, Federal Highway Administration,
1988 or 1989.

Updegrove, Mark K. *Second Acts: Presidential Lives and Legacies After the
White House*. Guilford, CN: Lyons Press, 2006.

Walch, Timothy, and Dwight M. Miller, eds. *Herbert Hoover and Harry
S. Truman: A Documentary History*. Worland, WY: High Plains
Publishing Company, 1992.

Weber, Ralph E., ed. *Talking with Harry: Candid Conversations with
President Harry S. Truman*. Wilmington, DE: SR Books, 2001.

Weingroff, Richard F. "From Names to Numbers: The Origins of the U.S. Numbered Highway System." Federal Highway Administration Web site. www.fhwa.dot.gov/infrastructure/numbers.htm (retrieved July 5, 2008).

Weingroff, Richard F. "The Man Who Loved Roads." *Public Roads*, Vol. LXV, No. 6 (May/June 2002). (Retrieved from www.tfhrc.gov/pubrds/02may/08.htm.)

Whitman, Arthur. "Take a Tip from Harry: 'Wake Up and Walk!'" *This Week*, June 4, 1961.

Woods, Edward F. "Harry Truman, Private Citizen." *St. Louis Post-Dispatch*, February 1, 1953.

Writers' Program of the Work Projects Administration in the State of Missouri. *Missouri: A Guide to the "Show Me" State*. New York: Hastings House, 1954.

Wynn, Anita. "The Story of Nemesis and Negro Mountain." *Anthropology News*, October 2006.

Yenne, Bill. *UFO: Evaluating the Evidence*. Glasgow, Scotland: Saraband, 2007.

Index